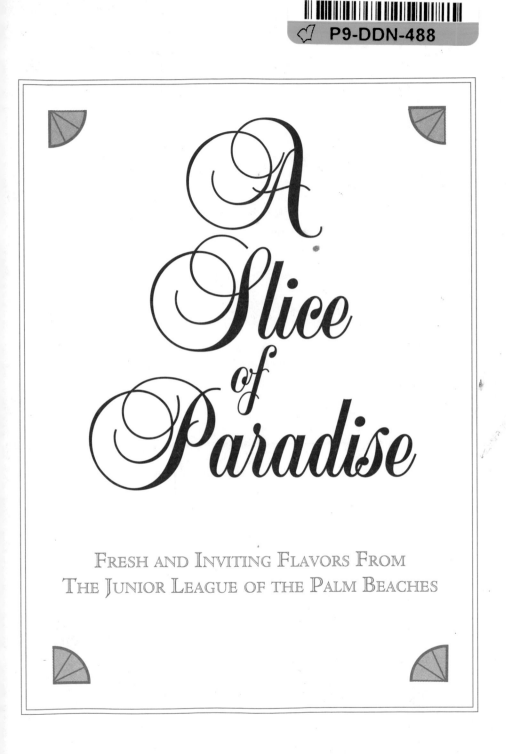

A Slice of Paradise

FRESH AND INVITING FLAVORS FROM
THE JUNIOR LEAGUE OF THE PALM BEACHES

The Junior League of the Palm Beaches, Inc. is an organization of women committed to promoting volunteerism and to improving the community through the effective action and leadership of trained volunteers. Its purpose is exclusively educational and charitable. The Junior League reaches out to all young women regardless of race, religion, or national origin who demonstrate an interest in and commitment to volunteerism.

First printing, November 1996, 15,000 copies.
Second printing, September 1997, 20,000 copies.

Information on obtaining additional copies of *A Slice of Paradise* may be found at the back of the book or by contacting:

The Junior League of the Palm Beaches, Inc.
470 Columbia Drive, Suite F101
West Palm Beach, Florida 33409
561-689-7562

Library of Congress Catalog Card Number:
96-78698

International Standard Book Number
0-9608090-1-5

Printed in the USA by

The Wimmer Companies
Memphis

A Slice of Paradise is a collection of treasures from the Palm Beaches. Each recipe, painting and thought is a little piece of our paradise which we, the Junior League of the Palm Beaches, Inc., would like to share with you. The fresh and inviting flavors of our triple tested recipes represent the varied backgrounds of our residents and provide a unique Floribbean flare. They were carefully chosen to appeal to cooks of all levels, satisfy the palates of the health conscious and fit into all varieties of schedules. The thoughts, information and original artwork define our region of South Florida. The proceeds support the many projects of the Junior League of the Palm Beaches, Inc., making our community a better place for all who live here. Step into the pages of this book and enjoy a slice of paradise!

The Junior League of the Palm Beaches, Inc. wishes to thank the following for contributing and testing thousands of recipes, writing, word processing, editing, proofing, researching and spending countless hours in the production of this book:

Pamela Adams
Kristen Ahrens
Ann Aiken
Marcie Alevizos
Shirley Anderson
Barbara Anderson
Barbara Angiuli
Annis Arasim
Lori Arcuri
Bobbie Arnold
Brenda Arnold
Judith Arnold
Jean Askwith
Nancy Atwater
Sara Ayres
Maria Bacinich
Karen Baer
Sheila Baldwin
Jayne Barkdull
Pauline Beain
Regina Bedoya
Marty Bender
Grace Benelli
Christine Bennett
Deborah Bennett
Lucy Berckmans
Naomi Berman
Melissa Bernard
Marilyn Beuttenmuller
Vicky Bidwell
Roz Bishop
Renee Blews
Kathy Blomqvist
Barbara Boerstler
Betsy Boggie
Martha Boruff
Theresa Bowman
Valerie Boyd
Colleen Bracci
Diana Brady
Susan Brattebo
Suzanne Brenner
Liz Brinson
Kim Brock
Chere Brodi
Kathy Bronstien
Aimee Brown
Judy Brown
Lynne Brown
Michael Bubis
Eileen Budnyk
Libby Bulkin
Lynda Burgy
Beth Burr
Barbara Bush

Marian Butler
Barbara Byron
Lynn Cain
Dawn Calder
Sylvia Camp
Eloise Campbell
Cindy Cantrell
Marlene Canzio
Candy Cappello
Kathy Carpenter
Diane Carron
Marieke Carter
Barbara Catalfumo
Kim Celedinas
Debra Cennave
Kimberly Chehrazi
Andrea Christiansen
Andrew Clark
Carolyn Clark
Christine Clark
Betsy Cohen
Brent Collins
Dean Collins
Jeff Collins
Karen Collins
Susan Collins
Robin Colton
Marguerite Compiani
Janet Converse
Cary Cook
Marci Cook
Missie Cook
Rosemary Cooney
Gail Cooney
C. Coppatio
Celeste Cordon
Catherine Corson
Mark Corson
Sandy Coster
Katie Couric
Jackie Cowell
Mary Cox
Carla Cramer
Suzanne Crawford
Michele Criser
E.J. Crittenden
Kathleen Cromwell
Diane Cronin
Jean Dahlgren
Jane Dahlmeier
Brenda Daley
Suzanne Dansby-Phelps
Bonnie Davis
Karen Davis
Margaret Davison

Dianna Dawson
Nita Deal
Allison Dean
Nancy Dee
Mary DeFilippo
Linda DeFrehn
Denise del Russo
Eileen Dempsey
Staci DiTocco
Kathy Dolbow
Ed Donahue
Eileen Donahue
Shannon Donnelly
Cathy Dorsey
Heather Dorsey
Wanda Doumar
Ed Downey
Julie Downey
Julie Dreyfoos
Becky Duke
Bobbye Duke
Cathy Duncan
Catherine Eaton
Cindy Eberly
Jane Eckler
Ann Eisenhart
Gail Eissey
Wendy Eissey
Peggy Ekberg
Barbara Eldridge
Susan Elhilow
Eriel Erickson
Pat Eskew
Cheryl Evatt
Peggy Evatt
Mary Fairbanks
Beth Farr
Cindy Farr
Sherry Farrell
Sara Fattori
Mary Ann Favaloro
Mary Fendrich
Lisa Ferguson
Julie Fiedor
Susie Fisher
Judy Fitzsimmons
Pat Fitzsimmons
Susan Fleming
Stephanie Florine
Sharon Flow
Charla Floyd
Cheryl Foreman
Judy Forsythe
Rita Forte
Mary Fountain

Howard Frankel
Suzanne Frankel
Robi Freeman
Jack Frost
Woody Gardner
Jamie Gerard
Elaine Gerlinger
Fran Gill
Merrily Goering
Beth Goetz
Connie Goldberger
Tillie Gonella
Jean Goodnight
Joni Gooley
Pam Gordon
Susan Gordon
Jennifer Gray
Kelli Greer
Chris Gregory
Julie Grieb
Sheila Griffin
Debbie Gryzbowski
Deborah Hale
Alice Hamilton
Pegi Hamner
Maria Hartley
Skippy Harwood
Candy Hatcher
Lisa Hawthorne
Lisa Hayes
Katie Heimbach
Susan Heintzman
Ali Henderson
Gail Henderson
James Henderson
Amy Hickman
Diane Higgins
Julie Hislop
Flo Holden
Terri Horrow
Ellen Hotz
Kathleen Houseman
Linda Hunt
Maureen Hurlbent
Elizabeth Hustad
Renea Hutchings
Teresita Iglesias
Becky Isiminger
P.K. Isiminger
Judy Ivins
Mary Jacobs
Beth Jacobson
Jim Jenkins
Wanda Jenkins
Linda Johnson

Shelley Johnson
Laura Johnson
Maureen Johnston
Phillis Jones
Suzanne Kairalla
Cheryl Kalokerinos
Virginia Kara
Kristen Kenney-Knight
Laura Kent
Ellen Kinard
Dawn Kiner
Sharon King
Dora Kino
Jennifer Kintz
Don Kitchings
Susan Knight
Ann Kohlmeyer
Charlotte Krag
Kathy Krinsky
Pam Kuhl
Nancy Kumpulainen
John Kurnick
Amanda LaBanz
Helen Lambert
Nancy Lambrecht
Leigh Ann Larosa
Susan Lazow
Joanne Leavitt
Debbie Ledwith
Bobbie Leek
Carri Leininger
Dotsey Letts
Carolyn Levine
Ray Levine
Shirley Lichtstein
Stasia Linton
Lynn Little
B.A. Lofton
Lucille Louderback
Allison Lovell
Heather Lyons
Joanne Manely
Beth Manno
Karen Marasco
Jay Marra
Tom Marra
Victoria Marra
Janice Marshall
Ann Mathews
Sharon McCormick
Pam McDulin
Kelly McFadden
Susan McGuire
Andrea McKalvey
Donna McMaster
Lynn McSherry
Anne Meijer
Marjorie Meijer
M.B. Mergerthaler
Anne Messer
Anne Methe

Colette Meyer
Debra Meyer
Jenny Miles
Shirley Miller
Elizabeth Molony
Lisa Molony
Judy Monteiro
Eugene Moore
Judy Moser
Jill Mross
Julie Mullins
Noelle Mullins
Todd Mullins
Suzanne Muntzing
Jeb Murphy
Kathy Murphy
Mary Murphy
Susan Murray
Hollie Myers
Judy Myers
Sherry Neal
Zan Nevels
Barbara Nicklaus
Jaye Norris
Nanette Norton
Linda Olsson
Beth Owen
Ellen O'Bannon
Joan O'Connell
Jean O'Connell
Nan O'Leary
Vicki O'Leary
Christine O'Shea
Diane Page
Elizabeth Parella
Laura Parrott
Sharon Pauly
Jodie Payne
Sandy Pepin
Lynda Pepper-Schwartz
Sherrie Perrelli
Michele Perry
Ann Petersen
Charlotte Petrokus
Deta Pfleger
Dora Pikounis
Allyson Pimentel
Gwen Pitcairn
Mary Polito
Carole Poncy
Susan Poncy
Staeci Porcher
Christy Potter
Diane Prange
Mona Prager
Mary Pressly
Ashleigh Price
Debbie Price
Donald Price
Kelly Price
Alison Pruitt

Lynn Pussic
Julie Quattlebaum
Leslie Randolph
Elizabeth Rank
Kathy Rapp
Jo Read
Kirsten Reback
Kim Reddington
Suzanne Redmond
Lorey Reese
Jeanne Reinig
Sheila Reynolds
Layne Reynolds
Paige Rhymes
Susan Ricci
Vicky Riley
Christine Rinker
Beverly Robinson
Lisa Rogers
Ann Marie Rollo
Bryn Rose
Lorraine Rosen
Ellen Royal
Lauren Rozowsky
Laurette Russell
Susan Salisbury
Emma Sams
Sherry Schattie
Laura Schiesz
Margaret Schuemann
Lynda Schwartz
Kimberly Seefeldt
Cheryl Seiler
Kim Sellers
Sheila Serraes
Allaire Sheehy
Lucinda Shenkman
Denee Shipley
Susan Shrier
Shawn Sipowski
Midge Smith
Marnie Smith
Marlena Smith
Susie Snayd
Barbara Sommers
Lisa Sowerwine
Tim Springer
Mary Sreenan
D. Stark
Marietta Stebor
Jack Steele
Kathy Steele
Lori Steele
Pam Steele
Terry Stone
Ruth Stott
Melissa Streisand
Corinne Stubeck
Debbie Suec
Valerie Sullivan
Susie Tamoney

Bess Taylor
Michele Telatovich
Kathy Theofilos
Connie Thomas
Pamela Thomas
Kara Thompson
Kay Thompson
Peggy Thorsen
Jeanne Tidwell
Kathy Tignor
Betsy Torres
Sherie Travers
Amy Triggs
Nils Turney
Tory Turney
Cathy Tyler
Brenda Upchurch
Christl Upchurch
Jan Utterback
Stephanie Valeche
Barbara Van DeVate
Susan Van Pelt
Joan Van Akin
Beth Vandenberg
Dennis Vandenberg
Kelly VanderWerff
Lacie Venzara
Sandy Vincent
Alex Vizoso-Saylor
Kim Warner
Karen Warshaw
Heidi Weiland
Marian White
Kelley Whitt
Rick Whitt
Ellen Wight
Mona Wiley
Gail Wilhite
Will Wilhite
Elizabeth Williams
Elyse Williams
Hunter Wilson
Poonam Wilson
Melissa Winchester
Montyne Winokur
Anne Winter
Suzanne Winzell
Ione Wiren
Barbara Wojciak
Janette Wojciak
Maury Wolfe
Linda Womack
Rebecca Woodcock
Janet Woodward
Roberta Yackira
John Yeend
Stephanie Young
Ida Yuille
Kitty Yundt
Daniel Zeigler
Marla Zeigler

THE COMMITTEE FOR THE DEVELOPMENT OF

A Slice of Paradise

CHAIRMAN:
Ali Henderson

ASSISTANT CHAIRMAN:
Lori Steele

COMMITTEE:

Annis Arasim
Lucy Berckmans
Renee Blews
Susan Brattebo
Beth Burr
Marlene Canzio
Betsy Cohen
Rosemary Cooney
Julie Downey
Sara Fattori
Merrily Goering
Susan Gordon

Kristen Kenney-Knight
Ann Kohlmeyer
Susan McGuire
Mary Murphy
Nanette Norton
Nan O'Leary
Laura Parrott
Sandy Pepin
Lynda Pepper-Schwartz
Dora Pikounis
Allyson Pimentel

Kim Reddington
Lisa Rogers
Bryn Rose
Beth Vandenberg
Kelly VanderWerff
Alex Visozo-Saylor
Kim Warner
Heidi Weiland
Janette Wojciak
Roberta Yackira
Marla Ziegler

ABOUT THE ARTISTS

Jim Guthrie is an architect with special interests in hotel design and historic preservation. Mr. Guthrie has degrees from Tulane and Columbia Universities. A native of Monroe, Louisiana, he has resided in West Palm Beach since 1993, after eighteen years in Hong Kong and Tokyo.

Sara Blitch Fattori is a native of Savannah, Georgia and is a graduate of the University of Florida with a Bachelor of Design Degree from the College of Architecture. Mrs. Fattori has worked as an interior designer and art consultant for over fifteen years in South Florida.

Contents

Appetizers 9
Beverages 28
Breads 35
Brunch 52
Soups 57
Salads 71
Sandwiches 97
Pasta 105
Vegetables 131
Side Dishes 151
Meats 159
Poultry 178
Seafood 196
Cookies 213
Cakes 221
Pies 232
Desserts 243
Paradise Guide 257
Roasting Peppers 259
Basic Pastry/Pie Crust 259
Herbed Extras 260
Stock 261
Nutrition Guide 264
Equivalent Measures 265
Fish Guide 266
Fruit Guide 268
Fruit Shipping 276
Index 277
Order Information 287

The Junior League of the Palm Beaches, Inc. gratefully acknowledges the following for their financial contributions in support of this book as a fundraiser to promote Junior League sponsored projects and volunteerism in our community:

Platinum Spoon Contributor

Cushman Fruit Company Inc.
West Palm Beach, Florida
(see page 276)

Golden Spoon Contributor

Golden Bear International, Inc.
North Palm Beach, Florida

Silver Spoon Contributor

Global Travel Management, Inc.
Palm Beach, Florida

Northern Trust Company
North Palm Beach, Florida

Appetizers & Beverages

POLO PONIES AND PRESTIGE

Women in exquisite hats and men in crisp linen suits listen for the growing rumble of the trained hooves and the sudden crack of a mallet. The announcer, with a hint of an accent, claims, "This will be the match of all matches!" Thus, an afternoon of polo begins.

Polo, a sport of the rich and famous, has found a home in the Palm Beaches. Since 1925, spectators have included movie stars, royalty, well-heeled old money sorts, as well as the average horse lover who enjoys watching the fast-paced sport. Fans turn out for sunny afternoons, often bringing their own tailgate picnics from champagne to fried chicken. Many matches are played to benefit local and international charities, attracting the most sought after celebrities and players.

Whether interested in the abilities of the horses and the players who ride them, or in the sport of people watching and festive fanfare, polo enthusiasts will find themselves in paradise as they experience the polo of the Palm Beaches.

BRUSCHETTA WITH ARUGULA AND SMOKED MOZZARELLA

1 large bunch arugula, washed, coarse stems discarded

½ pound smoked mozzarella cheese, finely chopped

2 tomatoes, seeded, finely chopped

Salt and pepper to taste

12 diagonally cut ½ inch thick slices Italian bread

2 garlic cloves, halved

¼ cup extra virgin olive oil, divided

*P*reheat broiler. Finely chop the arugula. In a bowl, combine arugula, mozzarella, tomatoes and salt and pepper to taste. Grill the bread slices in the broiler, 4 inches from the heat, turning once. Rub the toasts with garlic on one side and brush the same side with ½ of the oil. Spoon the arugula mixture onto the oiled sides of the toasts and drizzle the remaining oil on top.

Yield: 12 pieces

Nutrition Analysis per piece:

saturated fat -	3.2 g	sodium -	380 mg
calories -	167	fiber -	0.5 g
fat -	8 g	cholesterol -	16.6 mg
carbohydrate -	15.8 g	sugar -	3.6 g

CHILI RELLENOS SQUARES

4 cups shredded Monterey jack cheese

1 (4-ounce) can chopped green chili peppers

5 eggs, beaten

*P*reheat oven to 300°. Layer cheese and chilies in lightly greased 12 x 8 baking dish. Pour eggs over mixture. Bake for 45 minutes or until center is firm. Let cool for 10 minutes; cut into 2 inch squares.

Yield: 2 dozen squares

These tasty cheese squares are terrific served with tortilla chips and Snappy Sunshine Salsa. Place a cheese square on a tortilla and top with a spoonful of salsa.

Bruschetta with Matchstick Pepper Strips

1 red pepper
1 yellow pepper
1 green pepper
¼ cup extra virgin olive oil, plus extra for drizzling
1 small onion, thinly sliced
Sea salt and freshly ground pepper to taste
2 tablespoons capers
9 thick slices Italian or French bread, cut in half
2 large garlic cloves, cut in half
9 large fresh basil leaves, cut into strips

Cut peppers in half lengthwise. Remove core, seeds and white membrane and cut peppers into thin strips. Place in a medium sauce pan with the oil, onions, salt and pepper. Cook over low heat 12 minutes until peppers and onions are tender. Remove from heat and stir in capers.

Grill or lightly toast bread. Rub one side with garlic cloves and drizzle with olive oil. Spoon pepper mixture over bread and sprinkle with basil. Cut each slice into three pieces and serve.

Yield: 18 pieces

Nutrition Analysis per piece:

saturated fat -	0.2 g	sodium -	228 mg
calories -	96	fiber -	1.6 g
fat -	2.2 g	cholesterol -	0
carbohydrate -	13.1 g	sugar -	2.9 g

This recipe can be served as an appetizer or as an accompaniment to a main dish salad.

Smoked Salmon Spread

6 ounces cream cheese, softened
6 ounces thinly sliced smoked salmon, divided
1 teaspoon prepared white horseradish
2 teaspoons fresh lemon juice
1 teaspoon minced fresh dill
Bagel chips for serving

Combine cream cheese and ½ of the smoked salmon in a food processor until smooth. Add horseradish and lemon juice and process until smooth, scraping sides as necessary. Add dill and process briefly, until incorporated.

Finely chop the remaining salmon and stir it into the spread until evenly distributed. Transfer the spread to a small mold or bowl. Refrigerate, covered for at least 3 hours and up to 2 days. To serve, bring to room temperature, remove from mold and serve with bagel chips.

Yield: servings for 8

Hot Artichoke Crostini

1 French baguette
1 cup mayonnaise or salad dressing
1 cup grated Parmesan cheese
2 garlic cloves, minced
1 (14-ounce) can artichoke hearts, drained and chopped
1 (4½-ounce) can chopped green chilies
Chopped green onions for garnish
Chopped tomatoes or crumbled bacon for garnish

*P*reheat oven to 400°. Slice baguette into approximately 36 ¼-inch slices. Place slices on foil lined baking sheet. Bake for 5 minutes or until lightly browned. Combine mayonnaise, Parmesan cheese, garlic, artichoke hearts and chilies; spread on bread slices. Bake at 400° for 5 minutes or until cheese melts. Top with choice of garnish and serve immediately.

Yield: 36 pieces

Can be assembled ahead of time and placed in oven for final baking when guests arrive.

Gouda Cheese Puff

1 (8-ounce) can refrigerated crescent rolls
1 (7-ounce) wheel Gouda cheese, wax removed
¼ cup Dijon mustard
1 egg white, slightly beaten
1 tablespoon sesame seeds
Sesame crackers for serving

*P*reheat oven to 325°. Unroll crescent rolls and separate into 4 squares. Lay two squares side by side and seal perforations. Spread mustard on top and bottom of Gouda; place cheese on the center of sealed pastry squares. Wrap corners and sides up and over cheese and thoroughly seal all open areas. Place one of the remaining pastry squares on a greased baking sheet. Set the pastry-wrapped Gouda on top of the pastry on the baking sheet. Separate the remaining pastry square into 2 triangles at the perforation. Roll and twist each triangle and stretch across wrapped Gouda to form an X. Brush top with egg white and sprinkle with sesame seeds. Bake for 20-30 minutes until golden brown and cheese is heated through. Serve with sesame crackers.

Yield: servings for 8-10

SUMMER VEGETABLE MEDLEY

2 tubes refrigerator crescent rolls (8 rolls per package)

16 ounces cream cheese, softened

⅔ cup mayonnaise

1 small onion, grated

1-3 teaspoons dried dill weed or 9 teaspoons fresh dill

Favorite raw vegetables, shredded or chopped (3 cups suggested)

Shredded cheese of choice (½ cup suggested)

Preheat oven to 400°. Spread rolls on greased jelly roll pan, patting and pressing at seams to seal. Bake for 10 minutes or until crust is golden brown. Mix cream cheese, mayonnaise, onion and dill weed; spread over cooled crust. Top with your favorite raw vegetables, such as olives, shredded carrots, lettuce, green onions, chives, green pepper, mushrooms, radishes, broccoli, cauliflower or celery. Pat vegetables on top of cream cheese mixture and sprinkle with shredded cheese.

Yield: 20 pieces

Variation: Omit grated onion and dill weed. Add 1 package ranch dressing mix to cream cheese and mayonnaise mixture. Use ¾ cup each fresh finely chopped broccoli, green onions, radishes and peppers for vegetables. Top with ½ cup grated cheddar cheese.

HOT ARTICHOKE SPINACH DIP

10 ounces frozen chopped spinach, thawed and drained

1 (14-ounce) can artichoke hearts, drained

1 cup mayonnaise

1½ cups Parmesan cheese, shredded

1½ cups Monterey jack cheese, shredded

Garlic salt to taste

2 teaspoons Tabasco sauce

Melba toasts

Preheat oven to 350°. Squeeze excess water from thawed spinach. Finely chop artichoke hearts. Combine all ingredients and mix thoroughly. Pour into a 1½ quart, ovenproof dish. Bake for 30 minutes. Serve warm with crackers.

Yield: servings for 12

BASIL TOMATO TART

1 refrigerated
piecrust, unbaked

1½ cups shredded
mozzarella cheese,
divided

5 Roma or 4 medium
tomatoes

1 cup loosely packed
fresh basil leaves

4 garlic cloves

½ cup mayonnaise or
salad dressing

¼ cup grated
Parmesan cheese

⅛ teaspoon ground
white pepper

Fresh basil leaves to
garnish

*U*nfold piecrust according to package directions. Place in 9-inch quiche or pie plate. Flute crust edge and press with the tine of a fork. Pre-bake the crust according to package directions. Remove from oven and sprinkle with ½ cup of mozzarella cheese. Cool on a wire rack.

Cut tomatoes into wedges; drain on paper towels. Arrange tomato wedges on melted cheese in the pie shell. Combine basil and garlic in a food processor or blender until coarsely chopped; sprinkle over tomatoes.

Preheat oven to 375°. In a medium mixing bowl, combine remaining mozzarella cheese, mayonnaise, Parmesan cheese and pepper. Spoon cheese mixture over basil mixture, spreading to evenly cover the top. Bake for 35-40 minutes or until top is golden and bubbly. Garnish with basil leaves and serve warm.

Yield: 8 appetizer or 4 main dish servings

Nutrition Analysis per appetizer serving:

saturated fat -	3 g	sodium -	368.8 mg
calories -	296	fiber -	9 g
fat -	22.4 g	cholesterol -	25.3 g
carbohydrate -	13.7 g	sugar -	1.8 g

CHUTNEY CASHEW DIP

8 ounces cream
cheese, softened

⅔ cup sour cream

1 cup chutney,
chopped and
drained

1 cup cashew halves

3 teaspoons curry
powder

Golden butter
crackers

*C*ombine cream cheese, sour cream, chutney, cashews and curry powder until well mixed. Serve with golden butter crackers.

Yield: 2 cups

Quick, easy and always delicious!

Spicy Seafood Dip

1 large green pepper, chopped

1 tablespoon olive oil

1 pound small shrimp, shelled and deveined

2 tablespoons butter

2 (14-ounce) cans artichoke hearts, drained and chopped

2 cups mayonnaise

½ cup thinly sliced green onions

½ cup roasted red peppers, drained and chopped

1 cup freshly grated Parmesan cheese

2 tablespoons fresh lemon juice

4 teaspoons Worcestershire sauce

1 dash Tabasco sauce

3 pickled jalapeño peppers, minced

½ teaspoon salt

1 pound crabmeat

⅓ cup sliced almonds, lightly toasted

Pita triangles

Sauté green peppers in olive oil in large sauté pan over medium heat, stirring until peppers are soft; cool and set aside. Sauté shrimp in butter for 1½ minutes; set aside.

Preheat oven to 375°. In a large bowl, mix artichokes, mayonnaise, green onions, roasted peppers, Parmesan cheese, lemon juice, Worcestershire, jalapeño peppers, Tabasco sauce and salt. Gently stir in seafood and sautéed peppers. Transfer to a 2-quart buttered baking dish and sprinkle with almonds. Bake for 25-30 minutes. Serve in a chafing dish with lightly buttered pita triangles.

Yield: servings for 8-10

See page 259 for instructions on roasting peppers.

SMOKED FISH DIP

1 pound smoked fish

2 tablespoons grated onion

16 ounces cream cheese, softened

3 tablespoons lemon juice

3 tablespoons chopped parsley

℟emove bones and skin from fish; flake. Combine cream cheese, lemon juice and onion; whisk until smooth and fluffy. Stir in fish and parsley. Chill for one hour minimum or overnight.

Yield: 3½ cups

This is a favorite recipe of a West Palm Beacher who spent much of his youth near commercial fishing docks and smoke houses. Be creative! Add your favorite spices and seasonings for added zip!

VEGETABLES WITH AVOCADO ANCHOVY DIP

1 garlic clove, peeled and chopped

2 tablespoons chopped parsley

1 tablespoon tarragon vinegar

½ teaspoon dried tarragon or 1½ teaspoons fresh tarragon, chopped

6 anchovy fillets

¼ cup Dijon mustard

1 cup mayonnaise

1 very ripe avocado, peeled, seeded and mashed

3 tablespoons light cream

Salt and white pepper to taste

Vegetables for dipping (steamed asparagus, broccoli, mushrooms, cherry tomatoes)

𝒞ombine all ingredients, except salt and pepper, in the bowl of a food processor fitted with a steel blade. Blend, scraping down the sides as necessary. Add salt and pepper to taste and blend again. Place dip into a bowl, cover and refrigerate until serving. Serve with vegetables.

Yield: 2 cups

Nutrition Analysis per tablespoon:

saturated fat -	0.5 g	sodium -	134.5 mg
calories -	67	fiber -	0 g
fat -	6.8 g	cholesterol -	4.4 mg
carbohydrate -	0.9 g	sugar -	0.1 g

BULL'S-EYE CHILI DIP

1 pound ground chuck
¾ cup chopped onion, divided
1 (15-ounce) can stewed tomatoes
1 dash garlic powder
½ cup ketchup
3 teaspoons chili powder
1 teaspoon salt
1 (16-ounce) can kidney beans
½ cup chopped green olives
⅓ cup grated Cheddar cheese

*B*rown meat and drain. Add ½ cup onions, tomatoes and garlic powder. Cook until liquid has evaporated. Add ketchup, chili powder and salt. Mash beans with liquid and add to meat mixture. Heat through.

Empty onto a round plate. Cover top with ¼ cup onion, cheese and olives as follows: onion as inner circle, cheese as middle circle, olive as outer circle; bull's-eye style.

Yield: servings for 10

Nutrition Analysis per serving:

saturated fat -	1.2 g	sodium -	260.4 mg
calories -	80	fiber -	0.2 g
fat -	3.5 g	cholesterol -	12.9 mg
carbohydrate -	5.3 g	sugar -	2.3 g

This dip is loved by armchair quarterbacks during football season!

BAKED BRIE

1 sheet frozen puff pastry, pre-rolled
1 (16-ounce) wheel Brie cheese
1 (1½-ounce) box raisins
1 teaspoon cinnamon
¼ cup sliced almonds
¼ cup flour for rolling surface
Sliced apples for serving
Crackers for serving

*P*reheat oven to 350°. Thaw pastry sheet at room temperature for 20 minutes before gently unfolding. Flour rolling surface and rolling pin. Gently roll out pastry sheet. Place Brie in center of pastry. Sprinkle with raisins, cinnamon and nuts. Fold up sides of pastry around Brie; pinch closed or tie with a string. Place in a pie plate or quiche dish. Bake 25-30 minutes, until golden. Let stand ½-1 hour before serving. Serve with sliced apples and crackers.

Yield: 8-10 servings

Reuben Dip

8 ounces cream
cheese, cut into
pieces and softened

½ cup sour cream

1 cup sauerkraut,
rinsed, drained,
and chopped

½ pound cooked
corned beef, finely
chopped

2 teaspoons finely
chopped onions

1 tablespoon ketchup

2 teaspoons spicy
brown mustard

1 cup grated Swiss
cheese

Rye crackers for
serving

*P*reheat oven to 375°. In a large bowl, combine the cream cheese, sour cream, sauerkraut, corned beef, onion, ketchup, mustard and Swiss cheese. Transfer to a 2-quart casserole and bake, covered, for 30 minutes or until bubbly around the edges. Remove cover and bake for 5 minutes more or until golden. Serve warm with rye crackers.

Yield: servings for 8-10

Caramel Butter Brie

½ cup butter

½ cup brown sugar

½ cup sugar

½ cup heavy cream

¼ teaspoon nutmeg

1 (12-ounce) wheel
Brie cheese

⅛ cup sliced and
toasted almonds

*P*reheat oven to 225°. Melt butter, brown sugar and sugar in a saucepan over very low heat until sugars are dissolved. Gradually add cream, beating until smooth. Add nutmeg and continue to cook until thickened and caramelized. Place Brie in a pie plate and pour the caramel over the top. Bake for 10 minutes or until Brie softens to desired consistency. Remove from oven and sprinkle with almonds. Let stand 5 minutes before serving.

Yield: 8 servings

This is a real winner! Terrific when served on baquette slices.

PARADISE CHEESE BALL

15 slices bacon, cooked and crumbled, divided

¾ cup finely chopped pecans, divided

⅓ cup chopped fresh parsley

1½ tablespoons poppy seeds

2 cups shredded Swiss cheese

2 cups shredded sharp Cheddar cheese

8 ounces cream cheese, softened

½ cup sour cream

½ cup chopped onion

1 (2-ounce) jar diced pimento, drained

2 tablespoons sweet pickle relish

Salt and pepper to taste

Crackers for serving

Combine ¾ of the bacon, ½ of the pecans, parsley and poppy seeds; set aside. Combine the remaining bacon and pecans with the rest of the ingredients. Chill for 20-30 minutes.

Shape cheese mixture into 3 balls and roll each in the reserved pecan mixture to coat. Wrap the rolls separately in waxed paper or plastic wrap. Refrigerate for three or more hours to firm. Serve with crackers.

Yield: servings for 10-12

SHRIMP MOUSSE

1 can condensed
   tomato soup
8 ounces cream
   cheese
2 tablespoons
   unflavored gelatin
1½ pounds cooked
   shrimp, peeled,
   deveined, finely
   minced
1 cup mayonnaise
¾ cup finely chopped
   celery
½ cup finely chopped
   yellow onion
½ cup finely chopped
   green pepper
1 teaspoon
   Worcestershire
   sauce
1 teaspoon lemon
   juice
Butter crackers for
   serving

*H*eat tomato soup and cream cheese in top of double boiler until cheese melts. Cool slightly. Stir in gelatin; mix well. Add shrimp, mayonnaise, celery, onion, pepper, Worcestershire and lemon juice; mix well. Pour into a well greased 1 quart mold. Cover and refrigerate at least 8 hours. Unmold onto platter and serve with crackers.

Yield: 6 cups

Lobster can be substituted for the shrimp. A shell or fish mold makes an attractive presentation.

Layered Sun-Dried Tomato and Pesto Spread

8 ounces cream cheese, softened

1 (4½-ounce) wheel Camembert or Brie, rind removed, softened

½ cup whipping cream

1¼ cups fresh basil, firmly packed

½ cup grated Parmesan cheese

½ cup fresh parsley, firmly packed

⅓ cup pine nuts

1-2 garlic cloves

3 tablespoons olive oil

1 (7½-ounce) jar sun-dried tomatoes, drained

Water crackers

Spray a loaf pan with non-stick cooking spray; line with waxed paper, smoothing paper flat against side and bottom. Leave extra paper hanging over the sides.

Beat the two cheeses together until smooth. In a small bowl, whip the cream until soft peaks form. Gently fold the whipped cream into the cheese mixture and refrigerate until ready to use.

In a food processor or blender, combine the basil, Parmesan, parsley, pine nuts and garlic. Process until a paste forms. Gradually add oil and process to the consistency of soft butter. Remove from processor and set aside.

Wipe processor bowl and add sun-dried tomatoes. Process until smooth. Layer one half of the cheese mixture in the loaf pan and smooth with a spatula. Top first layer with one half of the basil mixture followed by all the tomatoes. Top tomato layer with remaining pesto followed by the remaining cheese. Be certain to spread all layers into the corners to keep an even shape. Cover pan with plastic wrap and refrigerate 4 hours or overnight.

To serve, invert pan onto serving platter and gently peel off waxed paper. Serve with water crackers.

Yield: servings for 20

If desired, sprinkle parsley on top of loaf for decoration.

PEPPERCORN SPREAD

16 ounces cream cheese, softened
½ pound blue cheese
½ cup butter
2 tablespoons limeade concentrate (optional)
2 tablespoons honey
¼ ground red pepper
¾ cup toasted chopped walnuts
1½ teaspoons chopped fresh basil
1½ teaspoons chopped fresh dill
red, green, and black peppercorns to cover (approximately 3 tablespoons each)

$\mathcal{C}$ombine all ingredients except peppercorns. Form into desired shape and roll in peppercorns to cover. Chill one hour and serve.

Yield: servings for 10-12

CRABMEAT IMPERIAL ON MELBA ROUNDS

½ teaspoon sugar
2 tablespoons lemon juice
2 tablespoons sherry
2 rounded tablespoons mayonnaise
1 pound backfin blue crab crabmeat
Melba rounds for serving
Green olives or pimentos for garnish

$\mathcal{P}$reheat broiler. Dissolve sugar in lemon juice. Add sherry and mayonnaise and mix well. Gently add crabmeat until evenly distributed. Place in a shallow baking dish and broil until bubbly and slightly brown. Spoon onto melba rounds and garnish with green olives or pimentos.

Yield: servings for 4-6

CRAB STUFFED MUSHROOMS

3 tablespoons butter
   or margarine
10-12 large mushrooms
6 ounces fresh
   crabmeat
Minced garlic to taste
½ Fresh lemon,
   squeezed
⅛ cup white wine
9-11 slices Monterey
   jack cheese
Fresh parsley and
   fresh lemon for
   garnish

*P*reheat oven to 350°. Remove one whole mushroom and finely chop. Remove stems from the remaining mushrooms and discard. In a small saucepan, sauté the cut up mushroom in butter or margarine. Add crab, garlic, lemon and wine. Cook on very low heat for 10-15 minutes or until liquid is absorbed. Stuff mushrooms with crabmeat mixture and top with one cheese slice each. Bake for 10 minutes or until cheese is melted and mushrooms are cooked. Garnish with fresh parsley and fresh lemon.

Yield: 10-12 mushrooms

WHITE CHEDDAR ROLLUPS

½ pound sharp white
   Cheddar cheese,
   finely grated
1 tablespoon Dijon
   style mustard
3 tablespoons
   mayonnaise
1 teaspoon butter,
   softened and 2
   tablespoons butter,
   melted
2 teaspoons
   Worcestershire
   sauce
18 slices very thin
   bread

*R*emove crust from bread. On a damp towel, roll out each slice and place in plastic bag to keep from drying out. Add mustard, mayonnaise, softened butter and Worchestershire to grated cheese; mix well.

Working with one slice of bread at a time, spread with cheese filling, roll up and cut into thirds. Quickly roll each piece in a pan with the melted butter, securing with a toothpick if necessary. Freeze in air tight container.

Preheat oven to 400°. Bake, frozen, on a baking sheet until light brown. Turn heat off and leave in oven 5 minutes longer.

Yield: 54 pieces

CHEDDAR ARTICHOKE CRESCENTS

1 package frozen puff
  pastry
½ cup mayonnaise
¾ cup grated Cheddar
  cheese
⅛ teaspoon onion salt
1 teaspoon dried dill
  weed or 3 teaspoons
  fresh minced dill
⅛ teaspoon lemon
  pepper
1 (6-ounce) jar
  artichoke hearts,
  drained
1 egg white, slightly
  beaten
½ cup flour for rolling
  and dipping

*T*haw puff pastry according to package directions. Preheat oven to 375°. Combine mayonnaise, Cheddar cheese, onion salt, dill weed and lemon pepper; chill. Cut each artichoke heart into six pieces. Roll out dough as thinly as possible on a lightly floured surface and cut into 24 pieces. Place one piece of artichoke on each piece of dough. Top each artichoke with ½ teaspoon mayonnaise mixture. Fold dough over filling, seal and dip in flour. Shape into crescent shaped tarts. Brush with egg white and bake for 12-15 minutes.

Yield: 24 pieces

CHEESE AND ONION ROLLS

3 tablespoons butter
  or margarine
½ cup melted butter,
  divided
3 large white onions,
  thinly sliced
8 ounces cream
  cheese, softened
1½ cups Swiss cheese,
  grated
½ teaspoon caraway
  seeds
1 package phyllo
  sheets

*S*auté onions in 3 tablespoons butter until limp. Remove from heat and combine with cream cheese, Swiss cheese and caraway seeds. Stack 2-3 sheets Fillo dough, brushing each layer lightly with melted butter. Spread ¼ of the onion cheese mixture on stacked sheets. Roll to enclose onion cheese mixture and place seam side down on baking sheet. Repeat steps, preparing three rolls. Brush each roll with melted butter. Place rolls in refrigerator and let chill for 30 minutes.

Preheat oven to 400°. Remove rolls from refrigerator and cut into 1 inch slices. Bake for 12 minutes or until browned.

Yield: 15 pieces

SNAPPY SUNSHINE SALSA

10 pounds tomatoes (approximately 5 quarts), (use a meatier tomato such as Romano, a few green tomatoes may be used)

2 large onions

1 large green pepper

½ cup white vinegar

2 teaspoons canning salt (use up to 2 tablespoons to taste)

½ tablespoon cumin

½ tablespoon coriander

1 tablespoon oregano

2-8 jalapeño peppers (to taste)

1 red pepper

Chili peppers, optional

1 garlic clove, minced optional

*B*lanch and peel tomatoes. Cut tomatoes into small pieces and add to 10 quart stew pot. Add vinegar and cook on medium low heat. Dice onions and peppers and add to pot. Slowly add remaining ingredients. Bring to a boil for 5 minutes. Reduce heat and simmer to desired thickness (approximately 1 hour; depends on juice of tomatoes). Refrigerate until ready to serve.

Yield: 3 quarts

Nutrition Analysis per tablespoon:

saturated fat -	0 g	sodium -	49.4 mg
calories -	6	fiber -	0.4 g
fat -	0	cholesterol -	0 mg
carbohydrate -	1.3 g	sugar -	0.8 g

This delicious salsa is best when made one day ahead. It also freezes well.

SWEET BACON WRAPS

1 pound bacon

1 box butter crackers

½-¾ cup brown sugar

*P*reheat oven to 350°. Cut bacon slices in half; wrap each around a cracker and overlap ends. Sprinkle well with brown sugar. Place on a broiler rack, seam side down, over a drip pan. Bake for 20-25 minutes. Best when served warm but may be served at room temperature.

Yield: 30 pieces

HERBED SPINACH BALLS

2 (10-ounce) packages frozen chopped spinach, drained

2 cups herbed stuffing mix, finely crumbled

¾ cup grated Parmesan cheese

¼ teaspoon nutmeg

1 teaspoon finely chopped garlic

1 medium onion, finely chopped

3 eggs, beaten

½ cup melted butter

Thaw spinach and squeeze excess liquid. Preheat oven to 325°. Mix well with remaining ingredients. Form into small bite size balls and place on a baking sheet. Bake for 15 minutes.

Yield: 80 pieces

To freeze: cool spinach balls and place in air tight plastic bags; freeze. To serve, thaw in refrigerator, bring to room temperature and heat in oven or microwave until warmed through.

ORIENTAL CHICKEN WINGS

24 chicken wings, cut in half

5 ounces soy sauce

1 teaspoon dry mustard

4 tablespoons brown sugar

½ teaspoon garlic powder

Combine soy sauce, mustard, brown sugar and garlic powder. Add chicken wings and marinate, refrigerated, over-night, turning chicken a few times.

Preheat oven to 375°. Remove chicken from marinade and place in shallow baking pan. Bake, covered, for 30 minutes. Uncover, turn chicken and bake 30 minutes longer, uncovered.

Yield: 48 pieces

FRESH LEMONADE

SYRUP BASE
1 tablespoon fresh, grated lemon rind
1½ cups sugar
½ cup boiling water
1½ cups fresh squeezed lemon juice

LEMONADE
2⅔ cups lemonade syrup base
5 cups cold water

*C*ombine lemon rind, sugar and boiling water in a jar. Cover and shake until sugar dissolves. Add lemon juice. Store tightly covered in refrigerator. Makes 2⅔ cups syrup base.

To make lemonade, combine syrup with cold water in a large pitcher and stir. Makes 1¾ quarts.

SEASIDE MIST

1 cup pineapple juice
1 banana, broken into 4 pieces
1 teaspoon lemon juice
2 teaspoons sugar
1½ cups crushed ice

*C*ombine all ingredients in a blender or food processor until well blended.

Yield: 2 servings

Nutrition Analysis per serving:

saturated fat -	0	sodium -	44.5 mg
calories -	138	fiber -	0.8 g
fat -	0.2 g	cholesterol -	0
carbohydrate -	25.8 g	sugar -	22.1 g

PINEAPPLE SMOOTHIE

¾ cup orange juice
1 (8-ounce) can crushed pineapple, undrained
2 medium bananas
2 teaspoons sugar
1 cup crushed ice
1 (8-ounce) carton plain yogurt

Combine all ingredients except yogurt in blender or food processor and process until smooth. Add yogurt and process until blended.

Yield: 4 servings

Nutrition Analysis per serving:

saturated fat -	0	sodium -	45.4 mg
calories -	150	cholesterol -	0
fat -	0.6 g	fiber -	0.8 g
carbohydrate -	34.4 g	sugar -	27.2 g

Start a great day with this nutritious drink!

FROSTED ORANGE DRINK

1 (6-ounce) can frozen orange juice
1 cup water
1 cup milk
½ cup sugar
¼-½ teaspoon vanilla extract
Ice

Combine all ingredients in a blender. Fill rest of blender with ice cubes. Blend until ice is crushed and drink is frothy.

Yield: 6 servings

This refreshing drink will bring back childhood memories of orange cream pops.

MANGO FROZEN DAIQUIRIS

2 cups ripe mango, peeled and cubed
2 tablespoons freshly squeezed lime juice
3 cups ice cubes
½ cup light rum
2 tablespoons sugar

Combine all ingredients in a blender. Blend until smooth.

Yield: 4 servings

Nutrition Analysis per serving:

saturated fat -	0.1 g	sodium -	2 g
calories -	158	cholesterol -	0
fat -	0.3 g	fiber -	0.8 g
carbohydrate -	24.6 g	sugar -	9.9 g

SUSTAINER SLUSH

1½-3½ cups bourbon whiskey (as desired)
1 (12-ounce) can frozen lemonade concentrate
2 tablespoons frozen orange juice concentrate
4½ cups water
Mint sprigs or maraschino cherries for garnish

*I*n a blender or food processor, combine the bourbon, lemonade and orange juice concentrates and water. Place in the freezer for 1 to 3 hours until the mixture freezes. Just before serving, mix in the blender or food processor until slushy. Pour into cocktail glasses. Add a sprig of mint and cherry to garnish.

Yield: 6-8 servings

*This popular recipe is featured in **The Junior League Centennial Cookbook**.*

RUBY FRUIT SANGRIA

750ml. dry red wine
1 ripe pear, unpeeled and cored, cut into ¼ inch slices
1 orange, unpeeled, sliced into ¼ inch rounds
1 cup green grapes, halved
3 tablespoons brandy
2 tablespoons sugar

*P*our wine into a large punch bowl. Stir fruit into wine along with brandy and sugar. Let sit at room temperature for at least one hour to allow flavors to mingle.

Yield: 8 servings

Nutrition Analysis per serving:

saturated fat -	0	carbohydrate -	19.1 g
calories -	115	cholesterol -	0
fat -	0.1 g	fiber -	1.0 g
sodium -	102.1 mg	sugar -	9.9 g

STRAWBERRY DAIQUIRI PUNCH

6 cups fresh strawberries, stems and caps removed (or 6 cups frozen unsweetened strawberries, undrained)

1 (6-ounce) can frozen limeade concentrate

¾ cup light rum (or unsweetened pineapple juice)

1 (16-ounce) bottle lemon-lime soda

2 cups ice cubes

*P*lace strawberries, half at a time, in blender or food processor. Cover and blend until smooth. Transfer blended berries to large non-metallic pitcher. Stir in limeade concentrate and rum or pineapple juice. Cover and chill until serving time.

Just before serving, stir in lemon-lime soda and ice. Garnish with whole berries, if desired.

Yield: 8-12 servings

CRANBERRY CINNAMON PUNCH

2 cups water

1½ cups sugar

4 cinnamon sticks

3 cups cranberry juice

2½-3 cups orange juice

1 cup lemon juice

42 ounces lemon-lime soda

Ice

Lemon, lime or orange slices for garnish

*S*immer water, sugar and cinnamon sticks over medium heat for 15 minutes. Set aside for several hours or overnight. Chill fruit juices and lemon-lime soda. At serving time, combine sugar syrup and fruit juices in a punch bowl. Slowly add lemon-lime soda. Add ice and garnish with lemon, lime or orange slices.

Yield: 30 servings

Nutrition Analysis per serving:

saturated fat -	0	sodium -	6.7 mg
calories -	87	cholesterol -	0
fat -	0	fiber -	0
carbohydrate -	20.8 g	sugar -	20.2 g

TROPICAL CHAMPAGNE PUNCH

2 cups cranberry juice
2 cups orange juice
¼ cup lemon juice
½ cup sugar
1½ cups white wine, chilled
1 bottle champagne, chilled
Orange slices for garnish

Combine juices and sugar. Stir until sugar is dissolved. Just before serving, add remaining ingredients and garnish with orange slices.

Yield: 18 servings

Nutrition Analysis per serving:

saturated fat -	0	sodium -	4.3 mg
calories -	92	cholesterol -	0
fat -	0	fiber -	0
carbohydrate -	13.3 g	sugar -	12.8 g

SUNRISE COFFEE PUNCH

4 quarts strong coffee, preferably chicory
1 quart whipping cream
5 tablespoons sugar
5 teaspoons vanilla
2 quarts vanilla ice cream

Early in the day or the day before, make coffee and refrigerate until chilled. Just before serving, whip cream, adding sugar and vanilla. Spoon or slice ice cream into large punch bowl. Add whipped cream. Pour cold coffee over and mix well. Serve in punch cups.

Yield: 50 servings

A wonderful brunch punch!

CHOCOLATE COFFEE ROYALE

½ cup vanilla ice cream
1-2 tablespoons coffee flavored liqueur
1-2 tablespoons Creme de Cacao
½ cup hot strong coffee
2 tablespoons whipped cream
¼ teaspoon shaved chocolate

Place ice cream in large 8-12 ounce tempered glass. Pour liqueurs over ice cream. Carefully and slowly pour coffee over ice cream. Top with whipped cream and sprinkle with shaved chocolate.

Yield: 1 serving

The perfect ending to a special meal; doubles as dessert and after dinner coffee.

Banana Zinger

1 very ripe banana
½ cup banana liqueur
¼ cup white Creme de Cacao
½ cup half and half
2 cups banana ice cream (may substitute vanilla)
3 ice cubes
Sliced bananas for garnish
Nutmeg for garnish

Combine all ingredients in a blender or food processor until smooth. Garnish as desired.

Yield: 4 servings

Can be made ahead and kept in refrigerator. Transfer to freezer about ½ hour before serving.

Toasted Almond

1 cup Kahlua
1 pint vanilla ice cream
1 cup half and half
⅛ teaspoon almond extract
Ice cubes

Combine Kahlua, ice cream, half and half and almond extract in blender. Add enough ice cubes to bring mixture to 6 cup level. Process until frothy and serve immediately.

Yield: 6 servings

Mocha Cream Liqueur

1 (14-ounce) can sweetened condensed milk
2 cups light cream
1 tablespoon instant coffee crystals
1 beaten egg yolk
1 cup Irish whiskey
½ cup coffee liqueur (Kahlua, Tia Maria)
3 tablespoons chocolate syrup

Combine first three ingredients in a heavy 1 quart saucepan. Cook and stir over medium heat until crystals are dissolved. Gradually stir ½ hot mixture into egg yolk; return all the mixture to saucepan. Bring to boiling. Cook and stir 2 minutes more. Remove pan from heat. Stir in whiskey, liqueur and syrup. Cool mixture and pour into container with airtight lid. Store in refrigerator up to 2 months.

Yield: 10 servings

Serve as an after dinner drink or over ice cream. Makes a nice holiday gift.

SPICED CRANBERRY TEA

¼ teaspoon nutmeg
¼ teaspoon cinnamon
¼ teaspoon allspice
4 tea bags
2½ cups boiling water
¾ cup sugar
1½ cups cold water
2½ cups orange juice
¼ cup lemon juice
1 quart cranberry
   juice cocktail

*P*lace spices and tea bags into boiling water. Cover and let steep 7 minutes; remove teabags. Add sugar; stir, cover and cool. Strain cooled mixture and combine with cold water, orange juice, lemon juice and cranberry juice cocktail. Chill for 24 hours.

Yield: 16 servings

MINT TEA

3 lemons
¾ cup sugar
20 mint sprigs
18 cups water, divided
10 tea bags
Ice

*J*uice the lemons and strain the juice. Boil the lemon juice, sugar, mint sprigs and 8 cups water for 10 minutes. Combine the tea bags and remaining 10 cups of water and boil for 3 minutes. Combine both boiled mixtures and cool. Serve over ice.

Yield: 10-12 servings

Breads
&
Brunch

PARTY PARADISE

*E*ntertaining is a way of life in the paradise of South Florida. The mild climate invites year-round cookouts and lawn parties. The catch of the day is invariably a reason for neighbors to gather around the barbecue at sunset. Visiting northerners are always a reason to celebrate.

Then, there is the "season." Beginning in November and ending in May, the season is a time when seasonal residents return to South Florida. The season brings an endless array of social activities and charitable galas. Private dinner parties may mean a jeweled pill box as a favor to all guests. Extravagant galas may have a formal structure or entertainment as lively as trapeze artists swinging from the ceilings. Whether held in an oceanside home or the exclusive club at Mar-a-Lago, parties in the Palm Beaches are unparalleled.

KEY LIME DANISH

PASTRY

6¼-6¾ cups all-
  purpose flour
1 cup granulated
  sugar, divided
2 packages active dry
  yeast
1½ teaspoons salt
1 cup water
1 cup milk
½ cup butter or
  margarine
1 egg

FILLING

8 ounces cream
  cheese, softened
½ teaspoon finely
  shredded lime peel
  (use Key limes
  when available)
3 tablespoons lime
  juice, divided (use
  Key limes when
  available)
½ cup sifted
  confectioners' sugar
1 teaspoon butter or
  margarine, melted

Combine 2 cups of flour, ½ cup granulated sugar, yeast and salt; set aside. In a saucepan, combine water, milk and butter or margarine. Heat, stirring, until warm and butter is nearly melted. Add to flour mixture. Add egg and beat for 30 seconds; scrape sides of bowl. Beat for 3 minutes longer. Stir in as much remaining flour as possible.

Turn dough onto a lightly floured surface. Knead in more flour to make a moderately stiff dough that is elastic (knead 6-8 minutes total). Shape dough into a ball and place in a greased bowl. Cover and let rise in a warm place until double (about 1 hour). Punch dough down and turn onto a floured surface. Divide in half. Cover and let rest for 10 minutes.

Meanwhile, combine cream cheese, lime peel, 2 tablespoons lime juice and ½ cup granulated sugar; set aside. In a separate bowl, combine confectioners' sugar, 1 tablespoon lime juice and 1 teaspoon butter or margarine; set aside.

Preheat oven to 375°. On a floured surface, roll each dough half into a 9 x 14 inch rectangle. Spread lightly with ¼ of the cream cheese mixture. Roll up from a long side and seal seams. Cut into 12 slices and arrange them 2 inches apart on a lightly greased baking sheet. Make an indentation on the top of each danish and fill with one teaspoon of the cream cheese mixture. Repeat with the remaining dough. Bake for 18-20 minutes or until golden. Let danish stand for 2 minutes then top with confectioners' sugar mixture. Serve warm or reheated.

Yield: 24 danish

If pressed for time, try substituting 2 (8-ounce) tubes of refrigerated crescent roll dough for the pastry. Seal seams and press out as directed.

ORANGE ROLLS

ROLLS
- 1 tablespoon dry yeast, or 1 square yeast cake
- 1½ cups lukewarm milk, divided
- 3 tablespoons butter or margarine
- ⅓ cup sugar
- ½ teaspoon salt
- 3 eggs, beaten
- 4½ cups flour

ORANGE FILLING
- Grated rind of 2 oranges
- 1 cup sugar
- ½ cup butter or margarine, softened

Add yeast to ½ cup of milk. Stir until dissolved. Beat with butter or margarine, sugar and salt. Add to well-beaten eggs and remaining milk. Add 2 cups of the flour and beat 2 minutes with beater at low speed. Let rise 2 hours or less (until bubbles form on top). Add remaining 2½ cups flour and mix well with spoon. Let rise 2 hours or less until double in bulk.

Mix together filling ingredients. Spoon one-half of dough onto a well-floured board. Roll into a large rectangle and spread with ½ of the orange filling. Roll up jelly roll fashion and fasten edges by pinching together. Cut in 1 inch slices and put in greased muffin tins. Repeat with other half of dough. Let rise in muffin tins in a warm place for 30 minutes or less. Preheat oven to 350°. Bake for 20-25 minutes or until golden.

Yield: 24 rolls

Try saving enough filling to put on top of rolls before baking (½ teaspoon on each). It makes them look as mouth watering as they taste!

Strawberry Orange Muffins

2 ¼ cups all purpose flour

2 teaspoons baking powder

1 teaspoon baking soda

½ teaspoon salt

¾ cup sugar

½ cup milk

½ cup sour cream

⅓ cup vegetable oil

1 egg

1 tablespoon orange zest

1 cup thinly sliced fresh strawberries

⅓ cup strawberry jam

*B*utter standard muffin tins. In a large bowl, stir the flour, baking powder, baking soda and salt; set aside. In a medium bowl whisk together the sugar, milk, sour cream, oil, egg and orange zest until mixed; stir in strawberries. Add to the combined dry ingredients and stir just until blended.

Preheat oven to 400°. Place a spoonful of batter in each prepared muffin tin. Top each with a scant teaspoon of strawberry jam. Spoon the remaining batter over the jam, filling each cup about ⅔ full. Bake until a toothpick inserted in the center comes out clean; 15-18 minutes. Cool in the tins for 5 minutes, then remove.

Yield: 16 muffins

Fantastic muffins! Good enough to wake up early for!

Caraway Soda Bread

2½ cups all-purpose flour

½ cup sugar

1½ teaspoons baking powder

¾ teaspoon salt

½ teaspoon baking soda

½ cup unsalted butter

1 cup raisins

1 tablespoon caraway seeds

1 large egg

1¼ cups buttermilk

¼ cup sour cream

*B*utter a 9-inch round cake pan. Preheat oven to 350°. Sift together the dry ingredients. Using a food processor with the steel blade or a pastry cutter, cut the butter into the flour mixture until it resembles small peas. Blend in the raisins and the caraway seeds. Beat the egg, buttermilk, and sour cream together until blended. Stir the egg mixture into the dry mixture just until blended. Transfer the batter to the pan and bake for 50 to 55 minutes, until a toothpick inserted in the center comes out clean.

Yield: 1 round loaf

BLUEBERRY ORANGE MUFFINS

2½ cups all-purpose flour

1 cup granulated sugar

2 teaspoons baking powder

1 teaspoon baking soda

½ teaspoon salt

½ cup margarine

¾ cup plain yogurt

1 small orange, peeled, seeded and finely chopped (discard excess juice)

2 teaspoons grated orange peel

2 large eggs, beaten

1½ cups fresh or frozen blueberries

*P*reheat oven to 350°. In a large bowl, combine flour, sugar, baking powder, baking soda and salt. Cut in margarine until mixture resembles fine crumbs. In a small bowl, combine yogurt, chopped orange and orange zest until blended. Stir in eggs. Make well in center of flour mixture. Pour in egg mixture and stir gently until lightly combined; fold in blueberries. Spoon batter evenly into prepared muffin cups, filling ⅔ full. Bake for 20 to 25 minutes, or until light brown.

Yield: 16 muffins

Nutrition Analysis per muffin:

saturated fat -	0	sodium -	327 mg
calories -	199	fiber -	1 g
fat -	5.0 g	cholesterol -	36 mg
carbohydrate -	34 g		

Florida Orange Bread

5 tablespoons butter
½ cup sugar
1 egg, beaten
2 tablespoons grated orange rind
1 cup orange juice
2 cups flour
4 teaspoons baking powder
½ teaspoon salt

*C*ream butter and gradually add sugar. Add the beaten egg and grated orange rind. In a separate bowl, sift together the flour, baking powder and salt. Add the orange juice and flour mixture alternately to the butter mixture. Mix thoroughly and put in a greased 4½ x 8½ loaf pan. Let stand 20 minutes before baking. Preheat oven to 350°. Bake for 55-60 minutes.

Yield: 10 slices

Nutrition Analysis per slice:

saturated fat -	4.1 g	sodium -	361.4 mg
calories -	220	fiber -	0.8 g
fat -	7.5 g	cholesterol -	71.3 mg
carbohydrate -	33.9 g	sugar -	12.3 g

Not too sweet. Very good served with dinner. Best when made with fresh Florida orange juice (see page 276 for ordering information).

Mango Nut Bread

1¾ cups all-purpose flour
2 teaspoons baking powder
¼ teaspoon baking soda
½ teaspoon salt
⅓ cup shortening
⅔ cup granulated sugar
2 eggs
1 cup ripe, mashed mangos
½ cup chopped pecans
½ cup raisins

*P*reheat oven to 350°. Sift flour, baking powder, baking soda and salt; set aside. Beat shortening and sugar with mixer at medium speed or by hand until creamed. Add eggs and beat until light and fluffy. Blend in flour mixture alternately with mangos, just until smooth. Add nuts and raisins and turn into a greased loaf pan. Bake for 1 hour. Cool in pan 10 minutes and remove. Cool completely before slicing.

Yield: 1 loaf

KEY LIME BREAD

⅔ cup melted margarine

2 cups sugar

4 eggs

1 teaspoon vanilla

3 Key limes, grated rind only

3 cups all-purpose flour

1 teaspoon salt

2½ teaspoons baking powder

1 cup milk

6 Key limes, juice only, divided

1 cup chopped pecans

⅔ cup confectioners sugar

Preheat oven to 350°. Blend margarine and sugar. Add eggs one at a time and beat after each one. Stir in vanilla and lime rind. Combine all dry ingredients, except confectioners sugar and add alternately with milk. Add one-half of the lime juice and nuts; stir well. Bake in two greased 8 or 9 inch loaf pans for 50-60 minutes. Cool until just warm and glaze with remaining key lime juice and confectioners sugar mixed together. Cool completely, then remove from pans. Do not slice for 24 hours.

Yield: 2 loaves

Freezes well. Nice tropical bread for brunch or afternoon tea.

TOASTED COCONUT BREAD

1 cup toasted coconut

1 cup milk

1 egg, beaten

¼ cup oil

1 teaspoon vanilla

2 cups all-purpose flour

1 tablespoon baking powder

½ teaspoon salt

¾ cup sugar

Preheat oven to 350°. In a large bowl, mix milk, egg, oil and vanilla. Add coconut, flour, baking powder, salt and sugar; stir until blended. Pour into a greased and floured 9 x 5 inch loaf pan. Bake for 1 hour. Cool on a rack.

Yield: 1 loaf

To toast coconut, spread on baking sheet and toast in a 350° oven for 10 minutes or until lightly brown.

APPLEANNA BREAD

½ cup plus 1 tablespoon shortening

1½ cups granulated sugar

2 large eggs, room temperature, slightly beaten

2 cups all-purpose flour

1 teaspoon baking soda

1 teaspoon baking powder

1 teaspoon ground cinnamon

1 teaspoon salt

2 ripe bananas, mashed

2 cups apples, peeled, cored, and finely chopped (or 2 cups chunky applesauce)

1 teaspoon vanilla

*W*ith 1 tablespoon shortening, grease and flour a 9" loaf pan. Preheat oven to 350°. Cream together ½ cup shortening and sugar until light and fluffy; add eggs. Sift together flour, baking soda, baking powder, cinnamon and salt; beat together with shortening mixture. Stir in mashed bananas, apples and vanilla. Pour the batter into prepared pan and bake for 1 hour, or until a knife inserted in the center comes out clean.

Yield: 10 slices

Nutrition Analysis per slice:

saturated fat -	3.1 g	sodium -	383.3 mg
calories -	362	fiber -	1.6 g
fat -	12.4 g	cholesterol -	54.8 mg
carbohydrate -	58.7 g	sugar -	36.3 g

TROPICAL LOAF

2 cups all-purpose flour
¾ cup sugar
1 teaspoon baking powder
1 teaspoon baking soda
½ teaspoon salt
1 egg
¼ cup vegetable oil
1 teaspoon vanilla
1 cup mashed, ripe bananas
1 cup crushed pineapple, undrained
1 cup chopped dates (optional)
½ cup chopped macadamia nuts or pecans

Preheat oven to 350°. In a large bowl, thoroughly stir together the flour, sugar, baking powder, baking soda, and salt. Beat egg in a small bowl; add oil, vanilla, banana and pineapple. Mix well. Add to dry ingredients until well moistened. Fold in dates and nuts. Pour batter into greased loaf pan. Bake for 1 hour or until toothpick inserted in the middle comes out clean (may also use a 9 x 9 cake pan, baking for 35-45 minutes). Cool in pan for 10 minutes; remove from pan and cool on wire rack.

Yield: 10 slices

Nutrition Analysis per slice:

saturated fat -	1.1 g	sodium -	261.6 mg
calories -	325	fiber -	2.2 g
fat -	8.8 g	cholesterol -	27.4 mg
carbohydrate -	57.2 g	sugar -	34.2 g

A "paradise" breakfast bread; perfect to eat while sipping morning coffee on a breezy terrace.

SWEET WALNUT BREAD

1 cup softened butter or margarine
2 cups sugar
4 eggs
4 cups all-purpose flour
½ teaspoon salt
2 teaspoons baking soda
1½ cups chopped walnuts
2 teaspoons vanilla
2 cups sour cream

Preheat oven to 350°. Cream butter or margarine and sugar until fully blended and fluffy. Slowly beat in eggs. Sift flour, salt and baking soda and add to egg mixture. Blend in nuts, vanilla and sour cream. Pour batter into two greased and floured 9 x 5 loaf pans. Bake for 45 minutes to 1 hour. Cool in pans 10 minutes, then invert on wire racks.

Yield: 2 loaves

This bread is delightful toasted and spread with butter or cream cheese.

STREUSEL COFFEE CAKE

CAKE
¾ cup margarine
1½ cups sugar
1½ teaspoons vanilla
3 eggs
1½ teaspoons baking powder
1½ teaspoons baking soda
1½ teaspoons salt
3 cups flour
1 pint sour cream

TOPPING
½ cup packed brown sugar
1 teaspoon cinnamon
½ cup chopped pecans

GLAZE
½ cup confectioners' sugar
1 tablespoon milk
1 tablespoon water

*P*reheat oven to 325°. Combine all cake ingredients except sour cream. Beat well and add sour cream. Pour ½ of the batter into a greased and floured bundt or tube pan. Mix topping ingredients and sprinkle on batter. Pour remaining batter into pan and bake for 1 hour. Invert pan onto serving plate and let cool. Mix glaze ingredients together and drizzle over cake.

Yield: 10-12 slices

CREAMY CARAMEL-PECAN ROLLS

1¼ cups sifted
confectioners' sugar

½ cup whipping
cream

1 cup coarsely
chopped pecans

2 (14-16 ounce)
loaves frozen white
or sweet bread
dough, thawed

3 tablespoons melted
butter or margarine

½ cup packed brown
sugar

1 tablespoon
cinnamon

¾ cup light or dark
raisins (optional)

*I*n a small bowl, stir together confectioners' sugar and whipping cream. Divide evenly between two 9 x 1½ inch round cake pans. Sprinkle pecans over topping mixture.

On a lightly floured surface, roll each loaf of dough into a 12 x 8 inch rectangle. Brush with melted margarine or butter. In a small mixing bowl, stir together brown sugar and cinnamon; sprinkle over dough. If desired, top with raisins. Roll up rectangles, jelly-roll style, starting from the long side. Pinch to seal. Cut each into 10 to 12 slices. Place rolls, cut side down, on top of topping mixture. Cover and let rise in a warm place until nearly doubled in size, approximately 30 minutes. (Or cover with oiled waxed paper, then with plastic wrap. Refrigerate 2 to 24 hours. Before baking, let chilled rolls stand, covered, 20 minutes at room temperature. Puncture any surface bubbles with a greased toothpick.)

Preheat oven to 375°. Bake, uncovered, until golden, allowing 20 to 25 minutes for unchilled rolls and 25 to 30 minutes for chilled rolls. If necessary, cover rolls with foil the last 10 minutes to prevent overbrowning. Cool in pans 5 minutes on wire rack. Invert onto a serving platter. Serve warm.

Yield: 20-24 rolls

For 8 Jumbo Creamy Caramel-Pecan Rolls: Prepare as directed, except use a 12 inch deep dish pizza pan or a 13 x 9 baking pan. Roll up each rectangle from the short sides; cut each into 4 slices. Let rise as directed. Bake, uncovered, in a 375° oven, allowing 25 to 30 minutes for unchilled and 30 to 35 minutes for chilled rolls. If necessary, cover with foil the last 10 minutes of baking. Cool. Invert onto serving platter.

Overnight Refrigerator Rolls

1 quart milk
1 cup sugar plus 1 tablespoon, divided
1 cup shortening
3 packages dry yeast
¼ cup warm water
12 cups all-purpose flour, divided
1 teaspoon baking soda
5 teaspoons baking powder
1 tablespoon salt
Vegetable oil for bowl preparation
Non-stick cooking spray

*B*ring milk to a boil and stir in 1 cup of sugar. Let cool until lukewarm. Meanwhile, melt shortening and set aside to cool to room temperature.

Dissolve yeast in the warm water. Add 1 tablespoon of sugar and stir. Pour into a large bowl and stir in the lukewarm milk mixture. Mix in four cups of flour and let stand for ½ hour.

Combine baking soda, baking powder and salt; add to the dough and stir in room temperature shortening. Gradually add six cups of flour. Knead, adding additional flour to make a soft dough (2 cups). Place dough in a large bowl oiled with vegetable oil. Cover tightly and place in the refrigerator overnight. Dough may be frozen at this point.

On the second day, take ¼ of the dough and divide it into 12 pieces. Separate one piece into two or three small pieces and form them into balls. Place the two or three small balls of dough in one cup of a muffin tin sprayed with non-stick cooking spray. Repeat with the other 11 pieces of dough. Cover and let rise (approximately one hour). Preheat oven to 350°. Bake for 20 minutes or until golden brown on top. Cool for 1 minute then remove from tin and serve. Repeat for remaining dough.

Yield: 42–48 rolls

This wonderful tasting hearty bread is a great do-ahead for entertaining a crowd.

Caramel Cinnamon Rolls

Overnight Refrigerator Roll Dough (on the second day, unbaked)*

1 cup heavy cream

1½ cups butter plus 9 tablespoons melted butter, divided

3 cups firmly packed light brown sugar, divided

6 tablespoons light corn syrup, divided

Melted butter to taste

Cinnamon to taste

Light brown sugar to taste

Divide the dough into thirds. Roll one third into a rectangle and spread it with 3 tablespoons melted butter, cinnamon and brown sugar to taste. Roll the dough up, jelly roll fashion, pressing the edges to seal. Slice the dough into 12 pieces and set aside.

Combine ⅓ cup heavy cream, ½ cup butter, 1 cup brown sugar and 2 tablespoons corn syrup in a small saucepan and cook over medium heat, stirring until smooth. Turn into a 13 x 9 inch pan. Place the sliced dough side by side in the pan; cover and let rise (approximately 1 hour). Preheat oven to 350°. Bake for 30 minutes or until golden brown. Cool for 1 minute then turn onto a cooling rack. Repeat for remaining two thirds of dough.

Yield: 36 rolls

See page 47 for Overnight Refrigerator Roll Dough recipe.

Focaccia

1 (14-16 ounce) loaf frozen white bread dough, thawed

2 tablespoons olive oil

4 garlic cloves, peeled and finely chopped

½ cup finely chopped onion

⅔ cup freshly grated Parmesan cheese

3 tablespoons fresh rosemary or basil, finely chopped

Roll or press dough into a 14 inch circle (you may have to allow the dough to rest during the rolling to get it to specified diameter.) Set on a greased cookie sheet or pizza pan. Brush the oil over the dough surface, then sprinkle on the remaining ingredients in the order given. Allow to rise, uncovered, for 30 minutes. Preheat oven to 400°. Bake for 15 to 20 minutes. Cut in wedges or squares and serve warm or at room temperature.

Yield: 16 wedges

Nutrition Analysis per 2 wedge serving:

saturated fat -	2.3 g	sodium -	412.3 mg
calories -	253	fiber -	1.2 g
fat -	11.7 g	cholesterol -	5.3 mg
carbohydrate -	31.0 g	sugar -	5.6 g

For a crispier focaccia, skip or shorten the rising time. Terrific with pasta or grilled chicken or served as an appetizer.

CHEDDAR DILL BREAD

5 cups unsifted bread flour, divided

2 packages rapid-rising dry yeast

3 tablespoons sugar

1 tablespoon dill seeds

1 teaspoon salt

2 cups warm water (120° to 130°F)

1 (8-ounce) package shredded extra-sharp Cheddar cheese, divided

½ cup chopped fresh dill

*I*n large electric mixing bowl, combine 3 cups flour, yeast, sugar, dill seeds and salt. With mixer at medium speed, beat in water to form a sticky batter. Reserve ¼ cup cheese and beat remaining cheese and the dill into batter until well mixed (about 4 minutes). With dough hook or wooden spoon, stir in 1½ cups flour to form a soft dough. Cover bowl with clean cloth and let rise in warm place, away from drafts, until double in size (about 45 minutes). With rubber spatula, stir dough down and sprinkle with ¼ cup flour to coat top; turn out onto floured surface. Knead dough, adding as much of remaining flour as necessary to prevent sticking, until smooth and elastic (about 5 minutes). If more flour is needed to reach the desired consistency, add up to ¼ cup more. Divide dough and shape each half into a ball. Using shortening, lightly grease two 1½ quart casseroles or souffle dishes. Place dough in greased casseroles. Cover with clean cloth and let rise 25 minutes.

Preheat oven to 375°. Bake for 30 minutes. Sprinkle the tops with remaining ¼ cup cheese and bake 10 to 15 minutes longer or until well-browned and loaves sound hollow when tapped on top. Remove loaves from casseroles and cool on wire rack at least 20 minutes before slicing.

Yield: 16 slices

Nutrition Analysis per slice:

saturated fat -	3 g	sodium -	224 mg
calories -	212	fiber -	1.0 g
fat -	5 g	cholesterol -	15 mg
carbohydrate -	33 g	sugar -	3.1 g

Flecked with cheese and dill, this aromatic bread is wonderful served with soup or salad.

Blue Cheese Bubble Bread

1 loaf French bread
2 tablespoons softened butter
2 tablespoons garlic spread
1 tablespoon paprika, divided
2 tablespoons dried parsley or 4 tablespoons freshly chopped, divided
¼-½ cup gourmet blue cheese dressing
¼-½ cup freshly grated Parmesan cheese

Preheat oven to 350°. Cut loaf of bread lengthwise and butter lightly. Lightly spread garlic spread over butter. Sprinkle with half of the paprika and parsley. Bake until lightly browned (10-12 minutes). Remove from oven and preheat broiler. Spread blue cheese dressing over bread. Sprinkle with Parmesan cheese and remaining paprika and parsley. Place under broiler, watching carefully. Remove from broiler when topping bubbles. Serve warm.

Yield: 10 servings

The quantity of ingredients in this flavorful bread can be easily changed to your own preference.

Jalapeño Cornbread

2 eggs
⅔ cup cooking oil
1 cup sour cream
1 cup yellow cornmeal
1 (8-ounce) can yellow creamed corn
1 small onion, grated
1 tablespoon baking powder
1½ teaspoons salt
4 fresh jalapeños, seeded and finely chopped, or 4 green chilies, chopped
1 cup grated sharp Cheddar cheese, divided

Preheat oven to 425°. Combine eggs, oil, sour cream, cornmeal, creamed corn, onion, baking powder and salt. Add chopped peppers or chilies and half of cheese. Spread in well-greased 13 x 9 inch pan and top with remaining cheese. Bake for 20-25 minutes.

Yield: 10 servings

Wash hands thoroughly or use rubber gloves when handling fresh jalapeños!

Herbed Buttermilk Biscuits

5 cups flour

⅓ cup sugar

1 tablespoon baking powder

1 teaspoon baking soda

2 teaspoons salt

1 cup shortening

1 teaspoon dried oregano

½ teaspoon celery seed

1 teaspoon dried chives

2 teaspoons herbs de Provence

2 teaspoons dried thyme

2 teaspons parsley flakes

2 packages dry yeast

¼ cup warm water (110 degrees)

2 cups buttermilk

*C*ombine flour, sugar, baking powder, baking soda and salt. Cut in shortening until mixture resembles coarse meal. Add herbs and mix well. Dissolve yeast in warm water; stir into buttermilk. Add yeast and buttermilk mixture to flour mixture and stir until well blended. On a floured surface, knead dough just until it holds together. Roll dough to ½-inch thick and cut with a biscuit cutter. Place biscuits on greased baking sheet and cover. Let rise for 1 hour. Bake at 450 degrees for 10 minutes

Yield: 32 biscuits

Pecan French Toast

4 eggs

⅔ cup orange juice

⅓ cup milk

¼ cup sugar

¼ teaspoon ground nutmeg

¼ teaspoon vanilla extract

½ loaf Italian bread, cut into 8 1-inch slices

⅓ cup butter, melted

2 tablespoons orange peel

½ cup pecan pieces

Confectioners' sugar

Warm maple syrup

Beat eggs, orange juice, milk, sugar, nutmeg and vanilla together. Put bread with edges touching in a single layer in a 13 x 9 inch baking dish. Pour milk mixture over bread; cover and refrigerate overnight, turning once.

Preheat oven to 400°. Pour melted butter on a jelly roll pan and spread evenly. Sprinkle orange peel and pecans on butter. Place bread on top and bake for 20-25 minutes. Serve with confectioners' sugar and warm syrup.

Yield: 4 servings

This easy yet elegant toast makes a beautiful brunch plate when served with sausage links and melon wedges.

Zucchini Frittata

3 cups thawed frozen egg substitute

1 cup heavy cream

2 garlic cloves, minced

½ cup finely chopped shallots

1 cup freshly grated Parmesan cheese

2 medium tomatoes, peeled and diced

Salt and pepper to taste

3 cups zucchini, cut in half lengthwise then thinly sliced

Preheat oven to 275°. Mix egg substitute, cream, garlic, shallots, Parmesan cheese, tomatoes, salt and pepper in a medium bowl. Let stand for ten minutes. Spray 9 x 9 inch baking dish with non-stick spray and spread zucchini on bottom of pan. Pour egg mixture over zucchini. Bake for 30 minutes. Cool and cut into squares.

Yield: 9 servings

CHEESE AND EGG STRATA

3 slices bread, cubed (approximately 2 cups)

½ pound grated sharp Cheddar cheese (2-2½ cups)

¼ cup diced green pepper

¼ cup diced celery

¼ cup diced onion

¼ cup sliced fresh mushrooms

3 eggs

2 cups milk

1 tablespoon prepared mustard

¼ teaspoon salt

Cayenne pepper to taste

2 tablespoons butter

*P*reheat oven to 325°. Place alternate layers of bread and cheese in a well greased 13 x 9 inch baking dish, ending with a layer of cheese. Combine green pepper, celery, onion and mushrooms and sprinkle over bread and cheese mixture. In a small bowl, combine eggs, milk, mustard, salt and pepper. Pour egg mixture over bread, cheese and vegetable mixture. Dot top with butter. Bake for 45-60 minutes. Let stand for 5 minutes before serving.

Yield: 6-8 servings

Nutrition Analysis per serving:

saturated fat -	9.8 g	sodium -	509.3 mg
calories -	282	cholesterol -	183 mg
fat -	17.6 g	fiber -	0.9 g
carbohydrate -	14.2 g	sugar -	5.8 g

RICOTTA CHEESE PANCAKES

1 cup part skim ricotta cheese

4 eggs

½ cup plus 1 tablespoon flour

½ teaspoon salt

*C*ombine cheese and eggs in food processor or blender until smooth. Add flour and salt; mix well. Ladle approximately 3 tablespoons batter onto preheated griddle or non-stick skillet for each pancake. Cook over medium heat until bubbles appear on surface; turn over and cook until golden on underside.

Yield: 4 servings

Nutrition Analysis per serving:

saturated fat -	4.8 g	sodium -	434.5 mg
calories -	234	cholesterol -	293 mg
fat -	10.7 g	fiber -	0
carbohydrate -	18.4 g	sugar -	0.9 g

Artichoke Quiche

1 9-inch pie crust, baked 10 minutes at 400° (see page 259 for recipe)

2 (6-ounce) jars marinated artichokes, chopped, drained, marinade reserved

⅓ cup finely chopped onion

1 garlic clove, minced

4 large eggs

¼ cup dry bread crumbs

Salt to taste

⅛ teaspoon pepper

⅛ teaspoon dried oregano

⅛ teaspoon Tabasco sauce

2 cups grated sharp Cheddar cheese

2 tablespoons chopped parsley

*P*reheat oven to 325°. Drain artichokes, reserving the marinade. Sauté onion and garlic in marinade for 5 minutes over medium heat. In a large bowl, beat eggs; add bread crumbs, salt, pepper, oregano and Tabasco sauce. Stir in cheese, parsley, artichokes and onion mixture. Pour into pastry shell and bake for 45 minutes.

Yield: 6-8 servings

Nutrition Analysis per serving:

saturated fat -	7.8 g	sodium -	441.1 mg
calories -	324	cholesterol -	207.1 mg
fat -	22.4 g	fiber -	0.5 g
carbohydrate -	19.2 g	sugar -	1.0 g

Seafood Quiche

1 9-inch pie crust, baked 10 minutes at 400° (see page 259 for recipe)

2 tablespoons butter

¼ cup minced onion

1 tablespoon tomato paste

¼ cup Marsala wine

½ pound raw shrimp, shelled, deveined, cut into 1-inch pieces

½ pound scallops, cut into ½-inch pieces

2 tablespoons minced parsley

2 tablespoons chopped chives

Salt and pepper to taste

1¼ cups grated Gruyere cheese

¾ cup whipping cream

¾ cup half and half

5 large eggs, lightly beaten

½ teaspoon dried basil or 1½ teaspoons fresh chopped basil

¼ teaspoon fennel seeds

Dash of cayenne pepper

Melt butter in a large skillet over medium heat; add onions and sauté until soft. Stir in tomato paste and wine; cook over high heat for 2 minutes or until sauce is reduced to 2 tablespoons. Add shrimp and cook over medium heat just until shrimp is pink. Stir in scallops, parsley, chives, salt and pepper. Cook one minute longer. Spoon seafood into pastry crust. Sprinkle with cheese. Preheat oven to 375°. Combine remaining ingredients and pour over cheese and seafood. Bake for 35-40 minutes until well puffed and set in center. Allow to cool on rack for 10 minutes before serving.

Yield: 8 servings

A quiche to beat all quiches!

Tomato and Basil Quiche

1 (7-ounce) package
   refrigerated
   breadstick dough
Vegetable cooking
   spray
1 teaspoon olive oil
1 cup chopped onion
1 garlic clove, minced
¾ cup shredded part
   skim mozzarella
   cheese
1 cup plum tomatoes,
   sliced ¼ inch thick
¼ cup shredded fresh
   basil
1 cup evaporated
   skim milk
1½ teaspoons
   cornstarch
¼ teaspoon freshly
   ground pepper
2 whole eggs
1 egg white

*U*nroll breadstick dough, separating into strips. Working on a flat surface, coil one strip of dough around itself in a spiral pattern. Add second strip of dough to the end of the first strip, pinching ends to seal. Continue coiling all strips of dough to make an 8 inch flat circle. Roll dough circle into a 13-inch circle and place into a 9-inch quiche or pie plate lightly coated with vegetable cooking spray. Fold edges under and flute. Set aside.

Heat oil in a skillet over medium heat until hot. Add onion and garlic and sauté for 8 minutes or until lightly browned. Spread onion mixture in bottom of prepared crust, sprinkle with cheese. Arrange tomato slices over cheese and top with basil.

Preheat oven to 350°. Combine milk, cornstarch, pepper, eggs and egg white in a blender or food processor until smooth. Pour over tomatoes. Bake for 45 minutes or until a knife inserted 1 inch from center comes out clean. Let stand 10 minutes before serving.

Yield: 8-10 servings

Nutrition Analysis per serving:

saturated fat -	2.3 g	sodium -	447.7 mg
calories -	294	cholesterol -	87.7 mg
fat -	9.1 g	fiber -	1.7 g
carbohydrate -	41.8 g	sugar -	9.4 g

Soups Salads & Sandwiches

FLORA PARADISE

Orchids, Hibiscus, Birds of Paradise... are these the flora of anywhere but the tropics? To the minds of many, these names conjure up a virtual paradise. For many of the fortunate population who call South Florida home, these flowers remind them of their backyards. Of course, there are tradeoffs. The seasons are depicted by the sporting events on television, and snow is something that is sprayed on windows. There are no apple orchards or peach trees to enjoy. Instead, citrus trees abound and can be found in most yards. There's also the more exotic fruits to brag about having: mangos, avocados and papaya, to name a few. Shade trees have a whole different appearance. Banyans, Poinciana and Ficus sound like foreign words to some, but in South Florida any park is bound to have its share of large old trees for children to play in and families to find reprieve from the heat. Last, but not least, is the infamous palm tree. Look closely and study them and you will find that not all palm trees are created equal. From the Foxtail and Queen Palm to the Royal Palm, each carries its own unique beauty for residents and visitors alike to share. Not anywhere but the tropics can such an abundant plant life be found. Florida... a better name could not have been chosen for such a glorious paradise.

LENTIL SOUP

¼ cup olive oil

2 large onions, chopped

4 garlic cloves, minced

6 celery stalks, chopped

3 carrots, chopped

1 teaspoon curry powder

1 teaspoon cumin powder

1 teaspoon salt

1 teaspoon pepper

1 teaspoon dried thyme

5 cups water

5 cups chicken broth

2 cups lentils

½ cup sherry

2 teaspoons brown sugar

2 teaspoons ketchup

3 cups canned tomatoes, chopped

2 bay leaves

*C*ook onions in a large heavy saucepan in olive oil until soft; add garlic, celery, carrots and cook until soft. Add remaining ingredients and simmer for 2 hours or until lentils are tender. Discard bay leaves before serving.

Yield: 8-10 servings

Nutrition Analysis per serving:

saturated fat -	1.1 g	sodium -	1071.5 mg
calories -	199	fiber -	4.2 g
fat -	7.1 g	cholesterol -	0
carbohydrate -	36.2 g	sugar -	9.6 g

Sweet Corn and Cheddar Chowder

3 tablespoons butter

1 large onion, chopped

1 celery stalk, chopped

1 carrot, chopped

2 teaspoons dry mustard

1½ cups chicken broth or stock

¾ pound potatoes, peeled and diced

1 tablespoon chopped fresh thyme leaves or 1 teaspoon dried, crumbled

1 large bay leaf

3 cups fresh corn kernels or frozen and thawed (approximately 3 medium ears)

¾ cup chopped fresh tomatoes

3 cups half and half or milk

2 cups shredded sharp Cheddar cheese, divided

1 green onion, thinly sliced

Salt and white pepper

Melt butter in heavy saucepan over medium heat. Add onion, celery and carrot, and sauté until vegetables begin to soften, about 5 minutes. Mix in dry mustard. Add chicken broth, potatoes, thyme and bay leaf. Bring mixture to a boil. Reduce heat to low, cover and simmer until potatoes are almost tender, about 10 minutes. Add 3 cups corn, tomatoes and half and half. Return soup to simmer. Cover sauce pan and cook until vegetables are tender, about 6 minutes. (Can be prepared 1 day ahead. Cover and refrigerate. Return soup to simmer before continuing.) Reduce heat to very low and add 1½ cups cheese, mixing until it is melted. Season soup to taste with salt and pepper. Ladle into deep bowls and garnish with remaining cheese and green onion.

Yield: 4-6 servings

Caution! Heat slowly; do not let half and half boil.

GOURMET SPINACH SOUP

5 tablespoons
  unsalted butter

¼ pound fresh
  mushrooms,
  washed, dried,
  trimmed and diced

1 scallion, chopped

5 tablespoons all-
  purpose flour

2 cups chicken broth
  or stock

2 cups milk

½ teaspoon salt
  (optional)

Black pepper, freshly
  ground

Ground nutmeg
  (optional)

4 ounces cream
  cheese, softened
  and cut into cubes

1 cup grated Swiss
  cheese

¾ pound fresh
  spinach, washed,
  trimmed, cooked
  and chopped

*M*elt the butter in a large saucepan. Slowly sauté the mushrooms and scallion until tender. Add flour and stir just until flour is cooked, a couple of minutes. Whisk in chicken broth, then milk, stirring until thickened. Add salt if desired, pepper, nutmeg if desired, cream cheese and Swiss cheese; stir until melted. Stir in spinach. Heat and stir very gently. Season to taste and serve hot.

Yield: 4-6 servings

TORTELLINI SOUP

1 tablespoon butter

4 garlic cloves, minced

2 (14-ounce) cans clear chicken broth

1 (9-ounce) package cheese tortellini

¼ cup grated Parmesan cheese

Salt and pepper to taste

1 (14-ounce) can stewed tomatoes

½ bunch fresh stemmed spinach

3 teaspoons fresh basil or 1 teaspoon dried basil

$\mathcal{M}$elt butter in large saucepan and sauté garlic over medium heat for 2 minutes. Stir in broth and tortellini. Bring to a boil. Mix in cheese and season with salt and pepper. Simmer 5 minutes. Add tomatoes, spinach and basil to soup. Simmer 10 more minutes and serve.

Yield: 4 servings

Nutrition Analysis per serving:

saturated fat -	5.2 g	sodium -	1483 mg
calories -	318	fiber -	1.2 g
fat -	10.5 g	cholesterol -	38.5 mg
carbohydrate -	38.8 g	sugar -	5.8 g

Cooked chicken can be added to soup. If so, add more chicken broth and enjoy!.

AVOCADO LAYERED SOUP

3 (10½ ounce) cans tomato madrilene

3 ripe avocados

3 tablespoons sour cream

3 tablespoons mayonnaise

1½ teaspoons minced onion

Salt and pepper to taste

2½ tablespoons lemon juice

$\mathcal{D}$ivide one can of the madrilene between 6-8 clear sherbet glasses, or small ramekins to make one layer. Place in refrigerator to set. Mash avocado with remaining ingredients and spoon half of it, divided among the glasses on top of the set madrilene. Smooth it to make a layer. Divide another can of the madrilene and carefully pour it over the soft avocado mixture using a teaspoon to "float" it on. Refrigerate this layer to set. Use the remaining avocado mixture to make another layer. Gently pour the third can of madrilene over the avocado mixture. Refrigerate until set. Garnish with leftover avocado mixture or a dollop of sour cream.

Yield: 6-8 servings

This may be made the day before; wait to garnish this impressive soup until serving time.

SHRIMP AND BASIL SOUP

3 tablespoons olive oil

1½ tablespoons butter

2 garlic cloves

1 small red onion, thinly sliced

2 stalks celery, cut into ¾ inch strips

3 small carrots, thinly sliced

1 tablespoon finely chopped fresh parsley

2 tablespoons finely chopped fresh basil

Salt and fresh ground pepper to taste

1 pinch cayenne pepper

1 pound medium uncooked shrimp, peeled and deveined

½ cup medium dry sherry

4 cups chicken broth or stock

2½ ounces small conchiglie pasta

¼ cup heavy cream

Fresh basil to garnish

*I*n a large saucepan heat oil and butter. Add garlic cloves and onion and sauté gently 2 to 3 minutes. Add celery and carrots and sauté until vegetables are golden; do not brown. Toss in parsley and basil, season to taste. Stir briefly, add shrimp, toss, then remove garlic cloves. Pour in sherry, increase heat and cook for 2 to 3 minutes. Add chicken stock, bring to a boil; lower heat and simmer for 5 minutes. Add conchiglie and simmer until pasta is al dente. Stir in cream, adjust seasonings to taste and garnish with fresh basil.

Yield: 4 servings

Nutrition Analysis per serving:

saturated fat -	0	sodium -	941 mg
calories -	530	fiber -	1.9 g
fat -	33.3 g	cholesterol -	159.4 mg
carbohydrate -	23.7 g	sugar -	3.3 g

Conchiglie is a delightful, shell shaped pasta.

COLD CREAM OF TOMATO SOUP WITH MINT, AVOCADO AND CUCUMBER

2 tablespoons butter

1 tablespoon olive oil

1 onion, diced

2 tablespoons flour

3 cups chicken broth or stock

5 tomatoes, peeled and diced

2 tablespoons tomato paste

Pinch of thyme, bay leaf and sugar

¾ cup heavy cream

1 avocado, diced

1 medium cucumber, diced

3 teaspoons chopped fresh mint

*I*n a large saucepan, sauté onion in butter and olive oil; add flour to make the roux. Stir flour and butter and cook until roux forms. Add the chicken stock and the remaining ingredients except for the cream, avocado, mint and cucumber. Simmer on very low for 10 minutes. Puree in food processor and refrigerate overnight. Before serving, add cream, avocado, cucumber and fresh mint, blending gently. Serve chilled.

Yield: 4 servings

VICHYSSOISE

3 cups peeled, sliced potatoes

3 cups sliced leek, white portions only

1½ quarts chicken broth or stock

salt to taste

½-1 cup whipping cream

Chopped chives as garnish

*S*immer vegetables in chicken broth until tender, approximately 15-20 minutes. Puree mixture in food processor until smooth. Stir in cream. Season to taste (slightly over-salt). Chill; serve with chopped chives as a garnish.

Yield: 6-8 servings

GAZPACHO

3 cups peeled, seeded, chopped tomatoes

1½ cups vegetable cocktail juice

½ cup chopped avocado

¼ cup peeled, seeded, chopped cucumber

¼ cup chopped green pepper

¼ cup chopped yellow pepper

¼ cup chopped sweet red pepper

¼ cup chopped onion

1 tablespoon minced garlic

1 teaspoon Tabasco sauce

¼ cup minced parsley

¼ cup minced fresh cilantro

2 tablespoons lemon juice

Ground black pepper to taste

Combine all ingredients in food processor except parsley, cilantro, lemon juice and black pepper. Using on-off pulses, process until coarsely chopped. Refrigerate until chilled. Transfer to bowls; add parsley, cilantro, lemon juice and black pepper.

Yield: 4 servings

Nutrition Analysis per serving:

saturated fat -	0.6 g	sodium -	344.9 mg
calories -	89	fiber -	2.5 g
fat -	4.1 g	cholesterol -	0
carbohydrate -	12.4 g	sugar -	7.0 g

With the wide availability of fresh vegetables in South Florida, gazpacho is a Floribbean "comfort food".

Turkey Vegetable Soup

¼ cup butter

2 medium onions, chopped

2 tablespoons flour

1 teaspoon curry

3 cups chicken broth or stock

1 cup chopped red potatoes, unpeeled

½ cup thinly sliced carrot

½ cup thinly sliced celery

2 tablespoons chopped fresh parsley

½ teaspoon dried sage or 1½ teaspoons fresh chopped sage

2 cups cooked turkey, cut into small pieces

1½ cups half and half

1 (10-ounce) package chopped spinach, cooked and drained

Salt and pepper to taste

Melt butter in large Dutch oven over medium heat. Sauté onions. Stir in flour and curry, continue to stir for 2-3 minutes. Add rest of ingredients except for turkey, half and half, and spinach. Bring to a boil, reduce heat, cover and simmer for 20 minutes. Add remaining ingredients, cover and simmer for 10 minutes. Add salt and pepper to taste and serve.

Yield: 4-6 servings

Cayenne pepper may be substituted for the curry for a zesty alternative!

Italian Sausage Soup

1¼ pounds Italian
sausage
2 medium onions,
chopped
3-4 garlic cloves,
minced
3 cups of tomatoes,
peeled and
chopped or 1 (28-
ounce) can Italian
tomatoes, chopped
1½ cups dry red wine
5½ cups chicken broth
or stock
1 tablespoon
chopped basil
1 tablespoon oregano
1 green pepper,
chopped
2 medium zucchini,
chopped
½ cup orzo pasta
Salt and pepper to
taste
3 tablespoons parsley
½ cup freshly grated
Parmesan cheese
Parsley for garnish
Freshly grated
Parmesan cheese
for garnish

*C*ut sausage into ½-inch pieces and sauté until fat is removed. Remove sausage from pan. Leaving 2 tablespoons of fat in pan, add onions and garlic; sauté until tender. Add sausage, tomatoes, wine and chicken broth. Bring to a boil. Add basil and oregano and simmer uncovered for 15 minutes. Add remaining ingredients and simmer for 10 minutes. Garnish with parsley and grated Parmesan.

Yield: 12 servings

CRABMEAT CORN SOUP

Vegetable cooking
spray
1⅓ cups chopped red
onion
1⅓ cups chopped
celery
¾ cup chopped green
bell pepper
3 garlic cloves,
minced
1 tablespoon
Worcestershire
sauce
½ teaspoon salt
½ teaspoon dried
thyme
¼ teaspoon pepper
2 (10½-ounce) cans
low-salt chicken
broth
1 (16-ounce) package
frozen shoepeg
white corn
1 (10-ounce) can
diced tomatoes and
green chiles,
undrained
1 (6-ounce) can
tomato paste
4 cups water
1 cup sliced green
onions
1 pound fresh lump
crabmeat, shell
pieces removed and
drained

Coat a Dutch oven with cooking spray; place over medium heat. Add onion, celery, green pepper and garlic; sauté 5 minutes. Add Worcestershire sauce, salt, thyme, pepper, chicken broth, corn, tomatoes and tomato paste; bring to a boil. Reduce heat and simmer, uncovered, 1 hour. Stir in remaining ingredients; cook over medium heat 15 minutes.

Yield: 12 servings

Nutrition Analysis per serving:

saturated fat -	0.3 g	sodium -	365 mg
calories -	113	fiber -	2.5 g
fat -	1.6 g	cholesterol -	38 mg
carbohydrate -	15.6 g	sugar -	0

RED PEPPER SOUP

1 tablespoon olive oil
4 tablespoons butter
7 red bell peppers, seeded and chopped
1 carrot, sliced
3 shallots, sliced
1 garlic clove, minced
1-2 ripe pears, sliced or 1 (8¼-ounce) can pears, drained and sliced
4 (14½-ounce) cans chicken broth
2-5 drops Tabasco sauce
1 teaspoon sugar
Salt and pepper to taste
Sour cream to garnish

Heat oil and butter in large saucepan; sauté peppers, carrots, shallots, garlic and pears over medium heat for 10 minutes. Add chicken broth, Tabasco, sugar, salt and pepper. Bring to a boil and simmer for 30 minutes; let cool. Puree in food processor and serve hot or cold. Garnish with sour cream.

Yield: 10-12 servings

CREAMY DOUBLE CHEESE SOUP

6 tablespoons butter
5 tablespoons flour
4½ cups hot milk
1 cup heavy cream
9 ounces Gouda cheese, grated
4½ ounces smoked Edam cheese, grated
2 tablespoons Worcestershire sauce
1 teaspoon paprika
1 dash of Tabasco
Salt and pepper to taste

Melt butter and stir in flour. Over low heat, slowly add milk stirring constantly until thick. Add cream; be careful not to boil. Gradually add cheeses, stir until velvety and smooth. Add Worcestershire sauce, paprika, Tabasco, salt and pepper to taste.

Yield: 6 servings

Black Bean and Chicken Chili

24 ounces dried black beans, prepared as directed on package or 2 (15-ounce) cans black beans

3 tablespoons olive oil

6 garlic cloves, minced

6 chicken breast halves, skinless, boneless, cut into 1 inch pieces

1 medium yellow pepper, chopped

1 medium red pepper, chopped

1 large onion, chopped

¼ cup chili powder

2 tablespoons cumin

1 tablespoon ground coriander

2 teaspoons salt

8 plum tomatoes, cut into 1 inch cubes or 1 (28-ounce) can Italian plum tomatoes, drained and chopped

12 ounces beer

1 cup water

16 ounces sharp Cheddar cheese spread

1 cup chopped fresh parsley

Tabasco sauce to taste

Sour cream for garnish

Diced tomatoes for garnish

*R*inse and drain black beans and set aside. In a large soup pot or Dutch oven, heat oil and sauté garlic, chicken, yellow and red peppers and onion for 10 minutes or until chicken is almost cooked. Add chili powder, cumin, coriander and salt; cook 3 minutes longer. Stir in black beans, tomatoes, beer and water; bring to a boil. Simmer, uncovered, for 30 minutes, stirring frequently. Reduce heat to low. Stir in cheese and parsley; continue cooking until cheese is melted. Add Tabasco to taste and garnish with sour cream and diced tomatoes.

Yield: 10 servings

This is truly a favorite!

RED LEAF RASPBERRY SALAD

1 head red leaf
   lettuce
½-1 head Bibb or
   Boston lettuce
1 (½-ounce) package
   arugula
⅓ cup toasted pine
   nuts
¾ cup grated Swiss
   cheese
4-5 pieces bacon,
   cooked and
   crumbled
¾ cup fresh
   raspberries
Raspberry Vinaigrette

Wash, dry and gently tear all three lettuces into pieces. Divide among four salad or serving plates. Evenly divide the pine nuts, cheese, bacon and raspberries between the four plates. Top with Raspberry Vinaigrette to taste.

Yield: 4 servings

Divide two grilled and sliced chicken breasts among the four prepared salads to serve as a light main dish.

RASPBERRY VINAIGRETTE

⅓ cup salad oil
⅓ cup raspberry
   vinegar
¼ cup sugar

Combine all ingredients in a jar and shake vigorously until well mixed.

Almond Orange Garden Salad

1 cup sliced almonds
¼ cup sugar
½ head iceberg lettuce
½ head romaine
    lettuce
6 green onions,
    chopped
1½ cups fresh oranges,
    peeled and
    sectioned or
    2 (10-ounce) cans
    Mandarin oranges,
    drained
Sunlight Salad
    Dressing

Add sugar to frying pan with almonds and cook over medium heat, stirring and watching closely. When almonds are browned, pour them onto foil and let cool. Tear clean lettuce into bite sized pieces and place in a salad bowl. Add onions and oranges. Pour Sunlight Salad Dressing over salad to taste and toss lightly. Top with almonds and serve.

Yield: 8 servings

Sunlight Salad Dressing

1 cup vegetable oil
¼ cup white wine
    vinegar
¼ cup sugar
1 teaspoon salt
1 teaspoon black
    pepper
3 teaspoons freshly
    chopped parsley or
    1 teaspoon dried
    parsley

Combine dressing ingredients in a jar and shake until well mixed.

Try this delicious dressing on all of your salad favorites.

Summer Feta Salad

1 head romaine lettuce, torn
1 large bunch parsley, stems removed
1 cucumber, sliced
1 (4.5-ounce) can pitted black olives, drained
1 tomato, quartered
4 ounces feta cheese
½ cup olive oil
¼ cup white wine vinegar
⅛ cup lemon juice
Pepper to taste

Toss together lettuce, parsley, cucumber, olives and tomatoes. Crumble feta cheese and add to lettuce; set aside. Mix olive oil, vinegar and lemon juice together; toss, to taste, with salad. Add fresh ground pepper to season and serve.

Yield: 4 servings

Endive and Gorgonzola Salad

2 heads Belgian endive lettuce
4 ounces Gorgonzola cheese, crumbled
½ cup chopped walnuts
20 cherry tomatoes, halved
¼ cup balsamic vinegar
½ cup olive oil
Salt and pepper to taste

Place four or five lettuce leaves in a circular pattern on each of six salad plates. Divide cheese, walnuts and tomatoes evenly amongst each plate. Sprinkle with oil and vinegar. Add salt and pepper to taste.

Yield: 6 servings

CURRIED WATERCRESS AND ORANGE SALAD

1¼ pounds watercress
2 oranges
4 celery stalks, thinly sliced
1 tablespoon fresh lemon juice
1 tablespoon white wine vinegar
1 tablespoon curry powder
Salt
Freshly ground pepper
5 tablespoons olive oil

*R*emove the tough stems and leaves from the watercress and arrange in a salad bowl. Peel the oranges eliminating the white membrane. Slice the oranges crosswise and remove seeds. Add sliced oranges and celery to the watercress.

In a small bowl combine the lemon juice, vinegar, curry powder, salt and pepper to taste until well mixed. Add the olive oil and stir vigorously until blended. Pour the dressing over salad, toss well and serve.

Yield: 4 servings

Nutrition Analysis per serving:

saturated fat -	2.3 g	sodium -	93.3 mg
calories -	181	fiber -	4.9 g
fat -	18.1 g	cholesterol -	0
carbohydrate -	11.6 g	sugar -	6.7 g

Vary the amount of curry to your taste preference.

DRIED CHERRY AND GOAT CHEESE SALAD

1 large head green leaf lettuce
1 large head red leaf lettuce
6 ounces goat cheese
½ cup dried cherries
½ cup toasted chopped pecans
Raspberry Vinaigrette Dressing (see page 71 for recipe)

*T*ear clean salad greens into bite size pieces in large bowl. Crumble goat cheese and add to greens with cherries and pecans. Add Raspberry Vinaigrette Dressing to taste.

Yield: 6-8 servings

Sunset Salad

1 cup shredded
purple cabbage

1 cup shredded
carrots

½ cup shredded
Colby cheese

½ cup raisins

½ cup cashew pieces

¼ cup sesame seeds

1 cup alfalfa sprouts

1 banana, peeled and
sliced

1 cucumber, peeled
and sliced

Honey Dressing or
any oil and vinegar
dressing

Layer all ingredients, except dressing, on a serving plate in the order listed. Serve with Honey Dressing to taste.

Yield: 4 servings

A medley of ingredients that will tantalize your taste and surprise your palate!

Honey Dressing

½ cup sugar

1½ teaspoons paprika

1½ teaspoons salt

1 teaspoon dry
mustard

½ cup vinegar

1 cup oil

Combine sugar, paprika, salt and dry mustard in a blender or food processor. Slowly add vinegar and oil; process until well blended.

Yield: 1 pint

SPLENDID RASPBERRY SPINACH SALAD

2 tablespoons raspberry vinegar
2 tablespoons raspberry jam
⅓ cup vegetable oil
⅔ (10-ounce) package of fresh spinach, washed and torn
¾ cup coarsely chopped macadamia nuts, divided
1 cup raspberries, divided
3 kiwi, peeled, sliced and divided

Combine vinegar and jam in a blender or food processor. Add oil in a thin stream, blending well; set aside. Toss spinach, ½ of the nuts, ½ of the raspberries and ½ of the kiwi. Add dressing and toss again. To serve, place on platter or in flat salad bowl and top with remaining nuts, raspberries and kiwi.

Yield: 4-6 servings

Nutrition Analysis per serving:

saturated fat -	3.6 g	sodium -	144.6 mg
calories -	347	fiber -	8.9 g
fat -	27.9 g	cholesterol -	0
carbohydrate -	24.3 g	sugar -	12.0 g

Strawberry vinegar and strawberries may be substituted for the raspberry vinegar and raspberries.

BLUE CHEESE COLESLAW

1 (2-pound) head cabbage, shredded
8 ounces blue cheese, crumbled
⅓ cup cider vinegar
¼ teaspoon dry mustard
1 teaspoon celery seeds
2 garlic cloves, minced
½ teaspoon salt
½ teaspoon freshly ground white pepper
2 tablespoons sugar
¼ cup minced white onion
¾ cup vegetable oil

In a large bowl, combine cabbage and blue cheese; chill, covered, for at least one hour. While the cabbage mixture is chilling, whisk together the vinegar, mustard, celery seeds, garlic, salt, pepper, sugar and onion. While continuing to process, add the oil in a stream until the dressing is emulsified. Chill dressing, covered, for at least one hour. To serve, pour the dressing over the cabbage mixture and toss until it is well combined. Serve immediately.

Yield: 8-10 servings

GOLD COAST SPINACH SALAD

1 (10-ounce) bag of spinach

1 large red apple, peeled and chopped

Juice from one fresh lemon

1 quart strawberries, sliced

4 ounces sliced almonds or ½ cup walnuts

8 strips bacon, cooked and crumbled

1 (10-ounce) can Mandarin oranges, drained or 1-2 fresh oranges, peeled and sliced, membrane removed

Poppy Seed Dressing

*W*ash and dry spinach leaves; tear into pieces and place in a bowl. Place chopped apple in a separate bowl; sprinkle with fresh lemon juice to prevent browning. Add strawberries, nuts, bacon, oranges and apple to spinach. Pour Poppy Seed Dressing over salad to taste and serve.

Yield: 6-8 servings

POPPY SEED DRESSING

1 cup sugar

2 teaspoons dry mustard

2 teaspoons salt

⅔ cup white vinegar

1 small onion, chopped

1½ cups vegetable oil

3 tablespoons poppy seeds

*I*n a blender or food processor, combine sugar, dry mustard, salt, vinegar, onion and oil. Process for one minute. Add poppy seeds and process for 5 seconds. Refrigerate until ready to use.

This dressing may be stored up to 2 weeks when refrigerated.

Fresh Spinach Salad

¼ cup sugar

1 teaspoon salt

1 teaspoon dry mustard

1 teaspoon poppy seeds

1 tablespoon onion juice

⅓ cup cider vinegar

1 cup salad oil

¾ cup cottage cheese

2 pounds fresh spinach, washed and torn, heavy stems removed

½ pound bacon, crisply fried, crumbled

2-3 eggs, hard boiled, chopped

¼ pound fresh mushrooms, sliced

Shake sugar, salt, dry mustard, poppy seeds, onion juice, cider vinegar, salad oil and cottage cheese in a jar and refrigerate overnight.

In a large bowl, toss spinach and dressing to taste. Add bacon, eggs and mushrooms. Toss again and serve immediately.

Yield: 8 servings

Dressing can be tightly covered and stored up to 1 week in the refrigerator. Shake well before adding to salad.

Fruit Salad with Celery Seed Dressing

2 grapefruit,
   sectioned
1 avocado, peeled
   and sliced
½ cup halved seedless
   grapes
1 cup halved
   strawberries
Lettuce leaves
Celery Seed Dressing

Arrange grapefruit and avocado alternately on lettuce leaves divided among 4-6 salad plates. Top each with grapes and strawberries. Pour dressing over top to taste and serve.

Yield 4-6 servings

Perfect for hot, balmy afternoons. Use any of your favorite fruits.

Celery Seed Dressing

½ cup sugar
1 teaspoon salt
1 teaspoon dry
   mustard
¼ medium onion,
   grated, or 2-3 green
   onions, chopped
⅓ cup red wine
   vinegar
1 cup vegetable oil
1 tablespoon celery
   seed

Mix sugar, salt, mustard and onion. Add a small amount of vinegar and oil and blend well. Beat dressing with an electric mixer adding the rest of the vinegar and oil alternately in small amounts. Add the celery seed and mix well.

CRUNCHY CABBAGE SALAD

2 (3-ounce) packages vegetable flavored Ramen noodles

1 head cabbage, torn into bite size pieces (approximately 6 cups)

4 scallions, sliced

2 green bell peppers, seeded and chopped

½ cup toasted sunflower seeds

½ cup sesame seeds

½ cup sliced and toasted almonds

½ cup vegetable oil

3 tablespoons white or apple cider vinegar

2 tablespoons sugar

½ teaspoon salt

½ teaspoon pepper

Remove seasoning packages from Ramen noodles and set aside. Crush noodles and combine with cabbage, scallions, green peppers, sunflower seeds and sesame seeds. In a separate bowl, combine one Ramen seasoning packet with almonds, oil, vinegar, sugar, salt and pepper. Mix with a wire whisk and pour over cabbage mixture. Toss gently to coat. Cover and chill. Serve promptly after chilling.

Yield:10-12 servings

Always a big hit! An interesting combination of tastes and textures.

AVOCADO SALAD WITH SPICY DRESSING

2 ripe avocados, peeled, cut into small pieces

2 small tomatoes, cut into wedges

1 cup pitted black olives

1 head lettuce

Spicy Dressing (see page 81)

Place avocados, tomatoes and olives in a medium bowl. Pour Spicy Dressing over and mix lightly. Let marinate for at least ½ hour in the refrigerator. Drain marinade, if desired, and serve on a bed of lettuce.

Yield: 4 servings

Roasted Red Pepper Salad

4 medium red bell peppers, roasted (see page 259 for roasting instructions)

1½ pounds fresh snow peas, ends removed

2 teaspoons salt

3-4 green onions, sliced

2 tablespoons Dijon mustard

4 tablespoons red wine vinegar

1 teaspoon ground cumin

salt and pepper to taste

½ cup olive oil

¼ cup fresh parsley or cilantro, finely chopped

*B*oil water in a medium to large pot with the salt. Add snow peas to water and blanch for 2 minutes. Drain snow peas, run under cold water and drain again.

Cut peppers lengthwise into strips. Layer the peppers and snow peas in a glass serving bowl. Sprinkle green onions over top; cover and refrigerate.

In a separate bowl or blender, combine mustard, vinegar, cumin, salt and pepper. Slowly whisk in olive oil. Stir in parsley or cilantro and pour over peppers and pea pods; toss until coated. Allow salad flavors to blend for a minimum of 30 minutes prior to serving.

Yield: 8 servings

Nutrition Analysis per serving:

saturated fat -	1.9 g	sodium -	693 mg
calories -	170	fiber -	3.6 g
fat -	13.8 g	cholesterol -	0
carbohydrate -	9 g	sugar -	5.7 g

For variety, try yellow or orange peppers!

Spicy Dressing

⅓ cup olive oil

Juice of 1½ lemons

2 tablespoons tomato paste

1 teaspoon salt

1 teaspoon chili powder

½ teaspoon ground cumin

Pinch of black pepper

*P*lace all ingredients in a blender or food processor and process on low speed for one minute.

Sweet Bell Pepper and Feta Salad

½ cup olive oil

¼ cup raspberry vinegar

1 rounded teaspoon Dijon mustard

2-3 teaspoons sugar

Salt and pepper to taste

4 cups assorted lettuce leaves, torn into bite size pieces

1 large red bell pepper, seeded and sliced

1 large yellow bell pepper, seeded and sliced

1 (16-ounce) can hearts of palm, drained and sliced

½ small red onion, thinly sliced

2 ounces feta cheese, crumbled

*T*o prepare dressing, whisk oil, vinegar, mustard, sugar, salt and pepper together until smooth; set aside. Combine lettuce, peppers, hearts of palm and onion in a large salad bowl. Toss with ½ of the dressing and add additional dressing as desired. Garnish with crumbled cheese and serve immediately.

Yield: 6-8 servings

Nutrition Analysis per serving:

saturated fat -	2.3 g	sodium -	204.9 mg
calories -	130	fiber -	2.5 g
fat -	9.7 g	cholesterol -	7.1 mg
carbohydrate -	5.8 g	sugar -	3.1 g

BLACK BEAN AND CORN SALAD

¾ cup Italian salad dressing

¾ teaspoon Tabasco sauce

½ teaspoon chili powder

1 tablespoon fresh lime or lemon juice

1 tablespoon cilantro

1 (12-ounce) can yellow corn, drained

1 (15-ounce) can black beans, rinsed and drained

1 red bell pepper, seeded and finely chopped

½ cup thinly sliced green onion

½ cup finely chopped red onion

1 garlic clove, minced

1 medium tomato, finely chopped

1 jalapeño pepper, seeded and finely chopped

*C*ombine Italian dressing, Tabasco sauce, chili powder, citrus juice and cilantro in a jar and shake well; set aside. Combine remaining ingredients until evenly mixed. Cover salad with dressing and chill at least 4 hours (best if made the day before serving). Serve cool or at room temperature.

Yield: 12-15 servings

Nutrition Analysis per serving:

saturated fat -	0.3 g	sodium -	254.8 mg
calories -	66	fiber -	2.4 g
fat -	1.9 g	cholesterol -	0.9 mg
carbohydrate -	10.9 g	sugar -	2.0 g

CHICK PEA AND CHEESE SALAD

4 cups cooked or canned chick peas, drained

3 tablespoons olive oil

1 tablespoon white wine vinegar

1 teaspoon ground cumin

1½ teaspoons dried thyme or 3 teaspoons fresh chopped thyme

2 tablespoons chopped parsley

1 head lettuce, shredded

⅓ pound shredded Cheddar cheese

⅓ pound shredded Swiss cheese

¾ cup chopped scallions

4 small tomatoes, quartered

4 eggs, hard boiled, sliced

½ cup Italian salad dressing or Honey Dressing (recipe found on page 75)

Combine the chick peas with oil, vinegar, cumin, thyme and parsley. Marinate for 2 hours. In a large bowl, combine the chick peas with marinade, lettuce, cheeses and scallions; toss lightly. Spoon into serving dish and arrange tomatoes and eggs on top. Pour dressing over top and serve immediately.

Yield: 6 servings

Nutrition Analysis per serving:

saturated fat -	12.7 g	sodium -	364 mg
calories -	564	fiber -	8.1 g
fat -	33.3 g	cholesterol -	49.5 mg
carbohydrate -	37 g	sugar -	7.2 g

Beachfront Bean Medley

1 (12-ounce) can Ceci beans
1 (8-12 ounce) can black beans
1 (8-12 ounce) can kidney beans
1 (8-ounce) can Pigeon peas
1 (8-ounce) can green Pigeon peas
1 (8-ounce) can blackeyed peas
8 ounces cooked lentils
1-3 garlic cloves, finely chopped
2 stalks celery, finely chopped
1 medium onion, chopped
1½ cups gourmet broken rice mixture
1 large chicken bouillon cube
¼ cup sherry
1 bottle vinaigrette salad dressing

*D*rain all beans and rinse thoroughly. Place in a large bowl and add lentils, garlic, celery and onion; combine and set aside.

Cook rice in 3 cups boiling water with bouillon cube for 20 minutes. Add sherry to boiling water and rice mixture and cool.

Combine rice and beans thoroughly; add vinaigrette dressing to taste. Refrigerate overnight.

Yield: 6-8 servings

This is a great salad for a picnic or a day on the boat!

TORTELLINI CHICKEN SALAD WITH SUN-DRIED TOMATO VINAIGRETTE

4 ounces cheese tortellini or other pasta, cooked, drained, cooled

4 ounces grilled chicken, cut into bite sized pieces

2 frozen artichoke hearts, thawed and sliced

1 ounce fresh spinach, torn into pieces

2 ounces feta cheese

3 slices red onion

2 garlic cloves

12 sun-dried tomatoes, plumped in water

1 teaspoon dried oregano or 3 teaspoons fresh oregano

1 tablespoon tomato paste

6 tablespoons balsamic vinegar

Salt and pepper to taste

½ cup olive oil

Mixed greens

*I*n a serving bowl, combine the tortellini, chicken, artichoke hearts, spinach, feta cheese and onion. Toss well.

Puree the garlic, dried tomatoes, oregano, tomato paste, vinegar, salt and pepper in a blender or food processor. With the machine running, gradually add the oil to make a smooth emulsion. Combine enough dressing with the salad ingredients to moisten them and toss to coat well. Serve over mixed greens.

Yield: 2 main course servings

This salad was selected from Junior League cookbooks across the country and appears in **The Junior League Centennial Cookbook**.

Chicken and Spinach Pasta Salad

2 cups tri-colored
  rotini pasta
2½ cups shredded
  fresh spinach,
  washed with stems
  removed
2 cups cooked
  chicken, cut into
  bite sized pieces
1 large tomato, diced
1½ cups sliced fresh
  mushrooms
⅓ cup fresh Parmesan
  cheese, shredded
3 slices bacon, crisply
  cooked, crumbled
⅓ cup olive oil
3 tablespoons Dijon
  mustard
1 teaspoon lemon
  juice
¼ teaspoon garlic
  powder
¼ teaspoon salt
⅛ teaspoon pepper
1 tablespoon water

Cook pasta to "al dente". Rinse under cold water and drain well. In a large salad bowl combine pasta, spinach, chicken, tomato, mushrooms, cheese and bacon. In a separate bowl whisk together remaining ingredients until smooth. Pour dressing over pasta mixture and toss gently. Serve immediately.

Yield: 4-6 main course servings

CITRUS SALAD WITH BANANA POPPY SEED DRESSING

Salad greens
2 oranges, peeled and sectioned
2 grapefruit, peeled and sectioned
Banana Poppy Seed Dressing

Arrange salad greens and fruit on a platter or individual salad plates. Top with Banana Poppy Seed Dressing and serve.

Yield: 4-6 servings

This salad is perfect with fresh Florida citrus; to order see page 276.

BANANA POPPY SEED DRESSING

1 ripe banana
1 cup sour cream
¼ cup sugar
1 tablespoon poppy seeds
1 tablespoon lemon juice
1 teaspoon dry mustard
¾ teaspoon salt

In a small bowl, finely mash banana. Add remaining ingredients and mix well. Chill for at least thirty minutes before serving.

Dijon Asparagus Salad

8 ounces pasta
  (penne or rotini)

½ pound asparagus,
  cut diagonally into
  1½ inch pieces

10 cherry tomatoes,
  quartered

2 tablespoons
  chopped onion

⅓ cup Raspberry
  Poppy Seed
  Dressing

2 tablespoons Dijon
  mustard

¼ cup toasted
  almonds

Cook pasta according to package directions. Cook asparagus in boiling water for 2 minutes until crisp-tender; drain and rinse. Combine pasta, asparagus, tomatoes and onions in a large bowl. In a separate bowl, combine salad dressing and mustard; toss with pasta. Chill 2 hours. Add almonds and serve.

Yield: 8-10 servings

Nutrition Analysis per serving:

saturated fat -	0.2 g	sodium -	147.4 mg
calories -	136	fiber -	1.9 g
fat -	2.7 g	cholesterol -	0
carbohydrate -	20.6 g	sugar -	1.9 g

Add grilled chicken breast or shrimp to transform this sumptuous side salad into a main dish.

Raspberry Poppy Seed Dressing

½ cup sugar

1 teaspoon dry
  mustard

1 teaspoon salt

1-2 tablespoons poppy
  seeds

¼ cup raspberry
  vinegar

⅔ cup vegetable oil

Combine dry ingredients in a jar. Add vinegar and oil and shake until well blended.

Palm Beach Pasta Salad

1 pound thin spaghetti or vermicelli, broken into 1 inch pieces, cooked according to package directions

3 large tomatoes, diced

2 medium zucchini, diced

1 large cucumber, diced

1 medium green pepper, diced

1 sweet red pepper, diced

1 large red onion, diced

2 (2 ⅓-ounce) cans sliced ripe olives, drained

1 (16-ounce) bottle Italian salad dressing

¼ cup grated fresh Parmesan or Romano cheese

1 tablespoon sesame seeds

2 teaspoons poppy seeds

1 teaspoon paprika

½ teaspoon celery seed

¼ teaspoon garlic powder

Combine all ingredients in a large bowl; cover with plastic wrap and refrigerate overnight to blend flavors.

Yield: 10-15 servings

Nutrition Analysis per serving:

saturated fat -	0.9 g	sodium -	414.9 mg
calories -	221	fiber -	2.7 g
fat -	6.4 g	cholesterol -	4 mg
carbohydrate -	32.9 g	sugar -	5.2 g

MARINATED STEAK
AND SPINACH SALAD

¼ cup red wine
vinegar

¼ cup olive oil

1 garlic clove, minced

1 (6-ounce) jar
marinated
artichoke hearts,
sliced, liquid
reserved

1 teaspoon sugar

1 teaspoon salt

½ teaspoon black
pepper

½ teaspoon dried
oregano

½ teaspoon dried
rosemary

2 pounds boneless
T-bone steak,
1 inch thick, broiled
to medium,
thinly sliced

1 large red onion,
thinly sliced

1 dozen cherry
tomatoes, halved

1 cup fresh
mushrooms, sliced

5 cups fresh spinach,
washed and
drained

$\mathcal{W}$hisk vinegar and olive oil together. Add garlic, liquid from the artichoke hearts, sugar, salt, pepper, oregano and rosemary. Add steak, onion, tomatoes and mushrooms. Marinate for one hour. Arrange spinach in bowl; add marinated ingredients and artichoke hearts. Toss well and serve immediately.

Yield: 6 servings

Paella Salad

1 (10-ounce) package yellow rice

2 boneless chicken breasts cooked, cut into 1-inch pieces

⅓ pound shrimp, cooked, peeled

½ red pepper, chopped

½ green pepper, chopped

3 scallions, chopped, including stems

2 medium tomatoes, seeded and chopped

⅓ cup olive oil

1 garlic clove, minced

2 tablespoons tarragon vinegar

⅛ teaspoon dry mustard

Cook yellow rice according to instructions on package. Add chicken, shrimp, peppers, scallions and tomatoes; set aside.

In a jar, combine olive oil, garlic, tarragon vinegar and dry mustard; shake until well mixed. Pour over rice mixture. Serve at room temperature or warm.

Yield: 5-6 servings

Nutrition Analysis per serving:

saturated fat -	2.9 g	sodium -	832.1 mg
calories -	448	fiber -	1.5 g
fat -	18.2 g	cholesterol -	34.8 mg
carbohydrate -	45.8 g	sugar -	2.6 g

The flavors blend nicely when this salad is made 4-5 hours before serving. Try adding a few shakes of red pepper flakes for added "zip". For a striking visual effect, alternate spinach leaves and quartered tomatoes in a circular pattern and mound salad in the center.

Summer Shrimp and Olive Salad

1 pound medium shrimp, peeled, deveined and cooked

1 cup sliced ripe olives

1½ cups small fresh mushrooms, quartered

½ cup pine nuts

¼ cup chopped red peppers

Vinaigrette Dressing

1 head romaine lettuce

Orange or lemon slices to garnish

Combine shrimp, olives, mushrooms, pine nuts and red peppers in a bowl. Pour vinaigrette dressing over top and stir to coat. Refrigerate for 8 hours.

To serve, arrange lettuce on plates and top with shrimp mixture using a slotted spoon to drain excess marinade. Garnish with orange or lemon slices around edge of plate.

Yield: 3-4 servings

Any blend of fresh greens may be substituted for the romaine lettuce.

Vinaigrette Dressing

¼ cup tarragon wine vinegar

1 tablespoon Dijon mustard

½ teaspoon salt

½ teaspoon pepper

1 tablespoon chopped fresh parsley

½-¾ cup oil

3 tablespoons chopped green onions

Combine vinegar, mustard, salt, pepper and parsley to make a smooth paste. Add oil slowly, whisking until smooth and creamy. Add onions and serve.

SHRIMP AND ARTICHOKE VINAIGRETTE

2 pounds medium shrimp, shelled, deveined and cooked

2 (15-ounce) cans artichoke hearts, drained and quartered

1 pound mushrooms, halved

2 small yellow onions, sliced and separated into rings.

1 (3 ¼-ounce) jar capers, drained

1 envelope Italian dressing mix

2 envelopes cheese garlic dressing mix

Vinegar

Salad greens

Combine shrimp, artichokes, mushrooms, onions and capers in a large bowl; set aside. Prepare salad dressing mixes according to the package directions, substituting vinegar for the water required (do not use any water in the mixes). Pour dressing over shrimp mixture, cover with plastic wrap and refrigerate overnight. Drain well before serving over salad greens.

Yield: 4-6 servings

Seafood Salad with Dill Dressing

½ pound cooked medium shrimp, shelled and deveined

1 cup crabmeat

¼ cup sliced green onion

1 medium cucumber, chopped and seeded

1 (8½-ounce) can sliced water chestnuts, drained

2 avocados, peeled and sliced lengthwise

Dill Dressing

Salad greens

1 tomato, cut into wedges

In a large bowl, combine shrimp, crabmeat, green onion, cucumber and water chestnuts. Pour Dill Dressing over and toss until well coated. Cover and refrigerate at least 1 hour.

To serve, arrange salad greens on luncheon plates. Arrange avocados on greens and top with shrimp mixture. Garnish with tomato wedges.

Yield: 4 servings

A 6-ounce package of frozen, cooked crabmeat may be substituted for the fresh crabmeat; thaw, drain and remove the cartilage.

Dill Dressing

½ cup mayonnaise

¼ cup sour cream or plain yogurt

2 tablespoons lemon juice

1 teaspoon fresh dill or ¼ teaspoon dried dill

¼ teaspoon salt

Combine all ingredients until well blended.

Fresh Lobster Salad

2 cups lobster meat
  (or 2-3 medium
  crawfish tails)
Juice of 1-2 limes
½ cup finely chopped
  celery
¼ cup finely chopped
  onion
3 hard boiled eggs,
  chopped
3 tablespoons
  mayonnaise
¼ teaspoon salt
Tabasco sauce to taste
Crisp lettuce for
  garnish
Tomato slices for
  garnish

*C*ut lobster into small pieces and marinate in lime juice for ½ hour. Add remaining ingredients and toss lightly. Chill in refrigerator and serve garnished with crisp lettuce and tomato slices.

Yield: 4-6 servings

Shrimp and Scallop Salad

¾ cup cooking sherry
1 pound medium or
  large shrimp,
  peeled and
  deveined
1 pound scallops
1 (8-ounce) package
  frozen artichoke
  hearts
1 (18-ounce) can
  sliced water
  chestnuts
½ cup Caesar salad
  dressing
Romaine lettuce or
  various salad
  greens

*H*eat sherry in a large skillet over medium heat. When warm, add shrimp and scallops in a single layer. Cook 5-7 minutes until done. Drain seafood and run under cold water to stop cooking. Cook artichoke hearts according to package directions. Drain and chop into quarters. Drain water chestnuts.

In a large bowl combine seafood, artichoke hearts and water chestnuts. Add Caesar dressing and stir, coating all ingredients. Refrigerate several hours until very cold, stirring occasionally. Serve over romaine lettuce or green lettuce of your choice.

Yield: 4-6 servings

Open-Face Gorgonzola Cheese, Tomato and Basil Sandwiches

¼ pound Gorgonzola cheese
2 ounces cream cheese
Salt and pepper
4 slices sourdough bread
1 pound tomatoes, cored, sliced
12 basil leaves, washed, bundled and cut into thin ribbons

*C*ream the Gorgonzola cheese with the cream cheese and a few pinches of salt and pepper to make a soft spread. Toast the bread and spread each slice with cheese mixture. Layer the tomatoes over the cheese, overlapping them slightly; sprinkle with salt and pepper. Garnish with the basil ribbons and serve.

Yield: 4 open-faced sandwiches

Nutrition Analysis per sandwich:

saturated fat -	8.4 g	sodium -	721.8 mg
calories -	220	cholesterol -	36.5 g
fat -	9.2 g	fiber -	0.8 g
carbohydrate -	13.1 g	sugar -	1.4 g

Italian Crescent Sandwiches

7 eggs, divided
1½ cups grated cheese (freshly grated Parmesan, Romano or Monterey jack), divided
½ teaspoon cayenne pepper
2 (8-ounce) tubes refrigerator crescent roll dough, divided
½ pound ham, sliced
½ pound Provolone cheese, sliced
½ pound hard salami, sliced
3 (7.5-ounce) jars roasted peppers, drained, sliced

*P*reheat oven to 350°. Beat 6 eggs, ½ cup grated cheese and the cayenne pepper; set aside. Press 1 tube crescent roll dough in a 13 x 9 inch glass dish. Layer half of the ham, Provolone cheese, salami and peppers over rolls. Ladle half of the egg and cheese mixture on top. Repeat layers of ham, cheese, salami, peppers and egg mixture. Lay the remaining tube of crescent roll dough on top and press seams together. Beat remaining egg and brush on top of dough. Sprinkle remaining cup of grated cheese over top. Bake for 40-45 minutes. Let cool for 30 minutes before cutting into squares and serving.

Yield: 8 sandwiches

CURRIED LENTIL POCKETS

½ cup dried French green lentils

1 garlic clove, minced

½ medium onion, finely chopped

¼ cup bulgur wheat

1 tablespoon plus 1 teaspoon curry powder

2 tablespoons fresh orange juice

1 tablespoon mango chutney

Salt

2 tablespoons non-fat yogurt

1 tablespoon non-fat cream cheese

2 tablespoons chopped fresh mint

1 tomato, thinly sliced

1 Kirby cucumber, unpeeled, sliced into thin rounds

1 cup alfalfa sprouts

3 (2-ounce) pita breads, cut open

*P*lace 1½ cups water, lentils, garlic, and onion in a small saucepan over medium-low heat, cover and simmer for 20 minutes. Add bulgur; cover and simmer until water is absorbed, 20 to 25 minutes. Add curry powder, orange juice, mango chutney and salt to taste; mix and set aside. Whisk together yogurt, cream cheese and mint. Make sandwiches using 1 tablespoon of spread and ⅓ of the lentil mixture, ⅓ tomato, ⅓ cucumber and ⅓ cup sprouts for each.

Yield: 3 sandwiches

Nutrition Analysis per sandwich:

saturated fat -	0	sodium -	165 g
calories -	278	cholesterol -	1 mg
fat -	1 g	fiber -	8 g
carbohydrate -	53 g	sugar -	0

GRILLED MUSHROOM SANDWICHES

1 tablespoon butter or margarine

1 small onion, finely chopped

1 small garlic clove, minced

1 pound fresh mushrooms, finely chopped

6 ounces cream cheese, softened

½ teaspoon salt

½ teaspoon Worcestershire sauce

Dash of pepper

12 slices white or rye bread

Butter or margarine for grilling

*I*n medium saucepan melt 1 tablespoon butter or margarine. Add onion and garlic; sauté until onion is tender. Add mushrooms and cook 3 minutes; remove from heat. Add cream cheese, salt, Worcestershire and pepper; mix until smooth. Cool to room temperature. (Can be made ahead to this point. Store in covered container in refrigerator up to one week or freeze up to one month. Thaw at room temperature for two hours). Spread ¼ cup mushroom filling on bread; top with second slice of bread. Spread butter or margarine on both sides of sandwich and grill on a hot griddle until golden brown.

Yield: 6 sandwiches

RATATOUILLE SANDWICHES

1 red bell pepper, seeded, cut into eighths

1 small zucchini, sliced into ¼ inch rounds

1 red onion, sliced ¼ inch thick

1 small Italian eggplant, sliced into ¼ inch rounds

1 teaspoon herbes de Provence

½ teaspoon salt

1 teaspoon freshly ground pepper

1 tablespoon balsamic vinegar

Non-stick olive oil cooking spray

2 sun-dried tomato halves

4 Kalamata olives, pitted

2 tablespoons non-fat cream cheese

2 tablespoons non-fat sour cream

1 small garlic clove, finely chopped

4 (1-ounce) slices Tuscan bread or 2 (2-ounce) sections baguette, cut open lengthwise

1 small tomato, thinly sliced

8 fresh basil leaves

*P*reheat oven to 400°. In a medium bowl, combine red pepper, zucchini, onion, eggplant, herbes de Provence, salt, pepper and vinegar; toss to coat. Arrange in a single layer on a non-stick baking sheet and spray with the olive oil spray for 3 to 5 seconds. Roast for 25 minutes, turning once. Remove from oven and set aside. Meanwhile, rinse sun-dried tomatoes and olives in hot water to eliminate excess oil. If using dried sun-dried tomatoes, rehydrate in boiling water for 1 minute and dry on paper towels. Coarsely chop olives and tomatoes and place in a small bowl. Add cream cheese, sour cream and garlic and mix until smooth. Spread mixture on 2 slices of bread. Layer roasted vegetables and tomato slices on top of the spread. Top with basil leaves and remaining slices of bread.

Yield: two sandwiches

Nutrition Analysis per sandwich:

saturated fat -	0	sodium -	1050 mg
calories -	245	cholesterol -	3 mg
fat -	4 g	fiber -	5 g
carbohydrate -	44 g	sugar -	0

If you would like to make your own herbes de Provence, combine equal amounts of thyme, marjoram, rosemary, and sage.

ORIENTAL CHICKEN SALAD PITAS

4 whole boneless chicken breasts, poached and skinned

1 sweet red pepper, cored, seeded and sliced julienne

1 (5-ounce) can water chestnuts, drained and halved

5 scallions, julienned

4 dozen snow peas, trimmed and blanched

¾ cup toasted cashews

2 tablespoons minced fresh parsley

2 garlic cloves, minced

½ cup bottled teriyaki sauce

¼ cup sesame oil

¼ cup safflower oil

¼ cup Tahini (sesame paste)

2 tablespoons rice vinegar

2 tablespoons dry sherry

1 tablespoon brown sugar

2 tablespoons ground coriander

4 pita bread rounds

*S*lice poached chicken breasts into ¼ inch strips. Combine the chicken, red peppers, water chestnuts and scallions in a large mixing bowl. Add the snow peas and cashews. Process the parsley and garlic in a food processor with a steel blade. Add the teriyaki sauce, sesame seed oil, safflower oil, Tahini paste, vinegar, sherry, brown sugar, and coriander. Process until smooth. Pour the dressing onto the chicken mixture and toss thoroughly. Refrigerate several hours before serving. Stuff chicken mixture into pita bread and serve.

Yield: 6-8 servings

Nutrition Analysis per sandwich:

saturated fat -	4.1 g	sodium -	491.2 mg
calories -	413	cholesterol -	36.5 mg
fat -	25.5 g	fiber -	2.3 g
carbohydrate -	25.3 g	sugar -	0

Tahini (sesame paste) may be found at Oriental Groceries or Health Food Stores.

GRILLED CHICKEN BREAST SANDWICHES WITH COLESLAW

10 ounces green cabbage (approximately ¼ of a small head)

5 tablespoons low-fat yogurt

1 teaspoon Dijon mustard

1 tablespoon cider vinegar

Salt and freshly ground pepper

1 sprig fresh tarragon leaves, torn

2 chicken breast cutlets, ¼ inch thick

Non-stick olive oil cooking spray

2 (2-ounce) sections baguette, cut open lengthwise, or 4 (1-ounce) slices sourdough bread

Remove outer leaves and core from cabbage. Slice into the thinnest shreds possible; set aside. In a small bowl, whisk together yogurt, mustard, vinegar, salt and pepper to taste. Add to the cabbage along with the tarragon and toss to coat well. Season chicken cutlets with salt and pepper. Heat a cast-iron grill pan over high heat. Spray with olive oil spray and add chicken. Cook 2 to 3 minutes, turn, and continue grilling until browned and cooked through (approximately 2 minutes). Assemble sandwiches using a piece of chicken and ½ cup coleslaw for each.

Yield: two sandwiches

Nutrition Analysis per sandwich:

saturated fat -	0	sodium -	280 mg
calories -	294	cholesterol -	91 mg
fat -	6 g	fiber -	2 g
carbohydrate -	21 g	sugar -	0

Turkey and Roasted Pepper Sandwich

3 medium red bell peppers, stemmed, seeded, quartered

1 round loaf French or Pumpernickle bread

2 garlic cloves

2 cups firmly packed fresh basil leaves

3 tablespoons olive oil

½ pound thinly sliced turkey breast

1 medium tomato, sliced

¾ cup arugula

¼ pound sliced mozzarella cheese

4 red leaf lettuce leaves

Place bell peppers, skin side up on foil lined baking sheet and broil until charred (approximately 7 minutes). Cool in a zipped plastic bag; peel off skin and cut into 1 inch strips.

Cut a wide circle in top of bread loaf, 1 inch from edge. Carefully lift off lid. Pull out bread from top and bottom, leaving a ½-inch thick shell.

In a food processor or blender, combine garlic and basil. With motor running, pour in oil until thickened. Spread mixture inside bread shell and on underside of lid. Arrange half of pepper strips in shell followed by turkey, tomato, arugula, half of pepper strips, mozzarella and top with red lettuce leaves. Replace lid and press down firmly. To serve, cut into wedges.

Yield: 6 servings

Great for a picnic or family gathering.

GRILLED PINEAPPLE BURGERS

2 pounds ground beef
3 tablespoons Italian salad dressing
1 tablespoon salt
⅛ teaspoon pepper
1 (15-ounce) can sliced pineapple, drained
8 slices bacon, uncooked
1 cup barbecue sauce
⅓ cup packed brown sugar
⅓ cup honey
1 tablespoon lemon juice

Mix beef with salad dressing, salt and pepper; shape into 8 burger patties. Press pineapple slices into each burger. Wrap each burger with bacon and secure with a toothpick. Place burgers in a 13 x 9 inch dish.

Mix barbecue sauce with brown sugar, honey and lemon juice; pour over burgers. Cover and refrigerate for 2 hours.

Preheat grill. Grill burgers, pineapple side down, 4 inches from coals for 12-15 minutes. Turn and brush with barbecue mixture. Grill for 10-15 minutes more. Heat remaining sauce and serve with burgers.

Yield: 8 burgers

HERBED EYE ROAST SANDWICHES

1 tablespoon thyme
1 tablespoon coarsely ground pepper
1 tablespoon minced garlic
1 tablespoon caraway seeds
1 tablespoon paprika
1 tablespoon bread crumbs
Eye round roast
Cooking oil
Pumpernickel rolls

Mix all herbs together in a small mixing bowl. Rub oil over roast. Rub and pat mixed herb mixture all over meat, then wrap in waxed paper and let sit, for at least two hours and up to eight hours, in refrigerator to absorb flavors.

Preheat oven to 425°. Place roast in roasting pan and cook until meat thermometer registers medium rare. Cool meat and slice very thin and serve with buttered pumpernickel rolls.

Yield: variable

Try a horseradish and sour cream sauce as a condiment for these delicious sandwiches! The herb mixture may be halved or doubled to accomodate the size of the roast.

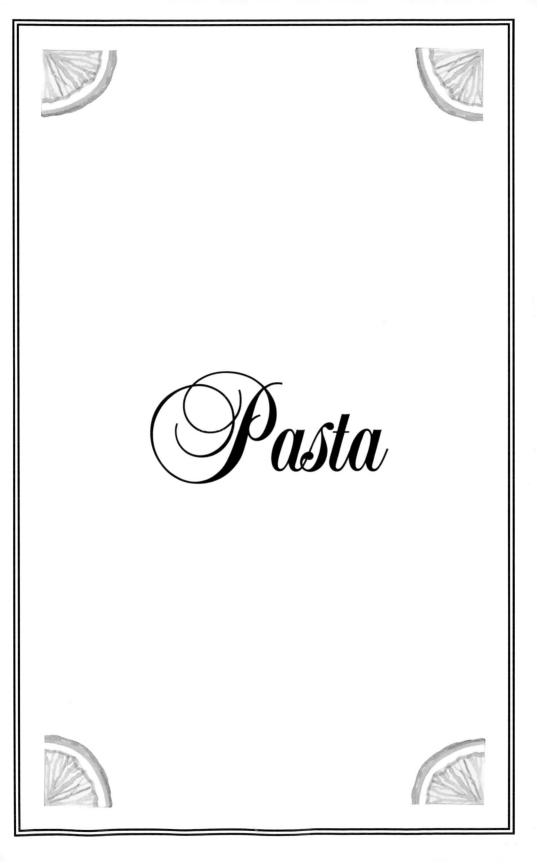

Pasta

STROLLING DOWN THE AVENUE

Worth Avenue, on Palm Beach, has long been known as the home of the most sought after treasures and trinkets, unique designs and personal service. Once comprised of locally-owned and seasonally-opened businesses, the shops of Worth Avenue now represent an array of local and international retailers catering to those with exclusive tastes.

Strolling down Worth Avenue is as much a pastime as meandering from shop to shop to find the perfect gift. The numerous vias, tucked in among the vine-covered archways, reveal the most distinct and delightful shops, the hidden treasures of the Avenue. Starting at the ocean's edge, Worth Avenue is an architectural wonder and a shopper's paradise.

Sun-Dried Tomato Fettucine

1 cup dry packed
   sun-dried tomatoes

½ cup olive oil

4 garlic cloves,
   minced

½ teaspoon dried red
   pepper

1 pound fettucine,
   cooked as directed
   on package

1 cup freshly grated
   Parmesan cheese

½ cup toasted pine
   nuts

*P*lace tomatoes in a small bowl and cover with boiling water. Let stand until soft; drain and chop.

Heat olive oil in skillet over medium heat. Add tomatoes, garlic and red pepper; sauté until garlic is golden brown (3 minutes). Transfer tomato mixture to a large bowl; add fettucine and Parmesan. Toss gently. Sprinkle pine nuts on top and serve.

Yield: 6 servings

Nutrition Analysis per serving:

saturated fat -	6.7 g	sodium -	473 mg
calories -	633	cholesterol -	11.2 mg
fat -	34 g	fiber -	5.7 g
carbohydrate -	61.7 g	sugar -	7.2 g

This is a quick and easy pasta with a lot of flavor!

Bow Ties with Spinach Sauce and Cheese

1 pound fresh spinach,
   washed, stems
   removed

3 tablespoons butter,
   divided

2 medium shallots,
   minced

1 cup whipping cream,
   divided

Freshly grated nutmeg
   to taste

Salt and black pepper
   to taste

8 ounces bow tie pasta,
   cooked according to
   package directions

1 cup finely shredded
   Gruyére cheese

*C*ook spinach in a large pan of boiling water until wilted (2 minutes); drain. Rinse in cold water and drain well. Chop and set aside.

Melt 1 tablespoon butter in medium saucepan over low heat. Add shallots and sauté until golden brown. Add spinach and cook 1 minute. Stir in ¾ cup cream, nutmeg, salt and pepper to taste. Cook and stir over low heat until heated through. Add remaining ¼ cup cream and bring to a simmer. Add remaining 2 tablespoons butter and heat until blended.

Place pasta in a heated serving dish. Add sauce and toss to blend. Add Gruyére cheese and toss. Serve immediately with additional cheese on the side.

Yield: 4 servings

ANGEL HAIR PASTA WITH FRESH TOMATO SAUCE

4 large tomatoes
⅓ cup fresh basil leaves, packed
¼ cup extra virgin olive oil
1 garlic clove, finely minced
Freshly ground pepper and salt to taste
1-1¼ pound angel hair pasta
Parmesan cheese to taste

𝒫lace 4-5 quarts salted water in a large pot over medium high heat. When the water is hot but not boiling, immerse tomatoes in hot water for 45 seconds and remove. Continue to heat water to boiling and cook pasta in it according to package directions. Slip the skins off the tomatoes and cut each in half. Remove seeds and pulp; coarsely chop tomatoes (3-4 cups).

Roll basil leaves and cut crosswise into strips; add to tomatoes with oil, garlic, salt and pepper. Top cooked pasta with tomato sauce and serve with grated Parmesan cheese.

Yield: 6 servings

Nutrition Analysis per serving:

saturated fat -	6 g	sodium -	90.5 mg
calories -	338	cholesterol -	0
fat -	5.8 g	fiber -	3.9 g
carbohydrate -	54 g	sugar -	4.9 g

Good tomatoes are the key to this wonderful sauce.

RIGATONI A LA VODKA

3 tablespoons butter
1 small onion, chopped
½ cup vodka
1 (6-ounce) can tomato sauce
1 cup heavy cream
8 ounces proscuitto, cut into 1 inch strips
Tabasco sauce to taste
⅔ cup grated Parmesan cheese
1 pound rigatoni pasta, prepared according to package directions
Fresh ground pepper to taste
Freshly grated Parmesan cheese to taste
Chopped fresh parsley to garnish

*I*n a skillet over medium high heat, sauté onion in butter until soft. Increase heat to high and add vodka; cook for 5 minutes stirring constantly. Reduce heat and add tomato sauce, cream, proscuitto and Tabasco. Simmer for 5 minutes; stir in Parmesan cheese and ground pepper. To serve, pour sauce over rigatoni and garnish with grated Parmesan and chopped parsley.

Yield: 4 servings

Béchamel Lasagna Rolls

LASAGNA AND FILLING

- 1 pound curly edge lasagna noodles
- 1 egg, beaten
- 1 pound ricotta cheese
- 8 ounces mozzarella cheese, grated
- 2 tablespoons salad oil
- 2 medium onions, chopped
- 2 large garlic cloves, minced
- 1 pound ground beef
- 1 cup plus 2 tablespoons fresh parsley, chopped
- 3 teaspoons fresh chopped basil
- 1½ teaspoons fresh oregano
- ¾ teaspoon salt
- ¼ teaspoon pepper
- 2 (15 ½-ounce) jars home-style spaghetti sauce

BÉCHAMEL SAUCE

- 2 tablespoons butter
- 2 tablespoons flour
- 1½ cups milk
- 1 cup plus 2 tablespoons grated Parmesan cheese, divided
- ½ teaspoon salt
- ¼ teaspoon pepper

Boil lasagna in 4 quarts salted water for 10 minutes or until tender but firm. Rinse lasagna with cold water and drain. Lay lasagna side by side on a towel to dry. In a bowl, combine egg, ricotta and mozzarella; set aside.

In a large skillet add oil and sauté onions and garlic over medium heat until tender. Add ground beef, cooking until brown; drain excess fat. Add 1 cup parsley, basil, oregano, salt and pepper. Add the egg and cheese mixture; stir until blended.

Pour 1 jar of spaghetti sauce into the bottom of an oblong 3 quart pan. Spread ¼ cup egg and meat mixture on each lasagna strip; roll up jelly-roll fashion. Place each roll in baking pan on its side.

To make béchamel sauce, melt butter in a saucepan over medium heat. Stir in flour, blending until smooth. Gradually stir in milk. Cook, stirring constantly until mixture boils and thickens. Stir in Parmesan cheese, salt and pepper.

Preheat oven to 400°. Spoon béchamel sauce over lasagna rolls. Pour remaining spaghetti sauce over the béchamel sauce. Sprinkle with the remaining parsley and Parmesan cheese. Cover with foil and bake for 20 minutes. Remove foil and bake an additional 10 minutes or until bubbly. Cool for 10 minutes prior to serving.

Yield: 8 servings

GORGONZOLA AND PISTACHIO
FETTUCINE

1 pound fettucine, cooked according to package directions

⅓-½ pound Gorgonzola cheese, crumbled

6 tablespoons light cream

4 tablespoons butter or margarine

6 tablespoons olive oil

2 garlic cloves, minced

6 tablespoons fresh parsley, finely chopped

4 ounces pistachio nuts, shelled

2 tablespoons pasta cooking water

6 tablespoons freshly grated Parmesan cheese

Freshly grated Parmesan cheese to taste

Mix Gorgonzola cheese and cream until thoroughly blended; set aside. Heat butter and oil in a skillet over medium heat. Add garlic and sauté until tender. Stir in parsley and pistachios. Cook and stir for 2 minutes; remove from heat. Add Gorgonzola mixture and stir until melted. Mix 2 tablespoons pasta water and Parmesan cheese into the sauce. Pour sauce over cooked fettucine and toss well. Serve with Parmesan cheese.

Yield: 4 servings

The secret of this recipe is to move quickly once the Gorgonzola has been added. Try adding sautéed, sliced Portabella mushrooms or fresh broccoli florets to the pasta. Also, pine nuts may be substituted for the pistachios.

Linguine with Garlic and Rosemary Oil

2 tablespoons olive oil

6 tablespoons unsalted butter

4 3-inch sprigs fresh rosemary

4 large garlic cloves, coarsely chopped

1 cup beef broth reduced to 2 tablespoons

12 ounces linguine

Freshly grated Parmesan cheese to taste

Fresh parsley or rosemary sprigs to garnish

In a small saucepan over medium heat, combine oil and butter. Add rosemary and garlic; cook until garlic begins to soften and brown lightly, about 5 minutes. Stir in reduced broth and set aside. Cook pasta in boiling salted water according to package directions; drain and place in a large serving bowl. Using a fine mesh sieve, strain infused oil over pasta. Toss and serve with freshly grated Parmesan cheese on the side. Garnish with fresh parsley or rosemary sprigs.

Yield: 6 side servings

Nutrition Analysis per serving:

saturated fat -	9.2 g	sodium -	225 mg
calories -	453	cholesterol -	37 mg
fat -	19.6 g	fiber -	2.7 g
carbohydrate -	53.4 g	sugar -	2.7 g

The flavor and aroma of this unusual pasta is delightful! The oil is also delicious brushed on bread and then grilled.

Fettuccine with Chardonnay Red Pepper Sauce

2 cups Chardonnay

2 large red peppers, roasted, peeled (see page 259 for instructions)

1 cup heavy cream

¼ cup fresh basil, packed

½ cup grated Parmesan cheese

12 ounces fettuccine, prepared according to package directions

Boil wine until it is reduced to ½ cup. Puree peppers and add to wine; stir in cream. Bring to a boil stirring constantly. Cut basil into strips and add to sauce. Add sauce to pasta and toss well. Top with Parmesan cheese and serve.

Yield: 4 servings

MARINATED CHICKEN BREASTS IN PEPPER SAUCE ON FETTUCINE

½ cup olive oil

½ cup minced fresh basil plus ¼ cup fresh basil cut into strips, divided

3 tablespoons fresh lemon juice

1 tablespoon crushed red pepper flakes

2 teaspoons minced garlic

2 pounds boneless chicken breast

5 tablespoons unsalted butter, divided

1 medium red bell pepper, cut into julienne strips

½ cup dry white wine

½ cup chicken broth or stock

2 cups heavy cream

1 cup sliced mushrooms

½ teaspoon salt

¾ cup Parmesan cheese

12 ounces spinach fettucine, cooked according to package directions

Combine olive oil, ¼ cup minced basil, lemon juice, red pepper flakes and minced garlic. Add chicken and stir to coat. Cover and refrigerate overnight.

In a skillet, melt 3 tablespoons butter over medium heat; add bell pepper and sauté for 2 minutes. Remove the pepper strips and set aside. Stir in wine and chicken broth. Increase heat to high and bring to a boil until sauce is reduced to 2 tablespoons (approximately 5 minutes). Lower heat, add cream and cook until sauce is reduced by half (approximately 4 minutes). In another skillet, melt 2 tablespoons butter over medium heat; add mushrooms and sauté until slightly browned. Add the reserved peppers, cream sauce and salt.

Preheat broiler. Drain chicken and discard marinade. Broil chicken 4 inches from heat, turning once, until juices run clear (you may also grill the chicken). Cut the broiled chicken into ½ inch strips. Stir Parmesan and ¼ cup basil into pepper sauce. On heated serving platter, arrange chicken on top of warm fettucine and pour sauce over the top to cover. Garnish with ¼ cup fresh basil strips and serve immediately.

Yield: 4 servings

The sauce may be made one day ahead, adding the Parmesan cheese and basil when reheating.

Pasta with Chicken and Peanut Sauce

8 ounces linguine

3 garlic cloves, minced

1 tablespoon red wine vinegar

1 tablespoon brown sugar

6 tablespoons chunky peanut butter

¼ cup soy sauce

6 tablespoons peanut oil

⅛ teaspoon Tabasco sauce

2 boneless, skinless cooked chicken breast halves

5 tablespoons toasted sesame seeds, divided

1 pound asparagus

3 scallions, white bulb and 3 inches green, cut into 2 inch strips

1 small cucumber, halved and cut into ¼ inch dices

Cook linguine according to package directions until just tender. Drain, rinse under cold water, drain again and set aside. In a food processor or blender, place garlic, vinegar, brown sugar, peanut butter and soy sauce. Process one minute. Continue processing and slowly pour in oil and Tabasco. Process until well blended. Cut chicken into bite sized pieces. Toss chicken and pasta together. Add sauce and 4 tablespoons sesame seeds. Blanch asparagus by placing in boiling water for one minute. Drain, rinse and pat dry. Place linguine and chicken into serving bowl and place asparagus on top. Sprinkle with scallions, cucumber and remaining tablespoon sesame seeds. Serve at room temperature.

Yield: 4 servings

Nutrition Analysis per serving:

saturated fat -	6.2 g	sodium -	980 mg
calories -	561	cholesterol -	43.5 g
fat -	40.5 g	fiber -	5 g
carbohydrate -	61 g	sugar -	8.8 g

Children love this one!

Chicken in Tomato Sauce with Dill and Feta Cheese

4 teaspoons olive oil, divided

½ cup finely chopped onion

1½ teaspoons minced garlic

1 teaspoon dried oregano leaves, crumbled

¼ cup dry white or red wine

1 (16-ounce) can crushed tomatoes

4 skinless, boneless chicken breast halves

¼ teaspoon salt

freshly ground pepper to taste

½ cup crumbled feta cheese

2 tablespoons chopped fresh dill or Italian parsley

¾ pound fresh pasta of choice, prepared according to package directions

Heat 2 teaspoons oil in a medium saucepan over medium high heat. Add onion and cook until lightly golden. Add garlic and oregano and cook 5 minutes longer. Pour in wine, add tomatoes and bring to a simmer for 10 minutes over low heat, until sauce is thickened.

Season chicken with salt and pepper. Heat remaining 2 teaspoons oil in a large skillet. Add chicken and cook over medium high heat until chicken is no longer pink at center. Add sauce to skillet and simmer 5 minutes longer. Place chicken and sauce on top of pasta and top with feta cheese and dill. Serve immediately.

Yield: 4 servings

CREAMY CHICKEN WITH ANGEL HAIR PASTA

12 ounces angel hair pasta, cooked according to package directions

6 tablespoons butter

½ teaspoon onion powder

½ teaspoon salt

¼ teaspoon white pepper

¼ teaspoon black pepper

¼ teaspoon thyme

2 boneless, skinless chicken breasts, cut into 1-inch pieces

½ cup green onions, chopped

2 cups half and half

*M*elt butter in skillet over medium heat; add onion powder, salt, white and black pepper and thyme. Add chicken and brown until almost cooked through. Add green onions and cream and simmer 2-3 minutes, until thick. Add pasta and toss until completely hot (2 minutes). Serve immediately.

Yield: 4 servings

VEGETABLE CARBONARA

10 ounces fettucini, cooked according to package directions

½ cup milk

½ cup mayonnaise

2 eggs, beaten

8 slices bacon, crisply cooked, crumbled

½ cup grated Parmesan cheese

¼ cup chopped parsley

1 cup sliced squash, steamed

1 cup broccoli florettes, steamed

*G*radually add milk to mayonnaise in a small saucepan. Cook over medium heat, stirring constantly, until hot. Remove from heat and stir in eggs. Toss with pasta until well coated. Add bacon, cheese and parsley. Toss lightly. Fold in squash and broccoli. Serve with additional cheese if desired.

Yield: 4 servings

A nice change from the usual carbonara.

Penne from Heaven

6 red peppers, quartered and seeded

4 tablespoons olive oil, divided

Salt and pepper to taste

½ cup Italian parsley, tightly packed

1 tablespoon fresh oregano

1 tablespoon fresh thyme

2 garlic cloves, coarsely chopped

1 pound large white mushrooms, cleaned and sliced

1 pound Italian sausage, sliced, casing removed

1 pound penne or other tube pasta

¼ cup reserved liquid from cooked pasta

Grated Parmesan cheese to taste

*P*reheat oven to 450°. Cut pepper quarters on the diagonal into ½-inch pieces and place in a 13 x 9 inch baking dish; drizzle with half the olive oil and add salt and pepper to taste. Bake peppers until tender and edges charred, stirring occasionally (15-20 minutes). Remove from oven and set aside.

Finely chop parsley, oregano, thyme and garlic together; set aside. Heat remaining oil in large non-stick skillet. Add mushrooms and stir over medium heat until mushrooms are tender and golden brown. Add herb and garlic mixture and sauté for 2 minutes. Sprinkle with salt and pepper to taste; transfer to another dish.

Wipe out skillet. Add sausage and cook over medium high heat until sausage is browned. Pour into colander to drain. Add mushroom mixture and sausage to baking dish with peppers. Keep warm in oven at lowest temperature.

Bring large pot of water to a boil. Add penne and cook, stirring frequently, until pasta is tender. Drain pasta and reserve ¼ cup cooking liquid.

On large, deep platter add pasta and red pepper mushroom mixture; stir gently to combine. Add cooking liquid as needed to moisten pasta. Sprinkle with grated cheese to taste. Serve immediately.

Yield: 6-8 servings

Nutrition Analysis per serving:

saturated fat -	5.4 g	sodium -	597 mg
calories -	517	cholesterol -	37 mg
fat -	22 g	fiber -	5.5 g
carbohydrate -	57.5 g	sugar -	6.8 g

Can be easily doubled. Try using green peppers or sun-dried tomatoes in place of red peppers.

LEMON DILL MEATBALLS IN CREAMY TOMATO SAUCE

2 tablespoons margarine
¾ cup chopped onion
2 garlic cloves, minced
2 (14½-ounce) cans Italian style stewed tomatoes
1 tablespoon fresh dill or 1 teaspoon dried dill
½ teaspoon sugar
¼ teaspoon salt
⅛ teaspoon pepper
1 egg, beaten
½ cup soft bread crumbs
2 tablespoons finely chopped onion
1½ teaspoons lemon peel, shredded
12 ounces ground beef
2 tablespoons cooking oil
¼ cup whipping cream
1 pound cooked linguine

Melt margarine in a saucepan over medium heat; add onion and garlic and sauté until onion is tender but not brown. Carefully stir in the undrained tomatoes, dill, sugar, salt and pepper. Bring to a boil and reduce heat. Simmer uncovered for 30-35 minutes or until sauce thickens, stirring occasionally.

Combine egg, bread crumbs, onion and lemon peel. Add meat and mix well. Shape into 1-inch balls (24 meatballs). In a large skillet, heat oil over medium high heat and add meatballs; cook for 8-10 minutes or until meat is no longer pink. Drain well. Stir meatballs into sauce. Slowly add whipping cream and cook 2 minutes longer or until heated through, stirring constantly. Serve over cooked linguine.

Yield: 4 servings

CRAB AND ANGEL HAIR PASTA

½ cup butter
2 tablespoons chopped onion
2 tablespoons minced fresh basil or 1 teaspoon dried basil
2 tablespoons minced fresh parsley
3 (16-ounce) cans peeled tomatoes, drained and chopped
½ cup dry white wine
1½ pounds crabmeat or 1 pound imitation crabmeat
1 pound angel hair pasta, cooked according to package directions
Freshly grated Parmesan cheese

*I*n a large skillet, melt butter over medium heat and sauté onion, basil and parsley for 2-3 minutes. Stir in tomatoes and heat to a boil. Add wine and simmer for 5 minutes. Add crabmeat and simmer 2-3 minutes longer. Remove from heat. Place warm pasta in a serving dish. Top with crabmeat mixture and serve with Parmesan.

Yield: 6-8 servings

Nutrition Analysis per serving:

saturated fat -	4.6 g	sodium -	1573 mg
calories -	449	cholesterol -	59 mg
fat -	19 g	fiber -	2.4 g
carbohydrate -	57 g	sugar -	8.7 g

CRAB AND LOBSTER LASAGNA

CREAM CHEESE MIXTURE

- ½ cup Parmesan cheese, freshly grated
- 1 pound cream cheese, softened
- ½ cup ricotta cheese
- 1 teaspoon crushed garlic
- ⅓ cup fresh basil, chopped
- 1½ tablespoons fresh oregano, chopped
- ⅓ cup heavy cream
- Salt and pepper to taste

MOZZARELLA MIXTURE

- 6 ounces mozzarella, grated
- 6 ounces Provolone, grated

SEAFOOD

- 1 live lobster (1¼-1½ pounds), cooked, meat removed, tail and claw shells reserved
- ¾ pound fresh crab meat

PASTA

- 1½ 12 x 18 inch sheets fresh pasta, cooked al dente and cut into three inch strips or 1 pound prepared lasagna noodles
- olive oil

*C*ombine all cream cheese mixture ingredients except basil; beat well and set aside. Combine mozzarella cheese mixture ingredients and set aside. To prepare shellfish stock, melt butter in a large saucepan over medium heat and sauté shells and vegetables until soft. Add wine, water, clam juice and spices. Bring to a boil; lower heat to simmer for 30 minutes. Season with salt and pepper. Strain and set aside.

Preheat oven to 400°. Combine lemon and butter; set aside. Spread cream cheese mixture evenly on cooked pasta (¼ inch thick). Lighty brush olive oil on the bottom of a lasagna pan. Place one third of the pasta on the bottom of the pan with the cheese side up. Place ½ of the crab and lobster on the first layer of pasta. Top this with half the mozzarella mixture and sprinkle with ½ of the basil. Repeat with second layer and top with third layer of pasta, cheese side down. Top with the lemon butter. Sprinkle remaining basil over pasta. Add 1½-2 cups shellfish stock to pan and cover with foil. Bake for 20 minutes.

Yield: 8-10 servings

SHELLFISH STOCK

- 2 tablespoons butter
- Reserved lobster shells
- ½ pound onion, chopped
- ¼ pound celery, chopped
- ¼ pound carrots, chopped
- 2 cups dry white wine
- 1 cup water
- 1 cup clam juice
- 1 tablespoon Hungarian paprika
- 1 teaspoon cayenne

LEMON BUTTER

- ½ cup butter, softened
- 2 ounces freshly squeezed lemon juice

Creamy Clam Sauce with Linguine

¼ cup margarine

1 cup sliced mushrooms

1 garlic clove, finely chopped

3 tablespoons flour

2 (6½-ounce) cans chopped clams, drained, liquid reserved

1 cup light cream

8 ounces fresh, whole clams

¼ cup grated Parmesan cheese

1 tablespoon dry sherry

1 tablespoon chopped parsley

¼ teaspoon pepper

1 pound linguine, cooked according to package directions

*I*n medium saucepan, melt margarine over medium heat. Add mushrooms and garlic, cooking until tender. Stir in flour. Gradually stir in clam liquid and cream. Cook, stirring until thickened. Add clams, cheese, sherry, parsley and pepper. Heat through and serve over linguine.

Yield: 6-8 servings

Nutrition Analysis per serving:

saturated fat -	9.6 g	sodium -	248 mg
calories -	586	cholesterol -	86.1 mg
fat -	26.5 g	fiber -	2.4 g
carbohydrate -	53.3 g	sugar -	3.2 g

Pasta with Shrimp and Jalapeño Orange Sauce

6 tablespoons
  unsalted butter

24 medium shrimp,
  peeled and
  deveined

2 tablespoons minced
  shallots

1 small jalapeño chili,
  seeded, thinly
  sliced

½ cup dry white wine

1½ cups orange juice

¾ cup whipping
  cream

Salt and pepper to
  taste

1 pound angel hair
  pasta

Fresh parsley to
  garnish

Melt butter in heavy large skillet over medium high heat. Add shrimp and cook until just pink, approximately one minute per side. Transfer shrimp to a plate. Add shallots and jalapeño to skillet and sauté 1 minute. Add wine and bring to a boil. Mix in orange juice and cream. Boil until reduced to thin sauce, stirring occasionally (approximately 10-15 minutes). Season to taste with salt and pepper.

Cook pasta in boiling salted water until tender; drain. Add shrimp to sauce and cook until heated through. Add pasta and toss well. Sprinkle with minced fresh parsley.

Yield: 6-8 servings

Nutrition Analysis per serving:

saturated fat -	13 g	sodium -	57 mg
calories -	486	cholesterol -	12.6 mg
fat -	21.7 g	fiber -	2.9 g
carbohydrate -	51 g	sugar -	7 g

Unique, easy and delicious!

PENNE AND FRESH TUNA WITH RAISIN AND ALMOND SAUCE

8 tablespoons butter, divided

1½ pounds fresh tuna steaks, cut into ¼-inch strips

3 tablespoons flour

¼ teaspoon nutmeg

Salt and white pepper to taste

1 cup white wine

3 tablespoons currants

⅓ cup raisins

¼ cup blanched almonds, slivered

1 tablespoon fresh lemon juice

1 teaspoon sugar

12 ounces penne pasta

½ teaspoon Tabasco sauce

2 egg yolks, beaten

Melt 2½ tablespoons butter in a large pan over medium heat and gently sauté tuna until medium rare. Transfer to a platter and keep warm.

Melt 5½ tablespoons butter in a saucepan over medium heat; stir in flour. Cook, stirring until smooth and golden. Add nutmeg, salt and pepper to taste and cook briefly. Gradually pour in wine, stirring constantly. When the sauce is smooth, stir in currants, raisins, almonds, lemon juice and sugar. Bring to a boil then reduce to a simmer over low heat for 20 minutes.

Cook penne in boiling salted water until tender; drain. Whisk Tabasco into the egg yolks. With the saucepan off the heat, whisk the egg mixture into the sauce; keep warm.

Transfer penne to warmed plates and top with tuna strips. Pour sauce over tuna and serve.

Yield: 4 servings

You will not want to miss this! An incredible mix of flavors!

Deep Sea Pesto Pasta

2 tablespoons olive
oil

1 garlic clove, minced

1 tablespoon minced
shallots

¼ cup red bell pepper,
cut into strips

¼ cup yellow bell
pepper, cut into
strips

¼ cup green bell
pepper, cut into
strips

8 ounces cooked
seafood (crab,
shrimp, scallops or
lobster)

¼ cup dry white wine

1 (9-ounce) package
linguine pasta

⅓ cup prepared pesto
sauce (see page 130)

*P*repare linguine according to package directions. While pasta is cooking, heat oil in a large
skillet over medium heat. Sauté garlic and shallots
for 1-2 minutes. Add red, yellow and green peppers
and sauté for 2 minutes. Add seafood and wine;
sauté 2-3 minutes. In medium bowl, toss pasta with
pesto and top with seafood mixture.

Yield: 4 servings

PENNE PASTA WITH BLACK BEANS AND MANGO

1 (14-ounce) can chopped tomatoes

1 small onion, sliced

3 garlic cloves, crushed

1 (15-ounce) can black beans, drained and rinsed

2 tablespoons olive oil

4 ounces penne pasta, cooked according to package directions

1 mango, peeled and cubed

½ cup fresh basil leaves, sliced

Salt and freshly ground black pepper to taste

*S*immer tomatoes, onion and garlic in a medium saucepan over medium heat for 10 minutes. Add beans and oil and cook one additional minute. Place pasta in a serving bowl and spoon bean sauce over top; add mango, basil, salt and pepper to taste. Toss and serve.

Yield: 2 servings

Nutrition Analysis per serving:

saturated fat -	2.6 g	sodium -	728 mg
calories -	338	cholesterol -	0
fat -	17 g	fiber -	14.2 g
carbohydrate -	106.8 g	sugar -	9.8 g

This is a quick, easy and nutritious pasta for busy schedules!

Vegetarian Pasta

½ pound spaghetti

3 tablespoons oil, divided

2 medium zucchini

2 scallions

2 garlic cloves, minced

3 carrots, chopped

1 green pepper, chopped into ¼ inch pieces

½ teaspoon salt

5 teaspoons soy sauce

Grated zest from 1 lime

1 tablespoon fresh lime juice

½ cup chopped roasted cashew nuts

Cook spaghetti in a pot of boiling salted water until tender. Drain and toss with 1 tablespoon oil; set aside. Quarter zucchini lengthwise and cut crosswise into ¼ inch slices. Chop white part of scallions and slice green tops. In a large frying pan, heat 2 tablespoons oil over medium high heat. Add zucchini; reduce heat to low and cook until starting to brown, approximately 5 minutes. Add garlic, scallions, carrots, green pepper and salt. Cover and cook until softened, 5-8 minutes. Stir in soy sauce, add spaghetti and heat through. Stir in lime juice, zest and scallion tops. Sprinkle with cashews and serve.

Yield: 4 servings

Pasta Primavera

¾ pound fresh
  asparagus

2 cups fresh broccoli
  florets

1 tablespoon olive oil

1 medium onion,
  chopped

2 large garlic cloves,
  chopped

1 large carrot, sliced

1 medium red
  pepper, chopped

1 medium yellow
  pepper, chopped

1 medium green
  pepper, chopped

½ pound fresh
  mushrooms, sliced

1 cup whipping
  cream

½ cup chicken broth

3 green onions,
  chopped

2 tablespoons
  chopped fresh basil
  or 2 teaspoons
  dried basil

½ teaspoon salt

8 ounces linguine,
  broken in half,
  cooked according to
  package directions

1 cup freshly grated
  Parmesan cheese

¼ teaspoon ground
  pepper

*S*nap off tough ends of asparagus. Remove scales with peeler or knife. Cut asparagus into 1½ inch pieces. Steam asparagus pieces and broccoli floretes for 6-8 minutes until vegetables are crisp-tender. Remove from heat and set aside.

Heat oil in a large skillet over medium heat and sauté onion and garlic until tender. Add carrots, peppers and mushrooms; sauté until crisp-tender. Remove from heat, drain, add to other vegetables and set aside.

Combine whipping cream, broth, green onions, basil and salt in a medium skillet. Cook over medium high heat for 5 minutes, stirring occasionally, until thick. Place linguine in a large serving bowl. Add reserved vegetables and whipping cream mixture; toss gently. Sprinkle with Parmesan cheese and pepper; toss gently. Serve immediately.

Yield: 8 servings

PESTO FETTUCCINE WITH CHICKEN AND ASPARAGUS

2 tablespoons olive oil, divided

1 medium red bell pepper, cut into thin strips

1 medium yellow pepper, cut into thin strips

½ pound asparagus, trimmed, cut into 1-inch pieces

8 oil-packed sun-dried tomato halves, thinly sliced

1 pound boneless chicken breasts, cut into ½-inch strips

Salt and pepper to taste

¾ cup pesto (see recipe below) or prepared pesto

6 tablespoons Parmesan cheese

1 pound dried fettucine

*H*eat one tablespoon olive oil in a large skillet over medium high heat. Add peppers and asparagus and sauté until lightly charred and softened, approximately 10 minutes. Transfer to a large bowl and toss with the sun-dried tomatoes.

Wipe out skillet and add remaining tablespoon olive oil; place over medium high heat. Salt and pepper chicken strips and add to skillet. Cook, stirring, until just cooked through, approximately 3 minutes. Transfer chicken to the bowl with vegetables. Toss together with ⅓ cup pesto and 2 tablespoons Parmesan cheese. Add salt and pepper to taste.

Prepare fettuccine according to package directions; drain. Toss fettuccine with remaining pesto and Parmesan cheese. To serve, place fettuccine on serving platter and spoon chicken mixture over top.

Yield: 4 servings

PESTO

4-6 garlic cloves, minced

2 cups packed fresh basil leaves

¼ cup Parmesan cheese

¼ cup pine nuts

½ cup olive oil

*P*lace garlic, basil, Parmesan cheese and pine nuts in a food processor. With motor running, slowly drizzle oil into processor and process until pureed. Do not heat; pour directly on drained warm pasta. If preparing ahead of time, refrigerate then bring to room temperature before using.

Yield: ¾ cup

Vegetables & Side Dishes

THE FLAGLER TRAIN

*S*parkling, turquoise waters surrounded by lush tropical wilderness inspired oil magnate Henry Morrison Flagler to call Palm Beach County a "veritable paradise." After visiting the small communities around Lake Worth in 1892 and becoming enchanted with the area, he built the world-class Royal Poinciana Hotel in Palm Beach. At that time, it was the largest resort hotel in the world. To provide a comfortable and timely means of transportation for his guests, Mr. Flagler extended his railroad, thus connecting South Florida to the nation.

The contributions Henry Flagler made to Palm Beach County continued with

the creation of the Palm Beach Inn, later renamed The Breakers, and the marble mansion, Whitehall, which he gave to his third wife as a wedding gift. The Flaglers shared their paradise with many guests, opening Whitehall to them and extending the most luxurious and extravagant hospitality.

Whether traveling to the Palm Beaches by rail, road, air or sea, the splendor of Whitehall, now the Henry Morrison Flagler Museum, and Henry Flagler's personal rail car can still be enjoyed today. Viewing these historic treasures, one can understand Mr. Flagler's desire to develop his slice of paradise.

Marinated Asparagus

2 tablespoons chopped fresh basil

2 tablespoons olive oil

2 tablespoons white wine or apple cider vinegar

½ teaspoon salt

¼ teaspoon sugar

⅛ teaspoon pepper

1 pound fresh asparagus

⅓ cup chopped tomato

Mix basil, oil, vinegar, salt, sugar and pepper. Refrigerate until ready to serve.

Cut ends off asparagus. Steam 4-6 minutes. Place asparagus on platter and top with chopped tomato. Pour vinaigrette on asparagus and serve.

Yield: 6 servings

Nutrition Analysis per serving:

saturated fat -	0.3 g	sodium -	164.8 mg
calories -	36	fiber -	1.2 g
fat -	2 g	cholesterol -	0
carbohydrate -	2.9 g	sugar 1.8 g	

Lemon Broccoli with Garlic

2 tablespoons olive oil

3 garlic cloves, finely chopped

3 large bunches broccoli, cut into large florettes (about 12 cups)

1 cup chicken broth

1 teaspoon grated lemon peel

1 tablespoon fresh lemon juice

Salt and freshly ground black pepper to taste

Heat oil in a large skillet over medium-high heat. Add garlic and cook 1-2 minutes until golden but not brown. Add broccoli; cook 3 minutes, turning frequently to coat with oil.

Add chicken broth and lemon peel. Reduce heat to medium; simmer, covered, 5-7 minutes until broccoli is tender but crisp. Sprinkle with lemon juice and salt and pepper to taste.

Yield: 12 servings

Nutrition Analysis per serving:

saturated fat -	0	sodium -	40 mg
calories -	68	fiber -	2.5 g
fat -	3 g	cholesterol -	1 mg
carbohydrate -	7 g	sugar -	1.4 g

Broccoli Puff

2 (10-ounce)
packages frozen
chopped broccoli
3 eggs, separated
1 tablespoon flour
⅛ teaspoon ground
nutmeg
1 cup mayonnaise
(may use reduced
fat)
1 tablespoon butter
or margarine,
softened
¼ teaspoon salt
¼ teaspoon pepper
¼ cup plus 1
tablespoon grated
Parmesan cheese

*C*ook broccoli according to package directions; drain well and set aside.

Beat egg yolks; add flour, mixing well. Stir in nutmeg, mayonnaise, butter, salt, pepper and cheese. Add broccoli, mixing gently and set aside.

Preheat oven to 350°. Beat egg whites at room temperature until stiff but not dry; gently fold into broccoli mixture. Pour into a lightly buttered 9 inch square baking dish. Bake for 30 minutes. Cut into squares to serve.

Yield: 9 servings

Scalloped Cauliflower

1 (10 ½-ounce) can
condensed cream of
celery soup
2 beaten eggs
½ cup shredded sharp
Cheddar cheese
½ cup bread crumbs
¼ cup chopped parsley
¼ cup chopped
pimentos, drained
1 tablespoon minced
onion
½ teaspoon salt
⅛ teaspoon pepper
2 (9-ounce) packages
frozen cauliflower,
thawed and drained

*P*reheat oven to 375°. Combine all ingredients except cauliflower and mix well. Fold in cauliflower until evenly mixed. Place in a greased 10 x 6 inch baking dish. Bake for 45 minutes.

Yield: 6-8 servings

This delightful dish can be prepared ahead and refrigerated prior to baking; bring to room temperature before baking and serving.

GINGER CARROTS

3-4 cups diagonally sliced carrots
1 cup orange juice
½ cup chicken broth
3 whole cloves
¾ teaspoon ground ginger
1½ teaspoons grated lemon zest
3 tablespoons sugar

*P*lace all ingredients except sugar in saucepan and bring to a boil. Stir in sugar. Cover and simmer for 30 minutes until carrots are tender. Serve immediately.

Yield: 6-8 servings

Nutrition Analysis per serving:

saturated fat -	0	sodium -	31.3 mg
calories -	50	fiber -	2.5 g
fat -	0.3 g	cholesterol -	0
carbohydrate -	10 g	sugar -	7.7 g

CURRIED CORN AND SWEET PEPPERS

8 ears fresh corn, or 4⅓ cups frozen whole corn kernels
4 tablespoons unsalted butter
½ cup diced sweet yellow pepper
½ cup diced sweet red pepper
½ cup diced green pepper
2 teaspoons curry powder
Salt and freshly ground pepper to taste
2 tablespoons unsalted butter
½ cup heavy cream

*S*huck the ears of corn and discard the husks and silks. Bring enough water to boil to cover the ears of corn. Drop the corn into the water. When the water returns to a boil, cover and remove from heat. Let stand five minutes only. Drain and let cool. Cut the corn from the cobs (about 4½ cups).

Heat butter in a skillet and add all of the peppers; sprinkle with curry powder. Cook, stirring, about one minute. Add the corn, salt and pepper to taste. Stir in two tablespoons of butter and the cream. Bring to a simmer, stirring continually. Serve hot.

Yield: 6 servings

Paraguayan Corn Souffle

1 cup water
½ tablespoon salt
2 medium onions, chopped
½ cup margarine
3 eggs
8 ounces mozzarella cheese, diced
18 ears corn, kernels removed and pureed in food processor
¾ cup milk

*I*n a medium saucepan, boil water with salt and onions for 10 minutes. Allow to cool but do not drain. Preheat oven to 375°. In a large bowl, whip the margarine until creamy; add eggs one at a time. Add the cheese, onions with water, corn and milk. Blend thoroughly and pour into greased 13 x 9 inch baking dish. Bake for 1 hour and 15 minutes.

Yield: 10 servings

Eggplant Casserole

½ medium onion, chopped
½ green pepper, chopped
3 stalks celery, chopped
2 tablespoons cooking oil
1 (16-ounce) can tomatoes, drained
½ teaspoon Worcestershire sauce
½ teaspoon salt
⅛ teaspoon pepper
1 large eggplant
¼ pound Cheddar cheese, grated
3 tablespoons butter, cut into pieces, softened

*S*auté onion, pepper and celery in cooking oil over medium high heat until onion is golden. Add tomatoes, Worcestershire sauce, salt and pepper. Leave to simmer while peeling and cubing eggplant. Cook eggplant in salted boiling water until cooked but still firm. Drain and add to simmering tomato mixture. Simmer 5 minutes longer.

Preheat oven to 350°. Turn eggplant mixture into a buttered casserole. Stir in most of the grated cheese, reserving a small amount to sprinkle on top. Dot top with butter and bake for 15 minutes.

Yield: 8-10 servings

Green Beans in Basil and Walnut Sauce

1½ pounds fresh green beans

¾ cup finely minced green onions

3 tablespoons finely minced parsley

4 tablespoons finely minced fresh basil

3 tablespoons vinegar or fresh lemon juice

1 cup coarsely chopped walnuts

¾ cup olive oil or vegetable oil

Salt and pepper to taste

Snap the ends off the beans and wash thoroughly. Bring a large pot of water to a boil. Add beans and cook for 6-8 minutes, until slightly tender. Drain and run under cold water. Drain, transfer to a medium serving bowl and set aside.

In a blender or food processor, combine the onion, parsley, basil, vinegar, walnuts and oil. Blend the mixture until smooth. Season with salt and pepper.

Pour sauce over beans and toss. Chill for 1 to 2 hours. Bring beans back to room temperature before serving.

Yield: 8 servings

For an interesting variation, add 1 cup diced plum tomatoes to the beans before adding sauce.

Oven-Baked French Fries

2 large baking potatoes

1 large sweet potato

1 egg white

1 tablespoon chili powder (or to taste)

½ teaspoon ground red pepper

Cut potatoes into thin fries. In a large bowl, lightly beat egg white with a fork until foamy. Stir in chili powder and pepper. Add potatoes and toss to coat well.

Preheat oven to 450°. Using a non-stick baking sheet or baking sheet coated with non-stick spray, spread potatoes in a single layer. Bake for 30-35 minutes or until potatoes are crisp and browned.

Yield: 4 servings

Nutrition Analysis per serving:

saturated fat -	0	sodium -	23.5 mg
calories -	143.5	fiber -	2.5 g
fat -	0.1 g	cholesterol -	0
carbohydrate -	32.5 g	sugar -	4.3 g

GREEN BEANS WITH WARM MUSTARD VINAIGRETTE

2 pounds fresh green beans, ends trimmed

2 shallots, minced

2 tablespoons Dijon mustard

2 tablespoons Balsamic vinegar

⅓ cup olive oil

Salt and pepper to taste

¼ cup chopped fresh dill

*H*eat large pot of water to boiling. Add green beans and cook until crisp-tender, approximately 2-4 minutes (or steam for 8 minutes using a vegetable steamer). Drain well.

While beans are cooking, place shallots, mustard, vinegar, oil, salt and pepper in small saucepan. Heat, whisking constantly, just until the mixture is hot to the touch.

Toss hot green beans with dressing to coat. Quickly add the dill and toss to combine. Serve immediately.

Yield: 6-8 servings

Nutrition Analysis per serving:

saturated fat -	1.6 g	sodium -	126.2 mg
calories -	112	fiber -	2.0 g
fat -	9.2 g	cholesterol -	0
carbohydrate -	6.6 g	sugar -	0.4 g

SWEET SCALLOPED ONIONS

3 medium sweet Spanish or Vidalia onions

¼ cup butter or margarine

¼ cup chopped green pepper

2 tablespoons diced pimento

1 cup grated cheese (Swiss or Cheddar), divided

1 cup cracker crumbs, divided

2 eggs, beaten

¾ cup light cream or evaporated milk

½ teaspoon salt

⅛ teaspoon white pepper

2 tablespoons butter or margarine, melted

*P*eel and slice onions to measure about 6 cups. Melt butter in skillet. Add onions and green pepper and sauté until onions are tender. Stir in pimento. Place half of onion mixture in shallow buttered baking dish (10 inch square). Sprinkle with ½ cup cheese and ½ cup cracker crumbs. Repeat layers of onions and cheese.

Preheat oven to 325°. Beat eggs with cream or evaporated milk and seasonings. Pour over onion mixture. Combine remaining cracker crumbs with melted butter. Sprinkle over top of onion mixture. Bake for 25-30 minutes until set.

Yield: 6 servings

For a sweeter variation, substitute red peppers for green.

SEASONAL PEAS AND ONIONS

9 tablespoons
  unsalted butter,
  softened, divided
1½ cups shredded
  Iceberg lettuce
  leaves
3 (17-ounce) cans
  early peas, drained,
  1 cup liquid
  reserved
1 pound frozen small
  white onions
½ teaspoon dried
  thyme
Salt and freshly
  ground black
  pepper to taste
1 tablespoon sugar
3 tablespoons flour
¼ teaspoon freshly
  grated nutmeg
¼ cup minced fresh
  parsley

*I*n 2-3 quart saucepan, melt 6 tablespoons butter; add the lettuce and stir until the leaves are wilted. Add the reserved liquid, peas, onions, thyme, salt, pepper and sugar. Toss to mix well. Simmer 15 minutes or until the onions are tender.

In a small bowl combine the remaining butter with the flour. Add to the peas with the nutmeg and stir until the liquid has thickened. Serve garnished with minced parsley.

Yield: 12 servings

May be prepared and refrigerated up to 24 hours in advance, reserving parsley for final heating.

GARLICKY POTATOES

6-7 small red potatoes,
  quartered
4 large garlic cloves,
  minced
2 tablespoons olive oil
½ teaspoon dried
  thyme or 1 teaspoon
  fresh chopped
  thyme
1 tablespoon dry
  white wine
Salt and freshly
  ground black pepper
  to taste

*P*reheat oven to 350°. Place potatoes in lightly greased 13 x 9 inch baking dish. Sprinkle garlic over potatoes; drizzle olive oil over potatoes. Sprinkle thyme then drizzle wine over potatoes. Cover tightly with foil and bake for 1 hour.

Yield: 2 servings

Nutrition Analysis per serving:

saturated fat -	1.9 g	sodium -	16.5 mg
calories -	349	fiber -	3.6 g
fat -	13.7 g	cholesterol -	0
carbohydrate -	51.2 g	sugar -	3.5 g

CARROT CUPS WITH SUMMER SAUCE

CARROT CUPS

3 medium carrots, peeled and cut into large pieces

2 small parsnips, peeled and cut into large pieces

1½ cups evaporated milk

4 eggs

½ teaspoon finely shredded orange peel

¼ teaspoon salt

⅛ teaspoon ground red pepper

SUMMER SAUCE

¾ cup fresh spinach leaves, washed, drained

1 green onion

½ cup evaporated milk

2 sprigs parsley

1 teaspoon crushed rosemary

¼ teaspoon salt

Fresh rosemary sprigs for garnish

*I*n a covered, medium saucepan, cook carrots and parsnips in water for 25-30 minutes until tender. Drain well. In a blender or food processor, combine carrots, parsnips, evaporated milk, eggs, orange peel, salt and red pepper. Blend until smooth.

Preheat oven to 325°. Place 6 greased 6-ounce custard cups in a 13 x 9 inch baking dish. Divide carrot mixture evenly among cups. Place baking dish on oven rack. Pour boiling water into dish around cups one inch deep. Bake for 30-35 minutes or until a knife inserted in the middle comes out clean.

While cups are baking, prepare Summer Sauce by combining spinach, onion, evaporated milk, parsley, crushed rosemary and salt in a blender or food processor. Blend until smooth. Transfer sauce to saucepan and heat and stir for 3-5 minutes to desired consistency. Serve while warm.

Loosen edges of custards, slipping point of knife down the sides. Invert cups onto dinner plates. Spoon Summer Sauce around carrot cups. Garnish with rosemary sprigs.

Yield: 6 servings

Rosemary Potatoes

18 small red potatoes, unpeeled
6 tablespoons olive oil
Salt and finely ground pepper to taste
6 tablespoons finely chopped fresh rosemary

*P*reheat oven to 350°. Place 3 potatoes each onto 6 x 6 inch pieces of aluminum foil. Sprinkle each serving with 1 teaspoon oil, salt, pepper and 1 tablespoon rosemary. Wrap tightly into foil bundles. Place on baking sheet and bake for 30-45 minutes until potatoes are tender. Serve immediately.

Yield: 6 servings

Nutrition Analysis per serving:

saturated fat -	1.1 g	sodium -	111.8 mg
calories -	256	fiber -	3.6 g
fat -	4.7 g	cholesterol -	0
carbohydrate -	51 g	sugar -	3.4 g

1 tablespoon dried rosemary may be substituted for every 2 tablespoons fresh. Dill, tarragon or thyme may be used in place of rosemary. Add 1 teaspoon minced shallot for variation in each foil pocket.

Gold Coast Sweet Potatoes

3 cups fresh cooked sweet potatoes
2 eggs, beaten
1 cup white sugar
⅔ cup melted butter, divided
½ cup milk
1 teaspoon vanilla
⅓ cup self-rising flour
1 cup coconut
1 cup chopped pecans
½ cup brown sugar

*P*reheat oven to 375°. Mix potatoes, eggs, white sugar, ⅓ cup melted butter, milk and vanilla with electric mixer until smooth. Pour into greased 13 x 9 inch baking dish. Combine remaining ingredients, including reserved ⅓ cup butter, and sprinkle over potato mixture. Bake, uncovered, for 25 minutes.

Yield: 8-12 servings

SPINACH, BACON AND MUSHROOM GRATIN

2 slices bacon, cut into ½ inch pieces

¼ pound mushrooms, thinly sliced

1 (10-ounce) package fresh spinach, washed and stemmed

¼ cup freshly grated Parmesan cheese, divided

1 large egg, lightly beaten

1½ teaspoons fresh lemon juice

14 saltine crackers, finely ground, divided

1 tablespoon unsalted butter, melted

Salt and pepper to taste

*I*n a large skillet, cook the bacon over moderate heat until crisp. Pour off all but one tablespoon fat. Add mushrooms to skillet and sauté over moderately high heat until the liquid has evaporated. Transfer the bacon and mushrooms to a bowl. Add the spinach to the pan and cook covered over moderately high heat for 3 minutes or until wilted. Drain well. Add spinach to the bacon and mushrooms. Add Parmesan (reserving one tablespoon), egg, lemon juice and 2 tablespoons of the cracker crumbs and mix well. Salt and pepper to taste.

Preheat oven to 425°. Spoon the spinach mixture into a 1½ quart buttered shallow baking dish. In a small bowl, combine remaining cracker crumbs with the butter and remaining Parmesan. Sprinkle over spinach and bake for 15 minutes or until top is golden.

Yield: 2-3 servings

This recipe can easily be doubled.

SAUTÉED PEAS WITH BASIL

2 slices bacon, chopped

½ tablespoon olive oil

2 garlic cloves, minced

2 tablespoons chopped green onion

1 (16-ounce) package frozen peas, thawed and drained

½ cup fresh basil, cut into thin strips

Salt and pepper to taste

*S*auté chopped bacon in a large skillet over medium heat until well done. Place cooked bacon on paper towels. Drain drippings from skillet, reserving 1 tablespoon. Stir tablespoon of bacon drippings and olive oil together in skillet. Add garlic cloves and green onions; sauté for 2 minutes. Add peas and basil; cook until heated through (approximately 5 minutes). Add bacon, salt and pepper and serve.

Yield: 6 servings

Apple Pecan Winter Squash

2 medium Acorn squash

¼ cup firmly packed brown sugar

¼ cup butter or margarine, melted

1 cup chopped, unpeeled Red Delicious apple

¼ cup chopped pecans, toasted

Preheat oven to 350°. Cut squash in half and remove seeds (microwave whole squash for two minutes to make cutting in half easier). Place squash, cut sides up, in shallow baking dish. Add ½-inch boiling water to pan. Combine brown sugar, butter and chopped apple and spoon into squash shells. Cover and bake for 1 hour (or microwave on high for 15-20 minutes covered with waxed paper) until squash is tender. Sprinkle with pecans and serve.

Yield: 4 servings

Nutrition Analysis per serving:

saturated fat -	2 g	sodium -	10 mg
calories -	267	fiber -	5.5 g
fat -	12.9 g	cholesterol -	0
carbohydrate -	39.0 g	sugar -	21.9 g

Try another variation; replace the apple with ½ cup crushed butter crackers and prepare as directed.

Herb Butter Zucchini Fans

⅓ cup butter, softened

2 tablespoons minced fresh parsley

½ teaspoon dried whole tarragon

⅛ teaspoon salt

⅛ teaspoon pepper

4 small zucchini

¼ cup water

2 tablespoons freshly grated Parmesan cheese

1 tablespoon soft bread crumbs

Preheat oven to 400°. Combine butter, parsley, tarragon, salt and pepper and set aside. Cut zucchini lengthwise into 4 slices but leave slices attached at stem end. Fan zucchini open and spread with the butter mixture. Place in 13 x 9 inch pan and add water. Bake for 20 minutes. Remove from oven and preheat broiler. Combine cheese and bread crumbs. Sprinkle over zucchini. Broil 4 inches from heat for 2 minutes and serve.

Yield: 4 servings

Nutrition Analysis per serving:

saturated fat -	10.6 g	sodium -	297 mg
calories -	340	fiber -	2.4 g
fat -	17.2 g	cholesterol -	45.7 mg
carbohydrate -	5.1 g	sugar -	4.9 g

Pumpkin Squash Bake

1 cup canned
  pumpkin
1 (10-ounce) package
  frozen winter
  squash, thawed
1½ cups applesauce
¼ cup brown sugar
½ cup heavy cream
2 eggs, beaten
½ teaspoon salt
⅛ teaspoon nutmeg
½ teaspoon pumpkin
  pie spice
4 tablespoons butter,
  melted
½ cup soft bread
  crumbs
⅓ cup ground
  almonds
2 tablespoons butter,
  melted

*I*n a large bowl, mix together pumpkin, squash, applesauce, brown sugar, cream, eggs, salt, nutmeg, pumpkin pie spice and 4 tablespoons melted butter. Place in shallow, buttered 2 quart casserole.

Preheat oven to 350°. Mix remaining ingredients and sprinkle over casserole. Bake, uncovered, for 45 minutes. Serve hot.

Yield: 8 servings

Stuffed Zucchini

2 medium zucchini
½ cup chopped onion
1 garlic clove, minced
4 tablespoons butter,
  divided
1 large tomato,
  peeled, seeded and
  chopped
½ cup soft bread
  crumbs
2 tablespoons freshly
  grated Parmesan
  cheese

*P*reheat oven to 350°. Wash zucchini and cut in half lengthwise. Hollow out shells, reserving pulp. In 2 tablespoons butter, sauté garlic and onion until soft. Add zucchini pulp and tomatoes and mix. Fill shells with mixture, rounding the top. Place in shallow buttered 2-quart baking dish. Melt remaining butter and mix with the bread crumbs and cheese. Sprinkle on top of stuffed shells. Cover with foil and bake for 30 minutes.

Yield: 4 servings

CONFETTI SQUASH CASSEROLE

2 pounds yellow
squash, sliced

1 can cream of
chicken soup

8 ounces sour cream

4 ounces chopped
pimento, drained

8 ounces sliced water
chestnuts, drained

1 large onion, finely
chopped

2 carrots, grated

½ cup butter

6 ounces garden herb
stuffing mix

Cook squash in salted water for 10 minutes; drain well. Combine all ingredients except butter and stuffing mix. Mix well, but gently. Preheat oven to 350°. Melt butter in a saucepan and add stuffing mix; mix well. Combine stuffing mix and squash mixture until blended. Pour into a greased 2 quart baking dish and bake for 30 minutes.

Yield: 8 servings

AuGRATIN TOMATOES

8 large tomatoes,
sliced

1½ cups herb stuffing,
uncooked

1½ cups grated
Cheddar cheese

½ medium onion,
chopped

½ cup butter, melted

Salt and pepper to
taste

Preheat oven to 350°. Layer ½ of the tomato slices on bottom of 13 x 9 inch pan; salt and pepper to taste. Layer ½ of stuffing, cheese and onion on tomatoes in that order. Layer remaining tomatoes and top with remaining onion, stuffing and cheese. Drizzle butter over top and bake, uncovered, for 50 minutes.

Yield 10-12 servings

This is a great do-ahead dish for dinner parties. Prepare without baking and refrigerate the morning of the party. Bring to room temperature prior to baking and enjoy your company.

Chevré Stuffed Tomatoes

2 large tomatoes,
  sliced in half
  horizontally or 4
  small tomatoes,
  cored and left
  whole
1 scallion, chopped
1 teaspoon olive oil
¼ teaspoon salt
⅛ teaspoon freshly
  ground black
  pepper
1 teaspoon finely
  chopped fresh basil
2 slices whole wheat
  toast, crumbled
3 ounces soft, mild
  Chevré (goat
  cheese)

*S*coop the seeds and pulp out of tomatoes, leaving only the thick, meaty shell. Reserve pulp. Turn tomatoes upside down and allow to drain.

Preheat oven to 425°. Combine pulp in a bowl with scallion, oil, salt, pepper, basil, toast and Chevré. Mix thoroughly. Stuff filling into shells and place in a 2-quart greased baking dish. Bake for 5 minutes. Remove from oven and preheat broiler. Return tomatoes to oven and broil for one minute, placing tomatoes as close as possible to the heating element. Serve hot.

Yield: 4 servings

Nutrition Analysis per serving:

saturated fat -	3.3 g	sodium -	460 mg
calories -	110	fiber -	1.9 g
fat -	6.2 g	cholesterol -	18.8 mg
carbohydrate -	8.0 g	sugar -	1.3 g

Tomato Pie

1 unbaked 9 inch
  deep dish pie crust
5 medium tomatoes,
  peeled, sliced and
  seasoned with salt
  and pepper
3 tablespoons
  chopped fresh basil
1 cup chopped
  scallions
1½ cups grated
  Cheddar cheese
½ cup mayonnaise
1 teaspoon Dijon
  mustard
¼ cup grated
  Parmesan cheese

*P*reheat oven to 450°. Prick holes in bottom of pie crust with fork. Bake for 10-15 minutes or until golden. Remove from oven and reduce heat to 325°.

Layer ½ of tomatoes on bottom of crust. Sprinkle with ½ of basil and scallions. Repeat layers. Mix Cheddar cheese with mayonnaise and mustard. Spread over pie. Sprinkle with Parmesan cheese to lightly cover. Bake for 45 minutes or until heated through and browned.

Yield: 6-8 servings

TOMATO CAPRESE

2 large tomatoes, peeled, cut into large sections

8 ounces fresh mozzarella, cubed (optional)

½ cup vegetable oil

3 tablespoons red wine vinegar

1 teaspoon Worcestershire sauce

¾ teaspoon salt

½ tablespoon sugar

⅛ teaspoon pepper

1 clove garlic, minced

2 tablespoons chopped fresh basil

1 pinch thyme

5 green onions, chopped

*P*lace tomatoes and mozzarella in medium bowl. Whisk together remaining ingredients and pour over tomatoes and mozzarella. Refrigerate for at least one hour.

Yield: 4-6 servings

Nutrition Analysis per serving:

saturated fat -	4 g	sodium -	453.8 mg
calories -	180	fiber -	0.7 g
fat -	28 g	cholesterol -	0
carbohydrate -	5.6 g	sugar -	3.8 g

GRILLED VEGETABLE SALAD

2 small eggplants
2 medium zucchini
2 medium yellow
   onions
2 red bell peppers
Olive oil
Salt and pepper to
   taste
Balsamic vinegar
Bamboo skewers

*P*reheat grill. Slice eggplants and zucchini into ⅓ inch thick rounds. Peel onions and cut into wedges ½ inch thick at outer edge. Core and seed peppers. Slice into 1 inch wide strips. Alternate vegetables on skewers. Brush vegetables on both sides with olive oil. Place on heated grill and cook for 5 minutes or until nicely browned. Turn and cook 5 minutes longer. Distribute among 4 salad plates and remove skewers. Sprinkle with salt and pepper and a few drops of balsamic vinegar. Serve warm or at room temperature.

Yield: 4 servings

Nutrition Analysis per serving:

saturated fat -	0.5 g	sodium -	152 mg
calories -	55	fiber -	2.4 g
fat -	3.8 g	cholesterol -	0
carbohydrate -	8.9 g	sugar -	5.9 g

Oven Roasted Vegetables

1 cup peeled baby
carrots

1 small onion,
chopped

2 tablespoons olive
oil

2 tablespoons fresh
lemon juice

1 clove garlic, minced

1 teaspoon dried
crushed rosemary

⅛ teaspoon ground
black pepper

½ small eggplant,
peeled, cut
lengthwise in half,
then into ½-inch
thick slices

1 medium red bell
pepper, seeded and
cut into ½-inch
wide strips

*P*reheat oven to 450°. Place carrots and onion in a shallow baking dish coated with non-stick cooking spray. In a small bowl mix together olive oil, lemon juice, garlic, rosemary and pepper. Drizzle 2½ tablespoons of the mixture over the carrots and onions in the pan. Roast in oven for 25 minutes, stirring occasionally. Add eggplant and red pepper. Drizzle with remaining oil mixture and toss. Continue to roast for another 15 minutes, or until vegetables are tender and slightly brown.

Yield: 4 servings

Nutrition Analysis per serving:

saturated fat -	0.5 g	sodium -	15 mg
calories -	61	fiber -	1.5 g
fat -	3.6 g	cholesterol -	0
carbohydrate -	7.2 g	sugar -	3.8 g

Baked Bananas

6 bananas, peels intact
¼ cup lemon juice
6 tablespoons brown sugar
Butter
½ cup rum

*C*ut bananas in half lengthwise, leaving peels on. Place halves in a shallow baking pan, sliced side up. Sprinkle with lemon juice and brown sugar. Dot with butter. Let sit for 30 minutes.

Preheat broiler. Pour rum over the bananas and broil for 10 to 15 minutes, basting once or twice.

Yield: 6 servings

Nutrition Analysis per serving:

saturated fat -	2.5 g	sodium -	6.5 mg
calories -	222	fiber -	1.8 g
fat -	4.7 g	cholesterol -	11 mg
carbohydrate -	31.2 g	sugar -	26.2 g

This delicious Floribbean side dish is wonderful served with meat or fish.

Hot Cranberry Casserole

3 cups chopped apples
2 cups whole raw cranberries
1 teaspoon lemon juice
1½ cups sugar
1⅓ cups uncooked, quick oats
1 cup chopped walnuts
⅓ cup packed brown sugar
½ cup margarine, melted

*S*pray a 2 quart casserole with non-stick spray. Preheat oven to 325°. Place chopped apples and raw cranberries in casserole. Sprinkle with lemon juice and cover with sugar. In a medium mixing bowl, blend oats, walnuts, brown sugar and margarine just until moist. Pour over fruit. Bake, uncovered, for 1 hour 15 minutes.

Yield: 8-10 servings

Nutrition Analysis per serving:

saturated fat -	2 g	sodium -	102.3 mg
calories -	456	fiber -	3.6 g
fat -	21.4 g	cholesterol -	0
carbohydrate -	64.5 g	sugar -	49.7 g

CHILI CHEESE CASSEROLE

2 (4½-ounce) cans chopped green chilies

1 pound Monterey jack cheese, coarsely grated

1 pound Cheddar cheese, coarsely grated

4 egg whites

4 egg yolks

1 tablespoon flour

½ teaspoon salt

¼ teaspoon pepper

⅔ cup evaporated milk

Fresh tomatoes, sliced

*P*reheat oven to 325°. Combine chilies and cheeses. Turn into a 2 quart buttered casserole. Beat egg whites until stiff but not dry. Beat egg yolks with flour, salt, pepper and milk until well blended. Gently fold whites into yolk mixture. Pour egg mixture over cheeses and chilies and mix gently. Bake for 30 minutes. Remove from oven and arrange slices of tomatoes around edge of casserole. Bake 30 minutes longer or until knife comes out clean.

Yield: 6 servings

FRIED RICE

3 strips bacon, diced

¼ cup chopped green onions

⅓ cup diced red pepper

¼ cup frozen green peas

4 cups cooked white rice

1 egg, beaten

3 tablespoons soy sauce

*C*ook bacon in large skillet over medium heat until crisp. Add onions, pepper and peas. Stir fry one minute then add egg and cook until egg is partially scrambled. Stir in rice and soy sauce; cook until heated through.

Yield: 6 servings

BAKED RICE, TOMATOES AND CHEESE

3 tablespoons butter

⅓ cup finely chopped onion

1 garlic clove, minced

1 cup rice, uncooked

½ cup diced tomatoes, fresh or canned

1 sprig fresh thyme or ¼ teaspoon dried thyme

½ bay leaf

1¾ cups chicken broth

3-4 tablespoons grated Parmesan cheese

3-4 tablespoons grated Gruyere cheese

1 tablespoon fresh chopped parsley

Melt the butter over medium heat in an ovenproof serving dish. Add onion and garlic and cook, stirring until onion is translucent. Add rice, tomatoes, thyme, bay leaf and broth. Stir until well mixed (may be prepared to this point and refrigerated one day ahead). Cover and bring to a boil. Remove cover. Preheat oven to 350°. Bake exactly 17 minutes. Remove from oven and remove bay leaf and thyme sprig. Stir in cheeses and parsley.

Yield: 6-8 servings

Nutrition Analysis per serving:

saturated fat -	4.1 g	sodium -	247.5 mg
calories -	142.5	fiber -	3.7 g
fat -	6.9 g	cholesterol -	18.2 mg
carbohydrate -	15.3 g	sugar -	0.8 g

CURRIED APPLE RICE

¼ cup butter

½ tablespoon curry

1 apple, peeled and cut into small pieces

1 medium onion, chopped

1 stalk celery, chopped

2½ cups apple juice

1 cup rice

¼ cup unsalted peanuts

Melt butter in saucepan over medium heat. Add curry and apples and sauté until apples are soft. Remove and reserve apples. Add onion and celery to same pan and sauté until soft. Add apple juice to onion and celery and bring to a boil. Add rice and cook until all liquid is absorbed; approximately 20 minutes. Add peanuts and apples and serve.

Yield: 4 servings

Nutrition Analysis per serving:

saturated fat -	6.1 g	sodium -	133.1 mg
calories -	256	fiber -	1.7 g
fat -	10.2 g	cholesterol -	26.4 mg
carbohydrate -	39.8 g	sugar -	23.6 g

VEGETABLE BROWN RICE

1 tablespoon butter or olive oil

½ cup chopped onion

2 tablespoons chopped parsley

1 green pepper, coarsely chopped

2½ cups beef broth

1 cup brown rice, uncooked

1 tablespoon thyme leaves

2 small zucchini, chopped

½ cup chopped red or yellow bell pepper

1 tomato, coarsely chopped

¼ cup cream

Salt and pepper to taste

*H*eat butter or oil in large saucepan and sauté onion, parsley and pepper until onion is translucent. Add broth and bring to a boil. Stir in rice and thyme. Cover tightly and cook over low heat for 40 minutes. Stir in zucchini and red or yellow pepper. Cover and continue cooking until all liquid is absorbed; about 10 minutes. Add tomato and cream and stir gently. Season to taste with salt and pepper.

Yield: 6 servings

Nutrition Analysis per serving:

saturated fat -	3.3 g	sodium -	332.3 mg
calories -	160	fiber -	1.5 g
fat -	5.8 g	cholesterol -	5.5 mg
carbohydrate -	21.8 g	sugar -	2.7 g

SAUSAGE GRITS

1 pound bulk pork sausage

2 cups shredded Cheddar cheese

3 tablespoons butter

3 cups hot, cooked grits

3 eggs, beaten

1½ cups milk

*I*n a heavy skillet, cook the sausage, stirring frequently, until brown. Drain and spoon into a 13 x 9 inch baking pan coated with non stick cooking spray.

Preheat oven to 350°. Add the cheese and butter to the hot grits and stir until melted. In a small bowl, combine the eggs and milk; stir into the grits. Pour the grits mixture over the sausage. Bake, uncovered, for 1 hour. Serve hot.

Yield: 8-10 servings

This southern specialty is a featured recipe in **The Junior League Centennial Cookbook.**

RICE AND BLACK BEANS

1 (15-ounce) can
black beans,
drained and rinsed

1 (12-ounce) can
whole kernel corn,
drained

1 cup uncooked
white rice

1 (16-ounce) jar
chunky mild salsa

1½ cups vegetable juice
cocktail

¼ teaspoon ground
cumin

¼ teaspoon ground
oregano

¾ cup shredded
Cheddar cheese

Sour cream and
cilantro for topping

*P*reheat oven to 375°. Lightly grease a 2 quart covered casserole. Combine beans, corn, rice, salsa, vegetable juice, cumin and oregano in casserole. Cover and bake for 60 minutes stirring after 30 minutes. Remove from oven and sprinkle with cheese. Cover and let stand for 5 minutes before serving. Top with sour cream and cilantro.

Yield: 8 side servings or 4 main dish servings

Nutrition Analysis per serving:

saturated fat -	2.3 g	sodium -	1121.3 mg
calories -	189	fiber -	5.5 g
fat -	4.2 g	cholesterol -	9.4 mg
carbohydrate -	26.3 g	sugar -	4.7 g

Saffron Rice with Avocado

3 tablespoons butter
1 small onion, finely chopped
1 small garlic clove, finely chopped
½ cup water
1 cup white rice
½ teaspoon saffron threads
2½ cups condensed chicken broth or stock, undiluted
Salt to taste
4 medium ripe avocados, peeled and diced

*M*elt butter over low heat. Add onions, garlic and water, cooking until water has evaporated and onion is soft. Add rice, continue to cook and stir until rice is opaque. Add saffron threads and broth. Bring to a boil. Cover and reduce to simmer for 20 minutes. Salt to taste. Fold in diced avocado just before serving.

Yield: 4 servings

Cinnamon Raisin Souffle

1 loaf cinnamon raisin bread, torn into pieces
1 (20-ounce) can crushed pineapple, undrained
1 cup butter
⅓ cup sugar
4 eggs

*P*reheat oven to 350°. Place torn bread pieces in a greased 13 x 9 inch pan. Pour pineapple over the bread and set aside. Cream together the butter and sugar. Add eggs to creamed mixture and mix well. Add creamed mixture to bread and pineapple. Bake, uncovered, for 40 minutes.

Yield: 8 servings

excellent!
Brunch

RISOTTO WITH
GORGONZOLA CHEESE

6 cups chicken or
beef broth or stock

6 tablespoons butter

1 small onion,
minced

2 cups Italian Arborio
rice

6 tablespoons
Gorgonzola cheese,
crumbled

2 tablespoons cream

Bring broth to a boil in a saucepan; reduce heat to keep at a slow boil. In a 2 quart saucepan, melt butter over medium heat; add the onion and cook until the onion has turned golden in color, stirring constantly. Add rice and stir for 3 minutes until every grain is coated with butter. Slowly add boiling broth to rice 1 cup at a time. Continue stirring over heat until all the liquid is absorbed and the rice is still moist. Remove from heat and stir in Gorgonzola cheese that has been combined with the cream. Cover the pan and let stand for 2-3 minutes before serving.

Yield: 8 servings

Nutrition Analysis per serving:

saturated fat -	8.1 g	sodium -	730 mg
calories -	331	fiber -	0.9 g
fat -	13.9 g	cholesterol -	35 mg
carbohydrate -	42.4 g	sugar -	1.1 g

EMBASSY RISOTTO WITH PORCINI

1½-2 cups sliced fresh porcini mushrooms
1 garlic clove, peeled
2 tablespoons olive oil
Salt and pepper to taste
½ small onion, chopped
6 tablespoons unsalted butter, divided
1 cup Italian rice (Arborio or Carnaroli)
¼ cup white wine
5 cups light beef broth, warmed
¾ cup grated Parmesan cheese
1 teaspoon chopped fresh parsley

Clean the mushrooms by running quickly under cold water. Dry immediately. Cut mushrooms julienne style.

Sauté the whole garlic in pan with olive oil. When the clove is lightly browned or golden, remove it and add the mushrooms to the seasoned oil. Sauté for 2-4 minutes. Add salt and pepper to taste and set aside.

In heavy enamel pan, sauté onion in half the butter until onion turns golden color. Add rice. After a minute, add the white wine and cook the rice, stirring constantly until the wine evaporates. While continuing to stir, add the warm broth, a ladle at a time, so that the broth just covers the rice. As the rice absorbs the broth, add more and stir gently.

When half the broth has been added, add the mushrooms. Continue to stir and add broth until it all has been absorbed by the rice. Once you start adding the broth, the whole process should take between 15-18 minutes. Turn off the heat. Add the remaining butter, Parmesan and parsley. Stir until smooth and creamy. Serve immediately.

Yield: 4 servings

Nutrition Analysis per serving:

saturated fat -	14.8 g	sodium -	1152.7 mg
calories -	395	fiber -	0.9 g
fat -	24.4 g	cholesterol -	61.5 mg
carbohydrate -	28 g	sugar -	0

May make ahead, double, halve, freeze or microwave. Any other kind of mushroom may be substituted for the porcini, but remember that mushroom types vary greatly in the amount of liquid they render during cooking. Adjust cooking time as necessary.

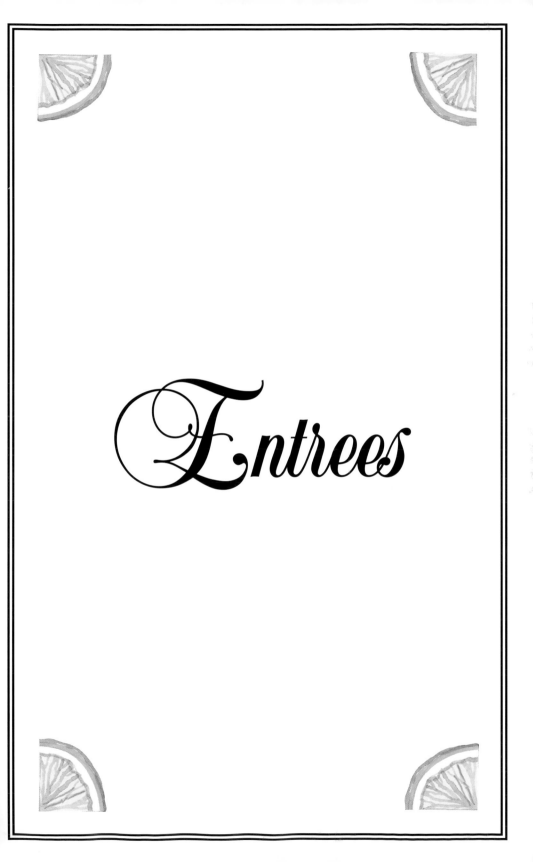

Entrees

BLUE AS BLUE

*B*ooks written, lyrics sung, memories made, all surrounded by water. Our Atlantic Ocean has been referred to as "she" which can explain its mystic serenity, violent temper and unyielding bounty. Never has mankind been so entranced by nature as it is by the ocean. The obvious reasons are many. The more obscure ones are romanticized. It grants us life with its fruit and steals lives with its fury, yet the ocean always remains both nemesis and friend without emphasis on either. The balance of its personality is seen in the faces of those who turn to it for serenity and pleasure. Walks on the beach calm and bond those who stroll its shores. Swimming and fishing are enjoyed by all who appreciate their right to use the seas. It is no wonder that people migrate to the water for pleasure and relaxation. Our duty as caretakers of the ocean is to see that it remains the clean and unscathed beauty we know her to be. Our future generations rely on us to maintain the right that is inherently ours to enjoy, the paradise of the sea, blue as blue can be.

VEAL ESCALLOPS WITH TOMATO BASIL CREAM SAUCE

3 tablespoons butter

1 tablespoon oil

12 veal escallops, cut ⅛ inch thick

2 tablespoons chopped shallots

¾ cup dry white wine

¾ cup chicken stock

¾ cup heavy cream

2 large peeled and seeded tomatoes, finely chopped

½ cup fresh basil leaves, chopped

Whole basil leaves to garnish

Salt and pepper to taste

Melt butter and oil in a large skillet over medium-high heat. Quickly sauté both sides of the veal escallops in batches until lightly browned. Remove to a warm platter and continue to sauté remaining veal. Cover veal with foil to keep warm. Pour off excess fat from pan, leaving 2 tablespoons. Stir in shallots and cook for 1 minute. Add wine and stock, bring to a boil and reduce to ½ cup. Add cream and boil until slightly thickened. Stir in tomatoes and chopped basil. Season to taste, if desired, with salt and pepper. Return veal to pan and heat gently just until warm. Divide among 6 plates and garnish with whole basil leaves.

Yield: 6 servings

Veal with Caramelized Onions

3 tablespoons butter
3 medium onions,
 thinly sliced
1 cup chicken stock
 or chicken broth
1 teaspoon sugar
4 (7-ounce) veal loin
 chops
Olive oil
Salt and pepper

Melt butter in medium saucepan or skillet. Add sliced onions and sauté over low heat until golden brown, approximately 30 minutes. Add chicken stock and sugar and simmer approximately 10 minutes or until all the liquid is absorbed. Preheat the broiler or grill. Brush veal chops with olive oil and season with salt and pepper. Broil or grill veal chops until done, approximately 5 minutes per side for medium. Spoon caramelized onions onto serving platter and place veal chops on top.

Yield: 4 servings

Nutrition Analysis per serving:

saturated fat -	13.0 g	sodium -	168.6 mg
calories -	400	fiber -	0.9 g
fat -	25 g	cholesterol -	124.7 mg
carbohydrate -	10.1 g	sugar -	8.6 g

Pork chops may be substituted for veal chops. If available, use vidalia onions for added sweetness.

Scallopini of Veal

12 veal scallopini
 Oil
 Flour
2 whole ripe
 avocados
12 slices of mozzarella
 cheese

In a sauté pan or large skillet place enough oil to cover the bottom of the pan. Dredge veal in flour. Heat skillet to almost smoking. Add scallopini to pan. Brown quickly and turn to brown the other side.

Remove scallopini and place on a baking tray. Peel avocados, cut in half and slice in wedges enough to make 12 pieces. You may have some leftover.

Preheat broiler. Place 2 pieces of veal together slightly overlapping; place two pieces of the avocados on top with two slices of cheese. Place under the broiler and melt the cheese, watching carefully.

Yield: 4-6 servings

Veal Escallops Stuffed with Crab

4 veal escallops
½ teaspoon paprika
Salt
4 ounces butter,
  melted and divided
Cooking oil
1 onion, finely
  chopped
½ pound Alaskan
  King crabmeat
1 egg, beaten
2 tablespoons bread
  crumbs
4 slices lean bacon
Chopped fresh
  parsley

*R*ub the paprika and salt into the veal escallops. Melt butter, reserving half. Cook the onions in an oiled skillet over medium heat until transparent. Combine onions with crabmeat, egg and bread crumbs.

Preheat oven to 350°. Divide crabmeat mixture equally among the escallops, roll into sausage shape and wrap the bacon around the whole escallop. Place bundles in a small roasting pan, pour the remaining melted butter over the bundles and bake for 20 minutes. Serve with the juices from the pan on the side; sprinkle with chopped parsley.

Yield: 4 servings

Steak Rolls in Red Wine Sauce

2 slices of bacon, cut
  in small pieces
1 small onion, finely
  chopped
1 hard boiled egg,
  sliced
4 slices of hard
  salami
4 slices of hard
  Romano cheese
4 garlic cloves
1 pound very thin
  round steak, cut
  into 4 strips
1 cup Burgundy wine
1 (8-ounce) can
  tomato sauce

*S*auté bacon and onion in a large skillet until lightly brown. Place one slice of hard boiled egg, one slice salami, one slice cheese and one garlic clove in each steak strip. Roll and tie each steak strip. Brown steak rolls in bacon and onion. Add wine, cook until liquid is nearly absorbed. Add tomato sauce. Simmer, covered on medium to low heat for approximately 1½ to 2 hours or until tender.

Yield: 2-4 servings

Terrific when served over egg noodles.

Ropa Vieja

1½ pounds flank steak
1 dash salt
1 teaspoon olive oil
2 cups white rice
2 tablespoons
vegetable oil
1 large onion, sliced
thin
1 (8-ounce) can
tomato sauce
1 teaspoon cumin
½ teaspoon salt
¼ teaspoon pepper

In a large pot of water, boil flank steak for 1½ hours or pressure cook for 20 minutes on medium-high heat. Remove steak from pot and shred using two forks. This will be easy to do provided the meat is thoroughly cooked.

Bring 2 cups of water, salt and olive oil to a boil. Add rice and reduce the heat to simmer; cover and cook for 20 minutes.

Meanwhile, heat a deep skillet and add the vegetable oil. Add the onions and sauté until softened. Add the meat, tomato sauce, cumin, salt and pepper; cover and cook for an additional 10 minutes. Serve beef over rice.

Yield: 4-6 servings

Nutrition Analysis per serving:

saturated fat -	8.8 g	sodium -	525.4 mg
calories -	389	fiber -	0.2 g
fat -	24.6 g	cholesterol -	97.2 mg
carbohydrate -	5.2 g	sugar -	2.7 g

GINGER-ORANGE BARBECUED BEEF BACK RIBS

3 pounds beef back ribs

⅔ cup orange juice

¼ cup lemon juice

¼ cup hoisin sauce

⅛ cup honey

1 tablespoon and 1 teaspoon dark soy sauce

1 tablespoon fresh ginger, peeled and grated

1 tablespoon garlic, peeled and minced

2 teaspoons grated lemon zest

1 teaspoon salt

Hot chili sauce

*T*rim excess fat from the ribs. Cut between the bones separating them into individual ribs. Combine remaining ingredients; mix well and pour over ribs. Marinate overnight, refrigerated, covered, but no longer than 24 hours.

Preheat oven to 425°. Remove ribs; reserve marinade in a saucepan. Place ribs on a rack over a pan of hot water in oven. Roast in oven for 30 minutes, turning once half way through the cooking until browned and crisp.

Reduce marinade by heating over medium high heat until it turns to a glaze-like consistency, approximately 10 minutes. Reduce oven heat to 375°. Brush ribs with glaze, roast 10 minutes, turn, brush with glaze and roast 10 minutes more. Garnish with lemon zest.

Yield: 4 servings

Hoisin sauce may be found in Oriental markets.

PICADILLO

2 pounds ground beef
2 tablespoons olive oil
1 medium onion, finely chopped
½ medium green pepper, finely chopped
1 large tomato, peeled, finely chopped
1 large garlic clove, minced
1 bay leaf
½ teaspoon dried oregano
½ cup raisins
3 tablespoons capers, rinsed and drained
¼ cup dry red wine
½ cup pimento stuffed green olives, thinly sliced
3 tablespoons tomato sauce
1 tablespoon red wine vinegar
1 teaspoon brown sugar
1 dash Tabasco sauce
1 pinch nutmeg
Salt to taste
¼ cup water
Pimento slices
5 cups cooked rice

*C*ook beef in a large skillet over medium high heat, stirring with a fork, until brown. Strain ground beef and dispose of grease. Reduce heat to medium and add olive oil to skillet. Add ground beef, stir in onion, green peppers, tomatoes, garlic, bay leaf, oregano, raisins and capers. Cover and cook for 10 minutes.

Add wine, olives, tomato sauce, vinegar, brown sugar, Tabasco sauce and nutmeg. Cook uncovered for 5 minutes. Blend in water. Reduce heat to low, cover and simmer for 30 minutes. Uncover and continue cooking until most of the liquid is evaporated. Add salt if needed. Serve over rice and garnish with pimento slices.

Yield: 8-10 servings

This is a flavorful Cuban standard, often referred to as Cuban Hash.

Mango Beef Stir-fry

1 pound New York Strip steak, trimmed of all fat

4 teaspoons light soy sauce, divided

3 teaspoons rice wine or dry sherry, divided

2 teaspoons cornstarch

1½ tablespoons peanut oil

2 teaspoons dark soy sauce

2 fresh mangoes, chunked

4-6 servings cooked rice

Cut beef into 2-by-¼ inch slices and put them into a bowl. Combine 1 teaspoon of the light soy sauce, 2 teaspoons of the rice wine vinegar and the cornstarch and mix well. Add to beef.

Heat a wok or large skillet, then pour in the oil. Add the beef and stir-fry for 2 minutes till brown. Add the remaining 1 teaspoon light soy sauce, the dark soy sauce, and the remaining 1 teaspoon rice wine and stir-fry for 30 seconds. Add the mango chunks and heat thoroughly. Give the mixture a final turn and serve at once with rice. The beef should be slightly undercooked, as it will continue to cook for a short time after it is removed from the wok or skillet.

Yield: 4-6 servings

Nutrition Analysis per serving:

saturated fat -	3.9 g	sodium -	306.6 mg
calories -	315	fiber -	0.9 g
fat -	12.9 g	cholesterol -	76.4 mg
carbohydrate -	15.4 g	sugar -	4.6 g

Beef Tenderloin with Peppercorns

2 (2½ to 3 pounds each) trimmed beef tenderloins

3 tablespoons Dijon mustard

1 tablespoon dried sage

1½ tablespoons white peppercorns, ground and divided

1½ tablespoons green peppercorns, ground and divided

1½ tablespoons black peppercorns, ground and divided

2 tablespoons butter or margarine, softened

Fresh spinach leaves for garnish

*P*reheat oven to 425°. Cut each tenderloin lengthwise to within ½ inch of 1 long edge, leaving edge intact. Open tenderloins out flat. Place heavy-duty plastic wrap over tenderloins; pound meat to flatten slightly, using a meat mallet or rolling pin. Remove plastic wrap; spread tenderloins evenly with mustard. Sprinkle tenderloins evenly with sage and 1½ teaspoons of each type of ground peppercorns.

Fold 1 side of each tenderloin back over, and tie each securely with heavy string at 3 inch intervals. Spread butter evenly over outside of tenderloins, and sprinkle with remaining ground peppercorns, gently pressing peppercorns into tenderloins. Place tenderloins, seam side down, on a greased rack in a roasting pan; insert meat thermometer into thickest portion of 1 tenderloin.

Bake for 30 to 45 minutes or until meat thermometer registers desired degree of doneness (rare 140°, medium-rare 150°, or medium 160°). Let stand 10 minutes before slicing. Arrange slices on fresh spinach leaves, if desired.

Yield: 12 to 14 servings

Nutrition Analysis per serving:

saturated fat -	4.3 g	sodium -	103.2 g
calories -	197	fiber -	0
fat -	10.1 g	cholesterol -	78.7 mg
carbohydrate -	0.1 g	sugar -	0

SAUTÉ DE BOEUF

4 tablespoons butter, divided

2 tablespoons oil, divided

½ pound sliced fresh mushrooms

3 tablespoons minced shallots

¼ teaspoon salt

1 pinch pepper

2 (½ pound) filets of beef

¼ cup Madeira wine

¾ cup beef stock or canned beef bouillon

1 cup whipping cream plus 1 tablespoon, divided

2 teaspoons cornstarch

2 tablespoons softened butter

Parsley sprigs for garnish

*H*eat 2 tablespoons butter and 1 tablespoon oil in heavy 9 or 10 inch skillet. Add mushrooms and sauté for 4 to 5 minutes. Stir in shallots and cook for a minute longer. Season the mushroom mixture with salt and pepper and set aside.

Remove all filament and fat from the filet and cut into 2 ounce pieces, about 2 inches across and ½ inch thick. Place 2 tablespoons butter and 1 tablespoon oil in the skillet and set over moderately high heat. When the butter foam begins to subside, sauté the beef a few pieces at a time for 2 to 3 minutes on each side to brown the exterior, keeping the interior rosy red. Set the beef aside.

Pour wine and beef stock or bouillon into the skillet and boil it down rapidly, scraping up coagulated cooking juices, until the liquid is reduced to about ⅓ cup. In a separate bowl, mix cornstarch with one tablespoon cream. Add one cup cream to beef stock in skillet, mixing well. Add cornstarch mixture and simmer one minute, stirring constantly. Add the sautéed mushrooms and simmer one minute more. Season the beef lightly with salt and pepper and return it to the skillet along with any juices. Baste the beef with the sauce and mushrooms. Add butter to sauce while basting the meat until it absorbs. Garnish with parsley.

Yield: 4-6 servings

Too good to be true!

PORK LOIN WITH ORANGE MARMALADE GLAZE

1 (3½ to 4 pounds) boneless center-cut pork loin
1 tablespoon olive oil
Salt and fresh ground pepper
2 teaspoons fresh rosemary leaves or 1 teaspoon dried rosemary
1 cup dry white wine
1 cup water
½ cup orange marmalade

*P*reheat oven to 350°. Place pork on rack in a shallow roasting pan. Brush meat with olive oil and sprinkle with salt, pepper and rosemary. Pour wine and water into the bottom of the roasting pan. Roast for 1 hour.

Remove pan from oven and spoon ½ cup of pan drippings into a small bowl. Add marmalade and mix well. Pour mixture over meat and return to the oven. Continue roasting for 30 to 45 minutes, basting 2 to 3 times with pan drippings until meat thermometer reaches 160°. Let meat rest 15 minutes before serving. Skim any fat from pan drippings and serve with roast.

Yield: 6-8 servings

CRANAPPLE AND HONEY BAKED PORK CHOPS

2 tablespoons olive oil
6-8 (½-inch thick) pork chops
¼ teaspoon minced garlic
¼ teaspoon nutmeg
¼ teaspoon salt
¼ teaspoon ground ginger or ½ teaspoon grated fresh ginger
¼ teaspoon dried basil or ½ teaspoon fresh chopped basil
2 tablespoons flour
¼ cup cranapple juice
½ cup honey

*H*eat oil in skillet over medium high heat; add chops, garlic, nutmeg, salt, ginger and basil; brown pork chops. Reserving drippings in skillet, place chops in a 13 x 9 inch baking dish. Preheat oven to 350°. Add flour, cranapple juice and honey to skillet and simmer until mixture thickens. Pour over chops and bake in oven, covered, until done (about 1 hour).

Yield: 8 servings

Nutrition Analysis per serving:

saturated fat -	0	sodium -	123.2 mg
calories -	364	fiber -	0
fat -	18.7 g	cholesterol -	81 mg
carbohydrate -	20.1 g	sugar -	18.4 g

Grilled Pork Tenderloin

½ cup peanut oil
⅓ cup soy sauce
¼ cup red wine vinegar
3 tablespoons Worcestershire sauce
3 tablespoons lemon juice
1 clove crushed garlic
1 tablespoon chopped fresh parsley
1 tablespoon dry mustard
1½ teaspoons pepper
2 (¾-1 pound each) pork tenderloins

Combine peanut oil, soy sauce, vinegar, Worcestershire sauce, lemon juice, garlic, parsley, mustard and pepper in a small bowl. Pour into a heavy zipped plastic bag; add tenderloins, turning to coat and chill for 4 hours, turning occasionally. Preheat grill. Grill with cover closed, 6 inches from coals, for 15 minutes or until done.

Yield: 6 servings

Stuffed Pork Chops

4 (1-inch thick) pork chops
2 ounces Fontina cheese
4 slices prosciutto
3 eggs
Salt and pepper to taste
1 cup dry breadcrumbs
3 tablespoons butter
2 tablespoons olive oil

Cut a 2-inch pocket in each chop. Cut Fontina cheese into pieces. Place cheese pieces and proscuitto slices into chop pockets. Secure with wooden toothpicks.

Beat eggs with salt and pepper. Dip pork into eggs, then breadcrumbs. Let stand 10 to 15 minutes. Melt butter and oil in large skillet. Brown pork chops over medium heat for 3 to 5 minutes on both sides. Preheat oven to 350°.

Place pork chops in baking pan and bake for 20 minutes or until thoroughly cooked.

Yield: 4 servings

For a lighter version, substitute egg whites for whole eggs.

HERBED PORK TENDERLOIN

2 tablespoons fresh parsley

2 tablespoons fresh oregano

2 tablespoons fresh rosemary

2 tablespoons fresh thyme

1 tablespoon chopped garlic

Salt and pepper to taste

¾ cup vegetable oil

2 pounds pork tenderloin

1 cup apricot preserves

½ cup Dijon mustard

¼ cup honey

¼ cup brown sugar

¼ cup apple cider vinegar

*I*n a small food processor or blender combine parsley, oregano, rosemary, thyme, garlic, salt and pepper. Add vegetable oil and mix thoroughly. Coat tenderloins with the marinade and refrigerate for 30 minutes.

Preheat grill to low. Combine apricot preserves, mustard, honey, sugar and vinegar in a blender or food processor. Grill tenderloins over low heat, approximately 20-30 minutes. Brush frequently with apricot preserve mixture while grilling, watching carefully.

Yield: 4-6 servings

Pork Tenderloins with Roasted Bell Peppers and Tomatoes

1 pound green or yellow bell peppers

2 cups cherry tomatoes

14 large garlic cloves, unpeeled

2 tablespoons olive oil, divided

3 tablespoons chopped fresh rosemary, divided

2 tablespoons grated lemon peel, divided

½ teaspoon salt, divided

¼ teaspoon freshly ground pepper, divided

1¾ pound pork tenderloin roast, trimmed and tied

3 tablespoons fresh lemon juice

Rosemary sprigs for garnish

*C*ut each bell pepper into quarters; remove seeds. Combine peppers, tomatoes and garlic in a large bowl. Add 1½ tablespoons olive oil, 1½ teaspoons rosemary, 1 teaspoon lemon peel, ¼ teaspoon salt and ⅛ teaspoon pepper. Toss well.

Preheat oven to 400°. Set pork in large heavy roasting pan. Rub with remaining rosemary, lemon peel, salt and pepper. Drizzle with remaining olive oil. Spoon vegetables around pork. Roast for 30 minutes.

Turn pork and gently stir vegetables. Cook pork an additional 30 minutes until meat reaches 170°. Sprinkle lemon juice over pork and vegetables. Let stand 5 minutes. Cut pork into ⅛ inch slices. Spoon vegetables and juices around pork. Garnish with rosemary sprigs.

Yield: 4 servings

This dish is wonderful served with toasted French bread slices!

Honey Grilled
Shoulder of Lamb

1 (3½ - 4 pound) shoulder of lamb, boned, rolled and tied

⅓ cup honey

½ cup dry white wine

½ cup finely chopped onion

½ cup finely chopped fresh mint or 1 tablespoon dried mint

2 tablespoons grated lemon peel

2 tablespoons lemon juice

1 teaspoon salt

¼ teaspoon ground pepper

*P*lace lamb in glass dish. Combine remaining ingredients; pour over lamb. Cover. Refrigerate several hours or overnight. Place lamb on spit over hot coals. Grill 1 to 1½ hours, or until meat thermometer registers 140° for rare, 150° for medium or 160° for medium-well. Brush occasionally with marinade. Heat leftover marinade to boiling and serve over sliced lamb.

Yield: 14-16 servings

Grilled Marinated Leg of Lamb

¼ cup soy sauce

¼ cup lemon juice

¼ cup honey

1 teaspoon pepper

1 fresh ginger root (1½-inches long), peeled and sliced or ½ teaspoon ground ginger

1 garlic clove

1 (4 - 7 pound) butterflied leg of lamb

*P*lace all ingredients, except lamb, in blender or food processor and blend until smooth. Place meat in glass casserole and pour marinade over lamb. Refrigerate, covered up to 12 hours; baste occasionally. Grill lamb 4 to 5 inches over charcoals or source of heat for 35 to 45 minutes or to desired doneness, basting occasionally.

Yield: 20 servings

Nutrition Analysis per servings:

saturated fat -	9.0 g	sodium -	263.7 mg
calories -	251	fiber -	0
fat -	16.1 g	cholesterol -	39.0
carbohydrate -	3.7 g	sugar -	3.5 g

Low-fat Lamb Kabobs

¾ cup plain nonfat yogurt

¼ teaspoon hot pepper sauce

2 large garlic cloves, finely minced or pressed

½ cup lemon juice (not from concentrate)

Mint to taste

¼ teaspoon paprika

1 pound lean leg or loin of lamb, cut into 1-inch cubes

*C*ombine all ingredients except for the lamb in a medium non-aluminum bowl and mix well. Add the lamb, coating well with the marinade. Turn into a shallow glass or ceramic pan and pierce with a fork. Cover the pan with plastic wrap and marinate in the refrigerator for 4 hours or overnight. Divide meat into 4 equal portions and thread on skewers. Discard leftover marinade. Place foil on bottom rack of oven to catch drippings. Broil lamb skewers 3 to 4 inches from heat for 10 minutes, turning once.

Yield: 4 servings

Nutrition Analysis per serving:

saturated fat -	4.5 g	sodium -	112.8 mg
calories -	242	fiber -	0
fat -	8.1 g	cholesterol -	51.8 mg
carbohydrate -	5.9 g	sugar -	2.9 g

Cranberry Orange Lamb Chops

4 lamb loin chops, cut 1½ inch thick

⅛ cup browning sauce

½ cup chopped onion

1 cup orange juice

1 cup fresh or frozen cranberries

½ cup sugar

1 tablespoon flour

1 tablespoon Dijon mustard

1 teaspoon grated orange peel

½ teaspoon allspice

*P*lace lamb in a 9 inch, shallow, round dish; brush with browning sauce and top with onions. Cook in microwave oven on medium-high (70% power) 12 minutes, turning once. Drain. Place remaining ingredients in large glass measuring cup. May freeze at this time. Cook on high 6 minutes or until it comes to a boil, stirring twice. Pour sauce over lamb. Cook on medium-high (70% power) 5 minutes.

From frozen: cook on defrost 10 minutes. Then cook on medium-high (70% power) for 15 minutes. Stir once, halfway through cooking time. Let stand covered 5 minutes.

Yield: 4 servings

PEACH GLAZED LEG OF LAMB

1 (8 pound) bone-in leg of lamb or 4 to 5 pound boned, rolled and tied shoulder roast
2 garlic cloves, cut into slices
2 tablespoons salad oil

PEACH GLAZE

2 (16-ounce) cans cling peach halves, liquid reserved
½ cup sherry
½ cup brown sugar
4 tablespoons butter or margarine
2 tablespoons cornstarch
1 teaspoon ground allspice
2 tablespoons grated lemon peel

PORTED GINGER PEACHES

1 (21 ounce) can cherry pie filling
2 tablespoons port wine
1 tablespoon chopped candied ginger
1 teaspoon grated orange peel

Cut small slits in surface of lamb; insert garlic slivers. Rub lamb with oil. Place leg on rack in roasting pan. Roast leg in preheated 450° oven for 15 minutes. Reduce temperature to 325° and continue to roast 1½ hours or until meat thermometer inserted into thickest portion registers 150° for medium. Brush roast with Peach Glaze the last 20 minutes of cooking.

To make the Peach Glaze, drain peach juice in 2 quart saucepan. Reserve peach halves for Ported Ginger Peaches. Add sherry, brown sugar, butter or margarine, cornstarch, allspice and lemon. Stir until cornstarch dissolves. Stir over medium heat until slightly thickened and smooth.

To make the Ported Ginger Peaches, place peaches in a 9 x 9 inch baking dish. Combine cherries with port, ginger and orange peel. Spoon cherry mixture into peaches. Bake at 350° for 15 minutes or until heated through.

Let roast stand 20 minutes before carving. Serve with remaining Peach Glaze and Ported Ginger Peaches.

Yield: 20 servings

JAMBALAYA

2 pounds chicken

2 cups canned chicken broth, divided

1 (14½-ounce) can stewed tomatoes, undrained and diced

1 small onion, finely chopped

½ cup diced red pepper

½ cup diced green pepper

1 tablespoon chili powder

¼ cup butter or margarine

1 tablespoon flour

2 shallots or whites of 2 large scallions, finely chopped

1 garlic clove, crushed

½ teaspoon dried oregano

½ teaspoon thyme

¼ teaspoon ground cayenne pepper

1 cup minute rice

4 ounces smoked ham, cubed

12 ounces large fresh shrimp, peeled, deveined and cooked

12 ounces precooked kielbasa, cut into ¼ inch slices, then cut each slice into quarters

*B*ake chicken at 400° until tender; remove from bone. Meanwhile, in 2 quart saucepan, bring to boil the following: 1 cup broth, tomatoes, onion, peppers and chili powder. Cover; simmer 20 minutes; set aside. In a small bowl, stir and blend butter, flour, shallots, garlic, oregano, thyme, and cayenne pepper. Set aside.

In an extra large, deep skillet, combine chicken, broth and tomato mixture, butter mixture and remaining 1 cup of broth. Bring to a boil over high heat. Add rice. Reduce heat and simmer 5 to 10 minutes until rice is cooked. Add ham, cooked shrimp and kielbasa and cook until heated through. If too thin, add more rice.

Makes 6 to 8 servings.

Don't let the number of ingredients deter you from making this wonderful dish; it's great!

Mandarin Almond Chicken

½ cup flour

¾ teaspoon salt

6 whole boneless chicken breasts

½ cup plus 1 tablespoon butter, divided

1 cup orange juice

¼ cup brown sugar

¼ cup cooking sherry

¼ cup honey

1 tablespoon cornstarch

1 tablespoon soy sauce

2 tablespoons lemon juice

¼ teaspoon ground ginger

1 (11-ounce) can Mandarin oranges, drained

¼ cup sliced almonds

1 tablespoon chopped parsley

*P*reheat oven to 350°. Combine flour and salt and coat chicken. Melt ½ cup butter and brush a small amount on bottom of 10 x 15 glass baking dish. Place chicken in dish and pour remaining butter on each piece. Bake chicken uncovered for one hour.

Combine orange juice, sugar, sherry, honey, cornstarch, soy sauce, lemon juice and ginger in a small saucepan. Place over medium heat, bring to boil, stirring constantly until sauce is smooth and thick. After chicken has cooked one hour, spoon sauce over chicken. Sprinkle Mandarin oranges over top and bake 15 minutes longer. Sauté almonds in 1 tablespoon butter until light brown; drain and salt lightly. Remove chicken from oven, sprinkle with almonds and parsley and serve.

Yield: 6 servings

ORANGE CHICKEN

1 chicken, cut up
6 tablespoons flour
Salt and pepper to
   taste
⅛ teaspoon dried
   basil
⅛ teaspoon dried
   oregano
⅛ teaspoon dried
   marjoram
2 tablespoons
   vegetable oil
1 (6-ounce) can
   frozen orange juice
   concentrate
¼ cup water
⅓ cup white wine
   vinegar
⅓ cup brown sugar
1 medium red onion,
   sliced

*M*ix flour, salt, pepper and spices together in a zipped plastic bag. Coat chicken in flour mixture; brown in the oil in a large skillet over medium for approximately 10 minutes. In a small bowl, mix orange juice, water, vinegar and brown sugar.

To prepare in skillet, pour orange juice mixture and onions over chicken in skillet and simmer for 1 hour. To prepare in oven, place the chicken in a large greased baking dish and cover with the onions and orange juice mixture. Bake, uncovered, at 325° for 1 hour.

Yield: 6 servings

BAKED CHICKEN PIQUANT WITH RICE

3 cups Burgundy wine
1 cup soy sauce
1 cup salad oil
1 cup water
4 garlic cloves, minced
1 teaspoon ginger
1 teaspoon oregano
¼ cup brown sugar
1 pound long grain
   rice
8 chicken breast halves

*P*reheat oven to 350°. Combine all ingredients except chicken and rice. Spread unprepared rice in bottom of 13 x 9 inch greased baking dish. Place chicken breasts on top of rice. Pour Burgundy mixture over all. Cover with foil and bake for 1½ hours.

Yield: 8 servings

Add water to rice if it becomes dry during the last ½ hour of baking.

RASPBERRY CHICKEN

2 whole boneless, skinless chicken breasts

2 tablespoons unsalted butter

¼ cup finely chopped yellow onion

4 tablespoons raspberry vinegar

¼ cup chicken broth

¼ cup heavy cream

1 tablespoon canned crushed tomatoes

16 fresh raspberries

Cut chicken breasts into halves. Melt butter in large skillet and add the chicken; cook 3 minutes per side or until lightly browned. Remove from skillet and set aside. Add onion to the remaining butter in pan and cook, covered, over low heat until tender, about 15 minutes. Add the vinegar, raise the heat and cook uncovered stirring occasionally, until vinegar is reduced to a syrupy spoonful. Whisk in chicken broth, cream and crushed tomatoes and simmer for 1 minute. Return chicken to pan and simmer in the sauce. Baste often until chicken is done and sauce has been reduced and thickened slightly, about 5 minutes. Do not overcook. Remove chicken with a slotted spoon and arrange on serving plate. Add raspberries to the sauce in the skillet and cook over low heat for 1 minute. Do not stir the berries, simply swirl them in the sauce. Pour sauce over chicken and serve immediately.

Yield: 4 servings

Unusual and delightful!

Arroz con Pollo

1 tablespoon cooking oil

1 whole chicken, cut up

1 green pepper, chopped

1 large onion, chopped

2 garlic cloves, minced

1 tablespoon cumin

1 teaspoon salt

¼ teaspoon pepper

½ teaspoon saffron

1 (8-ounce) can tomato sauce

2 cups water

1 chicken bouillon cube

2 cups white rice

Green peas or asparagus, optional

Brown chicken in deep pot with cooking oil. Add green pepper, onion and garlic; cook until onions are clear. Add cumin, salt, pepper, saffron and tomato sauce; stir for 5 minutes. Add water and bouillon cube and bring to a boil. Once at a boil add rice, stir well and cover. Reduce heat to simmer and cook for 20 minutes. Decorate with green peas or asparagus on top.

Yield: 4 servings

Nutrition Analysis per serving:

saturated fat -	4.8 g	sodium -	917.4 mg
calories -	542	fiber -	2.2 g
fat -	20.5 g	cholesterol -	109 mg
carbohydrate -	37.5 g	sugar -	4.8 g

A Cuban original; once tried, it will become a favorite!

CHICKEN RATATOUILLE

2 tablespoons olive or vegetable oil, divided

1 medium eggplant, peeled and cut into ½ inch cubes

2 large zucchini, sliced

1 medium yellow pepper, cut into ½ inch squares

1 small onion, chopped

3 garlic cloves, minced

4 large chicken breast halves, skin removed

½ teaspoon salt

¼ teaspoon pepper

1 teaspoon dried basil

4 large tomatoes, peeled and quartered, juice reserved

2 teaspoons cornstarch

*H*eat 1 tablespoon oil in a large dutch oven over medium heat. Add eggplant, zucchini, yellow pepper, onion and garlic; sauté until tender. Place vegetables in a bowl and set aside. Sprinkle chicken with salt and pepper; brown in remaining oil. Add basil and tomatoes; bring to a boil. Cover and simmer 45 minutes, or until chicken is tender. Remove chicken and place on a serving platter. Combine cornstarch with a small amount of juice from quartered tomatoes. Stir until blended. Stir cornstarch mixture back into tomatoes and add vegetables; bring to a boil. Reduce heat and simmer, stirring occasionally, for 5 minutes. Pour vegetables over chicken and serve.

Yield: 4 servings

Nutrition Analysis per serving:

saturated fat -	1.7 g	sodium -	379 mg
calories -	350	fiber -	5 g
fat -	12 g	cholesterol -	109 mg
carbohydrate -	17 g	sugar -	0

To peel tomatoes, place in boiling water for 30 seconds, then immediately place in ice water. Tomato skins should slide off easily.

CHICKEN CUTLETS ITALIENNE

1½ pounds chicken cutlets (¼ inch thick)

1 medium lemon

2 tablespoons flour

½ teaspoon salt

½ teaspoon oregano

3 tablespoons light corn oil spread, divided

1 medium onion, diced

3 medium zucchini, coarsely chopped

2 medium plum tomatoes, diced

1½ teaspoons chicken flavored instant bouillon

½ cup water

¼ cup chopped basil leaves

Fresh basil leaves for garnish

*S*lice each chicken cutlet crosswise in half. From lemon, grate peel and squeeze 2 teaspoons juice; set aside. In a shallow bowl, mix flour, salt, and oregano; dip cutlets in mixture to coat. Place 2 tablespoons corn oil spread in a non-stick 12-inch skillet over medium-high heat. Cook cutlets, half at a time, until browned on both sides, removing cutlets to warm plate as they brown; keep warm. Add 1 tablespoon light corn oil spread to drippings remaining in skillet. Set heat to medium-high and cook onion until golden. Add zucchini and cook, stirring occasionally until golden and tender crisp. Stir in tomatoes, lemon juice, lemon peel, chicken bouillon and ½ cup water. Increase heat to high and bring to a boil; boil 1 minute, stirring to loosen browned bits from bottom of skillet. Stir in basil. To serve, arrange cutlets on platter, spoon sauce over top. Garnish with basil.

Yield: 4 servings

A sensational blend of flavors!

BARBECUED CHICKEN MARINADE

CHICKEN MARINADE

1 (3-pound) chicken fryer, quartered

1 large garlic clove, crushed

1 teaspoon salt

½ teaspoon freshly ground pepper

1 tablespoon oil

3 tablespoons lemon juice

BARBECUE SAUCE

¼ cup cider vinegar

2¼ cups water

¾ cup sugar

½ cup butter or margarine

⅓ cup yellow mustard

2 onions, coarsely chopped

½ teaspoon salt

½ teaspoon pepper

½ cup Worcestershire sauce

2½ cups ketchup

6-8 tablespoons lemon juice

Cayenne pepper to taste

*P*lace chicken, garlic, 1 teaspoon salt, pepper, oil and lemon juice in a heavy zipped plastic bag. Shake to coat well. Refrigerate for 24 hours if possible, turning the bag several times.

Bring cider vinegar, water, sugar, butter, mustard, onions, ½ teaspoon salt and pepper to a boil in a saucepan over medium high heat. Reduce heat to low and cook for 20 minutes or until onion is tender. Add Worcestershire sauce, ketchup, lemon juice and cayenne pepper to taste. Simmer slowly for 45 minutes. Freeze or refrigerate until ready to use.

When coals are ready, place chicken on the grill, skin side up, basting with marinade. Cook until well browned before turning. Brush with Barbecue Sauce several times after turning. If baking in oven, bake at 400°, skin side down first.

Yield: 4 servings

A tried and true White House recipe from Barbara Bush. The Bush family has long enjoyed the sun and fun of south Florida.

LIME BARBECUED CHICKEN WITH BLACK BEAN SAUCE

MARINADE

¼ cup fresh lime juice

½ cup canola oil

½ teaspoon cayenne pepper

1 garlic clove, crushed

8 skinless, boneless chicken breast halves

BLACK BEAN SAUCE

2 tablespoons balsamic vinegar

½ cup orange juice

1 garlic clove, crushed

1 cup cooked, drained and rinsed black beans

Dash of salt and pepper

2 tablespoons chopped red onion

1 red bell pepper, diced

GARNISH

Red onion, sliced

Red pepper, sliced

Fresh cilantro, chopped

*M*ix all of the marinade ingredients except chicken and pour into a glass, ceramic or stainless steel bowl. Add chicken and marinate overnight or for 8 hours minimum. Preheat oven to 350° and preheat gas grill for 15 minutes. Quickly grill chicken on both sides to seal the juices and remove to a baking tray (chicken may be browned in a skillet if grilling is not possible). Place chicken in a shallow baking dish and bake in oven for 15 minutes to finish the cooking.

To make Black Bean Sauce, mix vinegar, orange juice, garlic and black beans and puree in a blender or food processor until smooth. Add salt and pepper to taste. Heat Black Bean Sauce until warm. Serve chicken topped with Black Bean Sauce. Garnish with red onion, red peppers and cilantro.

Yield: 8 servings

Nutrition Analysis per serving:

saturated fat -	1.4 g	sodium -	114 mg
calories -	167	fiber -	1.3 g
fat -	8.6 g	cholesterol -	36.5 mg
carbohydrate -	7 g	sugar -	2.8 g

BASIL GRILLED CHICKEN

¾ teaspoon coarsely
  ground pepper
4 chicken breast
  halves, skinned and
  boned
⅓ cup butter, melted
¼ cup chopped fresh
  basil
½ cup butter, softened
2 tablespoons minced
  fresh basil
1 tablespoon grated
  fresh Parmesan
  cheese
¼ teaspoon garlic
  powder
¼ teaspoon salt
⅛ teaspoon pepper
Fresh basil sprigs

*P*ress ¾ teaspoon pepper into sides of chicken breasts. Combine ⅓ cup melted butter and ¼ cup chopped basil; stir well. Brush chicken lightly with melted butter mixture. Combine ½ cup softened butter, 2 tablespoons minced basil, Parmesan cheese, garlic powder, salt and pepper in small bowl; set aside. Grill chicken over medium coals 8-10 minutes on each side, basting frequently with remaining melted butter mixture. Serve grilled chicken with basil butter mixture and garnish with fresh basil sprigs and a dollop of basil butter.

Yield: 4 servings

Grilled Chicken Kabobs

1 cup plain yogurt
Juice of one lemon
2 garlic cloves,
  chopped
1 tablespoon ground
  cumin
2 whole skinless,
  boneless chicken
  breasts cut into ½
  inch chunks
8 small yellow onions
3 tablespoons olive
  oil
Salt and pepper to
  taste
¼ cup chopped
  parsley
1 lemon, sliced
4 bamboo skewers

Combine yogurt, lemon juice, garlic and cumin. Add chicken chunks and refrigerate in a sealed container for 8 hours.

Preheat grill. Peel onions and cut into thick slices. Alternate chicken and onion onto bamboo skewers. Remove excess marinade. Brush with olive oil and season with salt and pepper. Grill approximately 10 minutes; turn once and cook until brown and cooked through. Garnish with parsley and one slice of lemon.

Yield: 4 servings

Nutrition Analysis per serving:

saturated fat -	2.2 g	sodium -	107 mg
calories -	320	fiber -	0
fat -	13.5 g	cholesterol -	73 mg
carbohydrate -	17.1 g	sugar -	11.2 g

Try serving these tasty kabobs with orzo!

CHICKEN AND ARTICHOKES

Salt and pepper to
   taste
Paprika to taste
4 skinless, boneless
   chicken breast
   halves
¼ cup butter
12 large fresh
   mushrooms, sliced
2 tablespoons flour
1 cup chicken broth
½ cup cooking sherry
   or white wine
1 (14-ounce) can
   artichoke hearts,
   drained, quartered

*S*prinkle salt, pepper and paprika over chicken breasts. Brown chicken in a skillet with ¼ cup butter over medium high heat. Remove chicken from skillet and set aside. Sauté mushrooms in same skillet until tender and liquid is absorbed. Add flour to chicken broth and whisk until smooth. Add chicken broth mixture and sherry to mushrooms; stir over medium heat until mixture begins to boil and is slightly thickened.

Preheat oven to 300°. Place artichoke hearts in bottom of 2-quart casserole; place chicken breasts over artichoke hearts. Pour mushroom, flour, chicken broth and sherry mixture over chicken breasts and artichokes. Bake, covered, for 30 minutes.

Yield: 4 servings

Nutrition Analysis per serving:

saturated fat -	8.8 g	sodium -	563.6 mg
calories -	344	fiber -	3.4 g
fat -	17.9 g	cholesterol -	96 mg
carbohydrate -	13.8 g	sugar -	6.5 g

For a pleasing presentation, serve on a bed of herb buttered noodles.

HONEY MUSTARD CHICKEN SAUCE

2 tablespoons honey
1 tablespoon Dijon
   style mustard
1 tablespoon lemon
   juice
½ teaspoon poppy
   seeds
¼ teaspoon pepper

*C*ombine all ingredients in a small bowl. Stir together well.

For a quick, low fat dish, broil 4 skinless chicken breast halves for 15 minutes per side, brushing chicken with Honey Mustard Chicken Sauce before the last 5 minutes of broiling.

CHICKEN BREASTS STUFFED WITH FETA AND DRIED TOMATOES

½ cup finely chopped red onion

2 tablespoons olive oil

1½ teaspoons minced garlic

¼ cup pine nuts, lightly toasted

½ cup oil-packed sun-dried tomatoes, drained, rinsed, dried and cut into thin strips

¼ pound feta cheese crumbled (approximately 1 cup)

2 tablespoons Parmesan cheese

1 tablespoon fresh marjoram or 1 teaspoon dried marjoram

2 whole boneless chicken breasts, halved

*S*auté onion in 1 tablespoon oil in a medium saucepan over moderate heat, stirring until softened. Add garlic and cook for 1 minute. Transfer to a bowl and let cool. Stir pine nuts, tomatoes, cheeses and marjoram into onion mixture; season with salt and pepper.

Preheat oven to 350°. Insert knife into thicker end of chicken breast and cut a lengthwise pocket, making it as wide as possible. Fill each breast with ¼ cup of filling. Secure opening with toothpicks, if necessary. Heat 1 tablespoon oil in large skillet until hot; brown chicken for 5 minutes. Place in shallow baking dish and bake for 20 minutes or until just cooked through.

Yield: 4 servings

Use any extra filling for garnish on the plate.

CHICKEN WITH TARRAGON AND WINE

2 whole large boneless chicken breasts

½ cup butter plus 2 tablespoons, divided

½ pound mushrooms, thinly sliced

1 medium carrot, cut into matchsticks

2 egg yolks

2 tablespoons dry white wine

1 tablespoon lemon juice

¼ teaspoon salt

1 teaspoon fresh tarragon or ⅛ teaspoon dried tarragon

Dash ground red pepper

*D*ivide chicken into 4 pieces. With a meat mallet, pound chicken breasts to ¼ inch thick. Brown each piece of chicken in a skillet with 2 tablespoons butter over medium-high heat. Remove chicken to a warm platter and set aside. In remaining drippings over medium heat, cook mushrooms and carrots until tender, stirring frequently. In a double boiler over hot (not boiling) water, beat egg yolks, white wine and lemon juice. Add ½ cup butter, 1 tablespoon at a time, beating constantly with a wire whisk until slightly thickened. Stir in the salt, tarragon and ground red pepper. Pour sauce over chicken. Top with mushrooms and carrots and serve.

Yield: 4 servings

This dish may be prepared ahead of time and warmed. Try serving over herbed egg noodles for added presentation to this unbelievable dish!

CHICKEN SAUTÉED WITH BALSAMIC VINEGAR

4 tablespoons olive oil

3 medium zucchini, thickly sliced

¾ pound mushrooms, thickly sliced

2 boneless chicken breasts, halved

2 tablespoons flour

2 medium onions, chopped

½ cup chicken broth or stock

1 (16-ounce) can tomatoes, undrained

3 tablespoons balsamic vinegar or red wine vinegar

½ teaspoon salt

*H*eat 1 tablespoon olive oil in a large heavy skillet over medium-high heat. Add zucchini and sauté until tender-crisp and lightly browned, approximately two minutes; remove to plate. In the same skillet, add one more tablespoon oil and sauté mushrooms until browned, approximately 2 minutes; remove to a bowl.

Coat the chicken with the flour. In same skillet, in 2 tablespoons hot oil, cook chicken until lightly browned and juice runs clear when pierced, approximately 10 minutes. Remove to the bowl with mushrooms. In the pan drippings over medium heat, sauté onion until tender and browned, 5-6 minutes; stir in chicken broth. Return chicken mixture to skillet; add tomatoes, balsamic vinegar and salt and heat to boiling. Reduce heat to low, simmer, uncovered, 5 minutes. Add zucchini, heat and serve.

Yield: 4 servings

CHICKEN PUFFS

3 ounces cream cheese, softened

2 tablespoons butter, melted

2 cups chicken or turkey, cooked and cubed

¼ teaspoon salt

⅛ teaspoon pepper

2 tablespoons milk

1 tablespoon chopped onion

1 tablespoon chopped pimentos

1 package of 8 refrigerated crescent rolls

Melted butter

Seasoned croutons, crushed

*P*reheat oven to 350°. Blend cream cheese and 2 tablespoons melted butter. Combine cream cheese mixture with chicken, salt, pepper, milk, onion and pimentos. Separate roll of crescent dough into 4 rectangles. On an ungreased baking sheet, press each piece of dough into a 6x5 inch rectangle. Firmly press perforations to seal. Spoon ½ cup of the chicken mixture onto the center of each rectangle. Pull the 4 corners of the dough to the top center of the chicken mixture mound and pinch seams together. Brush with melted butter. Cover with crushed croutons. Bake for 20-25 minutes, until dough is puffed and golden brown.

Yield: 4 servings

A puffed surprise and an elegant way to use leftover chicken or turkey!

MOORE-BETTY CHICKEN

1 (6-7 pound)
  roasting chicken
Coarse salt (sea salt)
4 garlic cloves
Fresh ground pepper
Juice from 2 lemons
1 cup water

*P*reheat oven to 400°. Rinse chicken; discard neck, gizzards and liver. Rub insides generously with sea salt. Peel and press garlic cloves and rub salted insides with garlic. Dust with pepper. Rub at least 2 tablespoons of sea salt on outside of chicken, followed up with the pressed garlic. Truss or tie up the chicken for the oven and stand chicken on a rack in a roasting pan. Pour half of the lemon juice inside the chicken and the remainder over the top. Dust with more coarse salt and pepper. Pour water in bottom of roasting pan. Bake for 1½ hours without basting.

Yield: 4-6 servings

Nutrition Analysis per serving;

saturated fat -	5.3 g	sodium -	355 mg
calories -	350	fiber -	0
fat -	19.9 g	cholesterol -	109.4 mg
carbohydrate -	1.6 g	sugar -	0

*This moist chicken is a garlic lover's dream! It is a revised favorite from the Junior League of the Palm Beaches' first cookbook, **Palm Beach Entertains**.*

Pecan Chicken

4 boneless skinless
  chicken breast
  halves
1 cup finely ground
  pecans
½ cup Parmesan
  cheese
½ teaspoon garlic salt
3 teaspoons minced
  fresh basil or ½
  teaspoon dried
  basil
1 cup lemon juice
2 tablespoons olive
  oil
Honey Mustard
  Chicken Sauce (see
  page 188)

*P*ound chicken breasts flat with a mallet until ¼ inch thick. Combine pecans, Parmesan cheese, garlic salt and basil. Dip chicken in lemon juice and then pecan mixture. Sauté in a skillet in olive oil over medium heat for 8 minutes per side or until cooked through. Serve with Honey Mustard Chicken Sauce.

Yield: 4 servings

Chicken Fajita Pizza

2 tablespoons
  vegetable oil
½ pound boneless,
  skinless chicken
  breasts
½ bell pepper, cut into
  thin rings
1 small onion, sliced
½ cup salsa or picante
  sauce
Pizza crust dough for
  one pizza
  (homemade or
  refrigerator dough)
1½ cups shredded
  mozzarella cheese

*M*ove oven rack to lowest position and preheat oven to 450°. Cut chicken breasts into strips ¼ to ⅛ inch thick. Heat a skillet to the point where a drop or two of water will bubble and skitter away when sprinkled on it. Add oil and rotate skillet to coat the bottom and sides. Add the chicken strips and cook, stirring for 3 minutes. Add the bell pepper and onion; cook and stir 3 to 4 minutes longer or until vegetables are crisp and tender. Remove from heat, stir in salsa and set aside.

Place pizza crust dough on pizza or jelly roll pan. Sprinkle ¾ cup of shredded cheese over the crust. Top with chicken and bell pepper mixture and sprinkle with remaining shredded cheese. Bake for 12 to 15 minutes or until crust is brown and cheese is melted and bubbly.

Yield: 4 main course servings or 8-10 appetizer servings

APRICOT CORNISH HENS

4-5 cups dried bread crumbs (from white fresh bread)

½ cup sliced celery

¼ cup chopped onion

½ teaspoon salt

¼ teaspoon pepper

¾ teaspoon marjoram leaves, divided

2½ cups apricot preserves

1¼ cups butter, divided

2-3 tablespoons chicken broth

4 Cornish hens

*I*n medium bowl stir together the bread crumbs, celery, onion, salt, pepper and ¼ teaspoon marjoram leaves. In a 1-quart pan, melt 1 cup preserves and ¼ cup butter. Stir into stuffing mixture; add 2 to 3 tablespoons of chicken broth to moisten stuffing (only if necessary).

Preheat oven to 375°. Rinse hens out and fill hens with stuffing. Secure opening with toothpicks. Place hens in a roasting pan, breast side up, uncovered. Bake for one hour.

Meanwhile, in the same 1-quart pan, combine ½ teaspoon marjoram leaves, 1½ cups apricot preserves and 1 cup butter. Cook over medium heat, stirring until melted. Brush hens with sauce several times throughout the baking process. If hens start to brown or darken on top from sauce, cover with foil. Bake until hens are tender (approximately 1 additional hour or 2 hours total). Serve with remaining sauce.

Yield: 4 servings

CRAB CAKES WITH MUSTARD SAUCE

1¼ cups dry bread crumbs, divided

1 pound crabmeat, flaked and picked over

½ cup finely chopped red pepper

⅓ cup mayonnaise

1 large egg, lightly beaten

¼ cup minced onion

¼ cup chopped green onions

2 tablespoons minced fresh parsley

2 tablespoons Dijon mustard

1 tablespoon fresh lemon juice

½ teaspoon minced garlic

½ teaspoon Worcestershire sauce

¼ teaspoon Tabasco sauce

⅛ teaspoon salt

3 tablespoons vegetable oil

Mustard Sauce (see page 197)

Place 1 cup bread crumbs in shallow dish. Combine remaining ¼ cup bread crumbs with remaining ingredients, except oil and Mustard Sauce, in large bowl until just blended. Shape mixture evenly into 8 patties. Coat each crab cake by turning carefully in the dish with the bread crumbs. Transfer to a cookie sheet lined with waxed paper; cover and refrigerate 2 hours.

Heat oil in a large non-stick skillet over medium heat. Cook crab cakes in batches for 4-5 minutes per side, until golden. Serve with Mustard Sauce.

Yield: 4 servings

Mustard Sauce

½ cup mayonnaise
1 tablespoon heavy cream
1¾ teaspoons dry mustard
1 teaspoon Worcestershire sauce
½ teaspoon steak sauce
Salt to taste

*C*ombine all ingredients with a whisk until smooth.

Blackened Pompano

2 tablespoons paprika
1 tablespoon salt
1½ teaspoons garlic powder
2 teaspoons cayenne pepper
1½ teaspoons white pepper
1½ teaspoons black pepper
¾ teaspoon dried thyme
¾ teaspoon dried oregano
4 (7-ounce) pompano fillets, ¾ inch thick, skinned and boned
1 cup butter plus 4 teaspoons, melted, divided
4 tablespoons butter, softened, in four pieces

*I*n a bowl, mix together all spices. Heat a 12 inch cast iron skillet until very hot. As the pan is heating, dip fish fillets in melted butter. Gently set buttered fillets in spices, lightly coating each side. Place fish into hot skillet with 1 teaspoon of melted butter on top of each fillet. Cook 2 minutes, until fish is charred; flip and repeat. Top each with 1 tablespoon of butter and serve.

Yield: 4 servings

Mahi Mahi with Mango Salsa

½ cup soy sauce

½ cup pineapple juice

½ cup merin or sake

2 tablespoons sesame oil

2 tablespoons lime juice

2 tablespoons minced ginger

1 tablespoon red pepper flakes

1 tablespoon minced lemon grass

1½ pounds Mahi Mahi (dolphin) fillets

Mango Salsa

Combine all ingredients, except fillets, in a shallow glass baking dish. Add the fish and marinate in the refrigerator for 3-4 hours, turning after 2 hours.

Preheat oven to 400°. Place the fish in a greased baking pan and pour excess marinade over the fish. Bake for 12 minutes or until center of the fish is opaque and flakes easily. Serve fish on warm plates with Mango Salsa.

Yield: 4 servings

Nutrition Analysis:

saturated fat -	1.3 g	sodium -	2043.2 mg
calories -	287	cholesterol -	85.3 mg
fat -	8.0 g	fiber -	1.3 g
carbohydrate -	27.1 g	sugar -	8.3 g

Mango Salsa

1 large ripe mango, peeled and diced

1 chili pepper, seeded and minced

½ cup red onion, minced

1 garlic clove, minced

1 tablespoon minced fresh cilantro

½ teaspoon salt

Combine all ingredients in a small bowl until well blended. Store refrigerated but serve at room temperature.

Tortilla Crusted Dolphin

8 flour tortillas
2 tablespoons chopped fresh cilantro
1 tablespoon ground cumin
1 teaspoon chili powder
1 teaspoon salt
1 teaspoon pepper
1 tablespoon cayenne powder
1 tablespoon tumeric
6 (8-ounce) fillets of dolphin or grouper
1 cup flour
2 eggs, lightly beaten
Olive or vegetable oil for sautéing
Vegetable Salsa

Tear tortillas into pieces and put into a food processor or blender. Process into pieces the size of corn kernels; set aside. Mix cilantro, cumin, chili powder, salt, pepper, cayenne powder and tumeric well; stir in the chopped tortillas.

Preheat oven to 375°. Dip fish fillets into flour then into eggs and roll in the tortilla crumb mixture to coat well. Heat oil in sauté pan over medium high heat and sauté fish pieces until golden brown. Place fish on a baking sheet and bake until fish is completely cooked yet still flaky. Serve with Vegetable Salsa.

Yield: 6 servings

Vegetable Salsa

1 red bell pepper
1 green bell pepper
1 yellow bell pepper
½ cup fresh cilantro
2 cucumbers
½ large red onion
1 large ripe tomato
3 jalapeño peppers, seeded
2 tablespoons lime juice
Salt and pepper to taste

Chop all ingredients in food processor or blender until pieces are ¼ inch in size. Refrigerate for 1 hour. Serve cold, warm or hot.

Baked Stuffed Lobster

2 (1½-pound) live
 lobsters
¼ cup margarine
½ pound crabmeat
½ pound small salad
 shrimp
¼ pound cooked
 lobster
⅛ cup lemon juice
¼ cup dry white wine
Dash Worcestershire
 sauce
Salt and pepper to
 taste
¾ cup dry bread
 crumbs

Boil or steam the lobster over high heat for 10-15 minutes. Meanwhile, melt margarine in medium saucepan. Add crabmeat, shrimp, cooked lobster, lemon juice, wine, Worcestershire sauce, salt and pepper. Cook over medium heat until heated through; add bread crumbs and mix thoroughly. Stuffing should be firm enough to form a ball, but not too wet.

Remove cooked lobsters from pot. Place lobsters on a cutting board and let cool 2-3 minutes. Remove claws and knuckles from body and chill for later use. Place each lobster, belly side up, on cutting board and extend tail. With a small sharp knife, cut down the center, starting mid-body between the swimmerets, until the knife grazes the back of the shell. Continue cutting to the end of the tail. Carefully split open the lobster body and tail.

Preheat oven to 425°. Stuff lobsters with stuffing, mounding well. Place stuffed lobsters on baking sheet and bake for 10 minutes, until top of stuffing has browned.

Yield: 2-4 servings

Poached Salmon with Raspberry Sauce

2 cups white wine
1 cup water
1 stalk celery, leafy top included
6 whole peppercorns
1 bay leaf
1 small onion, chopped
½ teaspoon salt
3 sprigs parsley
3 tablespoons lemon juice
4 salmon steaks
Raspberry Sauce
Fresh raspberries for garnish

Combine all ingredients except salmon in a large frying pan or fish poacher. Bring to a boil and simmer 5 minutes. Lower heat to medium low; add the salmon steaks. Simmer 8 minutes or until fish is flaky, yet moist (make sure salmon does not boil.) Place Raspberry Sauce on four dinner plates and arrange salmon on top. Garnish with fresh raspberries.

Yield: 4 servings

Nutrition Analysis:

saturated fat -	16.3 g	sodium -	600.9 mg
calories -	512	cholesterol -	130.6 mg
fat -	31.9 g	fiber -	0.9 g
carbohydrate -	12.5 g	sugar -	6.7 g

Raspberry Sauce

½ cup raspberry vinegar
¼ cup minced green onion
½ cup butter, cut into pieces
2 tablespoons seedless raspberry jam

Combine vinegar and onions in a small pan. Simmer, over medium heat, until reduced to 2 tablespoons and remove from heat. Whisk half of butter into vinegar and onions one piece at a time. Return pan to low heat and add the remaining butter while continuing to whisk. Add the raspberry jam and serve.

SALMON EN CROUTE

1 sheet frozen puff
  pastry
4 skinless salmon
  fillets, 4 inches x 2
  inches
½ tablespoon minced
  fresh parsley
½ tablespoon fresh
  tarragon
½ tablespoon fresh
  chervil
Salt and pepper to
  taste
1 egg beaten with 1
  teaspoon water

*O*n a floured surface, roll out pastry into a square and cut into 4 squares, 7" each. Season fillets with herbs, salt and pepper. Place one fillet on each square of pastry and wrap neatly around.

Preheat oven to 375°. Place wrapped fillets, seam side down, on ungreased baking sheet. Brush pastry with beaten egg and water. Bake for 20 minutes or until golden brown.

Yield: 4 servings

FLORIBBEAN SHRIMP

5 pounds fresh
  shrimp, unpeeled
1 bunch celery,
  chopped
3-4 garlic cloves,
  crushed
6 lemons, halved
2¼ tablespoons
  cracked black
  pepper
¼ cup Worcestershire
  sauce
1-2 tablespoons salt
  Dash Tabasco sauce
½ cup butter, cut into
  pieces

*P*reheat broiler. Place shrimp in a large foil casserole or shallow pan. Add celery, garlic, juice of the lemons, pepper, Worcestershire sauce, salt and Tabasco sauce. Stir until evenly mixed. Top with pieces of butter and lemon halves.

Place shrimp under broiler and broil, stirring several times, until butter melts and shrimp are pink, approximately 5 minutes. Reduce oven temperature to 350° and bake for 20-30 minutes, stirring often. Do not overcook. Place shrimp in bowls with some of the juice.

Yield: 10 servings

This is a terrific casual meal for a group of friends. Cover the table with newspaper; peel and eat!

BAKED SCALLOPS WITH CREAM

2 cups sliced zucchini
¾ cup carrots, cut into thin sticks, one inch long
2 tablespoons butter or margarine
¼ cup flour
⅔ cup whipping cream
1 pound scallops
5 tablespoons grated Parmesan cheese, divided
¼ teaspoon salt
¼ teaspoon white pepper
2 tablespoons dry white wine
1 (4-ounce) can crescent rolls
1 egg white, beaten

*I*n a large skillet, sauté zucchini and carrots in butter until crisp and tender, 3-4 minutes. Sprinkle flour over vegetables and toss lightly to coat. Cook one minute more over medium heat. Add whipping cream and cook one minute, stirring constantly, until thick. Add scallops, 2 tablespoons Parmesan cheese, salt and pepper; cook over medium heat until mixture comes to a boil. Remove from heat and stir in wine.

Preheat oven to 375°. Spoon hot mixture into ungreased 9 inch quiche or pie pan. Remove dough from can in rolled sections, do not unroll. Cut roll into 6 slices; cut each slice in half. Arrange halves around the outside edge of pan. Brush dough with beaten egg white then sprinkle with 3 tablespoons Parmesan cheese. Bake for 20-30 minutes. Let stand for 5 minutes before serving.

Yield: 6-8 servings

This is also excellent made with shrimp.

COCONUT FRIED SHRIMP

2 cups flour, divided
1½ cups milk
1½ teaspoons baking powder
1 teaspoon curry
½ teaspoon salt
2 cups shredded coconut
2 pounds large shrimp, peeled and deveined
Oil for frying

*I*n a 1-quart mixing bowl, combine 1½ cups flour, milk, baking powder, curry and salt. Place remaining flour and coconut in 2 separate shallow pans. Dredge shrimp in flour, dip in batter, then roll in coconut. Fry in hot oil at 350° until coconut is golden brown. Drain on paper towels then transfer to warming tray or warm plates. Serve hot.

Yield: 4-6 servings

This is wonderful served with a sweet and sour sauce.

Shrimp Enchiladas

2 tablespoons butter

1 cup diced onion

1 tablespoon chopped garlic

1 pound diced shrimp

2 tablespoons flour

1 teaspoon dried oregano

1 teaspoon dried basil

1 teaspoon dried thyme

½ teaspoon cayenne pepper

3 tablespoons chopped cilantro

2 teaspoons cumin

1 sliced jalapeño pepper

1 teaspoon salt

Pepper to taste

1 cup heavy cream

¾ cup grated Monterey jack cheese

12 corn tortillas (6-9 inches in diameter), room temperature

Grated cheese for baking

Taco or chili sauce

Heat butter in skillet over medium heat and sauté onion and garlic for 1-2 minutes. Add shrimp and sauté 1 more minute. Add flour and stir well; add seasonings and cream. Reduce until very thick; cool and fold in cheese.

Preheat oven to 350°. Place 2 tablespoons of the filling on each tortilla and roll up. Place rolled tortillas side by side in a baking dish and top with additional cheese to taste. Bake for 5 minutes until cheese is melted. Serve immediately with your favorite taco or chili sauce.

Yield: 4-6 servings

MILE MARKER SNAPPER

2 tomatoes, sliced

½ medium onion, thinly sliced

½ red pepper, cut into strips

½ yellow pepper, cut into strips

½ green pepper, cut into strips

3 tablespoons soft fresh bread crumbs

Salt and pepper to taste

1½ pounds snapper fillets

½ cup white wine

4 tablespoons butter

1 tablespoon lemon juice

Dash paprika

3 tablespoons Parmesan cheese

*A*rrange tomatoes in a lightly buttered 13 x 9 inch baking dish; layer onion and peppers over tomatoes. Sprinkle with bread crumbs and salt and pepper to taste. Place fillets over vegetables.

Preheat oven to 350°. Combine wine, butter and lemon juice in a small saucepan and heat until butter melts. Pour over fish and sprinkle with paprika and Parmesan cheese. Bake for 20 minutes.

Yield: 4 servings

Nutrition Analysis:

saturated fat -	8.6 g	sodium -	451.7 mg
calories -	307	cholesterol -	78.5 mg
fat -	15.1 g	fiber -	1.9 g
carbohydrate -	7.7 g	sugar -	3.5 g

This dish is also delicious with grouper. Soaking fish in milk prior to cooking keeps fish very moist.

Macadamia Crusted Yellowtail Snapper with Tropical Fruit Salsa

½ cup crushed macadamia nuts

¼ cup flour

Salt and white pepper to taste

4 (8-ounce) yellowtail snapper fillets, skin and bones removed

½ cup milk

½ cup vegetable oil or clarified butter

¼ cup white wine

¼ cup freshly squeezed orange juice

1 teaspoon chopped fresh chives

1½ cups Tropical Fruit Salsa (see page 207)

*M*ix nuts with flour, salt and pepper. Dip fillets in milk then dredge in nut mixture. Heat oil in sauté pan over medium heat. Place fish, flesh side down, in pan and sauté until lightly browned. Turn fish and sauté for 2 more minutes. Remove oil from pan, reserving 2 tablespoons; add wine and orange juice. Reduce by one half and add chives. Remove fillets to a plate. Spoon 1 tablespoon sauce over fish and top with 2 tablespoons of Tropical Fruit Salsa.

Yield: 4 servings

Tropical Fruit Salsa

2 cups mixed diced
  fruit (choose from
  mango, papaya,
  kiwi, carambola,
  pineapple,
  blackberry, orange,
  watermelon or any
  sweet tropical fruit)

Juice of one lime

2 tablespoons
  chopped fresh
  cilantro

1 teaspoon sugar

¼ cup freshly
  squeezed orange
  juice

½ chili pepper, finely
  diced, seeds and
  membrane
  removed (Serrano
  or Scotch Bonnet)

Salt and pepper to
  taste

½ small red bell
  pepper, finely diced

1 scallion, sliced into
  thin rounds

*P*lace fruit in a glass mixing bowl and add lime juice, orange juice, cilantro, sugar, peppers and scallion; mix well. Season with salt and pepper. Let sit for ½ hour before serving.

GRECIAN SNAPPER WITH FETA CHEESE

2 ounces feta cheese, crumbled
1 tablespoon olive oil
1 cup chopped onion
1 garlic clove, minced
3 medium tomatoes, peeled, seeded and chopped
¼ cup dry white wine
1 teaspoon dried whole oregano
¼ teaspoon salt
⅛ teaspoon pepper
6 (¼-pound) red snapper fillets
2 tablespoons chopped fresh parsley
1 tablespoon chopped ripe olives
Lemon twist for garnish
Fresh parsley sprigs for garnish

Place feta cheese in a colander and rinse under cold water for one minute; let drain 1 minute and set aside. Coat a large skillet with cooking spray; add olive oil and place over medium heat until hot. Add onion and garlic; sauté until tender. Stir in tomatoes, wine, oregano, salt and pepper. Bring to a boil; reduce heat and simmer, uncovered, 20 minutes.

Preheat oven to 350°. Rinse fillets with cold water and pat dry. Place in a 13 x 9 inch baking dish coated with cooking spray. Spoon sauce over fillets and bake for 15 minutes or until fish flakes easily with a fork. Sprinkle feta cheese, parsley and olives over fish. Garnish with lemon twist and parsley and serve immediately.

Yield: 6 servings

Nutrition Analysis:

saturated fat -	2.0 g	sodium -	235 mg
calories -	178	cholesterol -	71 mg
fat -	5.7 g	fiber -	1.1 g
carbohydrate -	5.8 g	sugar -	2.3 g

Mango Snapper

4 snapper fillets
2 teaspoons lime juice
3 tablespoons flour
¼ teaspoon salt
⅛ teaspoon white
  pepper
6 tablespoons
  unsalted butter,
  divided
1 tablespoon olive oil
1 large ripe mango,
  peeled and thinly
  sliced
2 tablespoons green
  peppercorns (1
  tablespoon whole, 1
  tablespoon
  crushed), divided
½ cup heavy cream
1 small bunch
  watercress

*R*ub snapper with lime juice and dust with flour seasoned with the salt and white pepper. In a large skillet, heat 3 tablespoons butter and the olive oil until hot, but not smoking. Add snapper and sauté 3-4 minutes on each side. Transfer to a warmed platter.

Wipe skillet clean and melt 2 tablespoons butter over medium heat. Add the mango slices and sauté for 1 minute on each side. Place slices on top of snapper fillets.

To the same pan, add 1 tablespoon butter and all peppercorns. Cook over medium heat 1 minute; add cream. Simmer over low heat for 3 minutes. Spoon over the mangos and fish. Garnish with sprigs of watercress.

Yield: 4 servings

Even those who do not like mangos will love this dish!

BROILED SWORDFISH WITH MINT AND LIME

Juice of one lime
1 tablespoon olive oil
1 tablespoon soy sauce
1 garlic clove, minced
2 tablespoons minced fresh mint leaves
1 pound fresh swordfish steaks
1 tablespoon fresh parsley, minced

Combine the lime juice, olive oil, soy sauce, garlic and mint in a shallow dish. Add the fish and marinate 20 minutes to 1 hour, turning several times.

Preheat oven to 425°. Spoon marinade over surface of fish and bake 12 minutes. Turn oven to broil and move rack as close to element as possible. Broil fish for 2 minutes. Remove from broiler and let stand for 1 minute. Divide on warmed plates and spoon marinade over top. Garnish with parsley.

Yield: 4 servings

Nutrition Analysis:

saturated fat -	0.9 g	sodium -	269.5 mg
calories -	163.1	cholesterol -	37.1 mg
fat -	6.1 g	fiber -	0 g
carbohydrate -	1.7 g	sugar -	0.8 g

This recipe is great with any firm fleshed fish.

GRILLED SWORDFISH WITH
AVOCADO SAUCE

1 small avocado,
  peeled, pitted and
  diced
1 tablespoon olive oil
1 tablespoon minced
  fresh basil
Dash lemon juice
⅛ teaspoon cayenne
  pepper
2 tablespoons sour
  cream
1 tablespoon capers
2 (4-ounce) swordfish
  steaks
2 lemon wedges

Combine avocado, olive oil, basil, lemon juice and cayenne pepper in a blender or food processor until smooth. Remove from container and mix in sour cream and capers; set aside.

Preheat grill. Brush swordfish steaks with a light coating of olive oil. Grill over hot coals until steaks turn white on both sides and are cooked through when checked with a knife. Top with avocado sauce and serve.

Yield: 2 servings

May also be prepared by broiling fish 4 inches from heat for 2-3 minutes per side until cooked through.

GRILLED TUNA WITH GINGER CREAM SAUCE

5 green onions, divided

1½ cups dry red wine

½ cup soy sauce

¼ cup red wine vinegar

¼ cup sesame oil

1½ tablespoons paprika

½ garlic head, cut in half to expose cloves

1 (9-inch) piece fresh ginger, divided (⅔ of the piece crushed, ⅓ thinly sliced)

6 (9-ounce) tuna steaks, 1 inch thick

1 cup dry white wine

1 cup rice vinegar

1 cup whipping cream

2 cups butter, chilled, cut into 32 pieces, divided

6 sprigs parsley or herb of choice for garnish

*P*reheat broiler. Place 4 green onions on broiler pan and broil 15 minutes until charred. Set aside.

Combine red wine, soy sauce, red wine vinegar, sesame oil and paprika in a non-aluminum pan. Add charred onions, garlic and crushed ginger. Add tuna turning once to coat. Let tuna marinate for 1 hour at room temperature.

While tuna marinates, dice the remaining green onion. In a saucepan, boil white wine, rice vinegar, diced green onion and sliced ginger over medium heat until liquid is reduced to a glaze. Add cream and boil until reduced by one half. Strain and put into a clean saucepan. Whisk in 2 pieces of butter. Place pan over low heat and whisk in remaining butter 1 piece at a time (remove pan from heat for a moment if drops of melted butter appear). Keep ginger sauce warm in top of double boiler over warm water.

Preheat grill or broiler. Arrange fish on grill or broiler pan. Grill or broil 9 minutes or until heated through. Spoon a few tablespoons of cream sauce on each of 6 dinner plates. Place fish on top of sauce and garnish with a sprig of parsley or herb of choice.

Yield: 6 servings

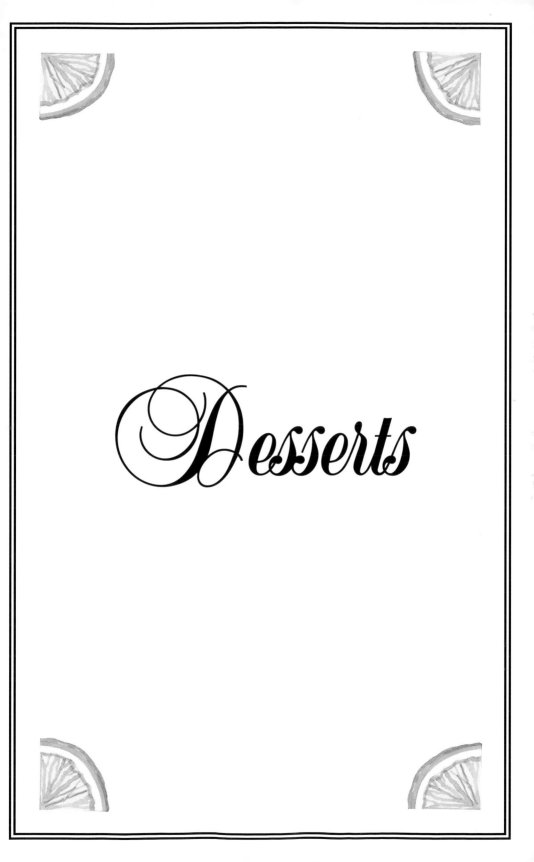

Desserts

THE LADY IN RED

The Jupiter Lighthouse is a majestic and elegant gateway to paradise, the Palm Beaches. She has guided floundering boats and ships through her challenging inlet for generations.

Her warm beacon that welcomes fishermen, boaters and vacationers alike is equally as beautiful as the blue waters beneath it. Her beaches are the home to children's sand castles, sunbathers, family picnics and local artists capturing her beauty.

The balmy breezes that guide the palm trees beneath her, flow gently across the sky. If you look closely, you may see a Roseate Spoonbill perching in preparation for flight. Or, one will be entranced by enjoying the tropical paradise found within the waters of the inlet which shimmer in her beam.

The Lady in Red's continued strength and courage shining bright will help to protect and guide future generations whose travels find them upon her shores.

Oatmeal Coconut Cookies

2 cups margarine
2 cups brown sugar
1½ cups granulated
    sugar
2 teaspoons vanilla
    extract
4 eggs
3 cups flour
2 teaspoons salt
2 teaspoons baking
    soda
5 cups quick oats
1½ cups flaked coconut
¾ cup chopped
    pecans or walnuts,
    optional

Preheat oven to 350°. Cream together margarine, brown sugar and granulated sugar. Add vanilla, then eggs, one at a time. Add dry ingredients to the mixture. Stir in oats, then coconut. If desired, add nuts to mixture. Drop dough by rounded teaspoonfuls 2 inches apart onto lightly greased cookie sheets. Bake for 10 to 12 minutes.

Yield: 4-5 dozen

A moist and chewy delight!

Coconut Crisps

2 cups all-purpose
    flour
¾ teaspoon baking
    powder
¼ teaspoon salt
¾ cup butter or
    margarine, softened
1 cup sugar
1 large egg
1 teaspoon vanilla
    extract
1½ cups shredded
    sweetened coconut

Preheat oven to 375°. Combine flour, baking powder and salt in a medium bowl. Beat butter and sugar in a large mixing bowl at medium speed until light and fluffy. Beat in egg and vanilla. With mixer at low speed, beat in dry ingredients just until combined. Stir in coconut. Drop dough by level tablespoonfuls onto ungreased cookie sheets. For each cookie, dip the flat bottom of a glass in flour and flatten cookie to ¼-inch thickness; press cookie with back of fork to form ridges. Bake for 10 to 12 minutes, until edges are golden. Transfer to racks to cool.

Yield: 3 dozen

Lime Delights

5½ tablespoons margarine or butter, softened

1 cup sugar, divided

1 cup flour plus 2 tablespoons, divided

2 eggs

3 tablespoons lime juice

½ teaspoon baking powder

⅛ teaspoon salt

2 teaspoons finely shredded lime peel

1 cup flaked coconut

Confectioners' sugar for garnish

Preheat oven to 350°. Beat margarine or butter and ¼ cup sugar until thoroughly combined. Add 1 cup flour and beat until mixture resembles fine crumbs. Press crumb mixture into the bottom of an ungreased 8 x 8 inch baking pan. Bake for 15 minutes.

Meanwhile, in the same mixing bowl, beat eggs until foamy. Add ¾ cup sugar, 2 tablespoons flour, lime juice, baking powder and salt; beat for 3 minutes. Stir in lime peel and coconut. Pour mixture over the partially baked crust. Bake for 20-25 minutes or until lightly browned around the edges and the center is set.

Cool in pan on a wire rack. Once cooled, lightly sift top with confectioners' sugar; cut into 20 bars. Store in refrigerator.

Yield: 20 bars

Chewy Brown Sugar Cookies

½ cup butter

2 cups brown sugar

2 eggs

1 teaspoon vanilla extract

1 cup flour

¼ teaspoon salt

1 cup chopped pecans or walnuts, divided

Preheat oven to 350°. Cream butter and sugar; add eggs one at a time, beating well. Add vanilla and blend. Sift flour with salt and add to butter mixture; stir in ½ of the nuts. Spread into greased but not floured 13 x 9 inch pan. Spread batter fairly thin; sprinkle with remaining nuts. Bake for 30 minutes. Cut while hot but leave in pan to cool.

Yield: 18-24 cookies

It is best to make two batches of these; they seem to disappear!

SUGAR AND SPICE COOKIES

¾ cup shortening
1 cup sugar
1 egg
¼ cup molasses
2 cups sifted flour
2 teaspoons baking soda
¼ teaspoon salt
¾ teaspoon ground cloves
¾ teaspoon ground ginger
1 pound confectioners' sugar

Preheat oven to 375°. In a large bowl, mix together shortening, sugar, egg and molasses thoroughly; set aside. Sift together dry ingredients and gradually add to the shortening mixture; blend well. Form into small balls and place 2 inches apart on a greased cookie sheet. Bake for 10 to 12 minutes. While still warm, roll cookies in confectioners' sugar to coat, then place on wire rack to cool.

Yield: 4-5 dozen

CRANBERRY AND WHITE CHOCOLATE CHIP COOKIES

½ cup butter, softened
1⅓ cups sugar
2 eggs, slightly beaten
1 tablespoon cinnamon
1¾ cups all-purpose flour, unsifted
1 cup rolled oats
1½ teaspoons baking soda
½ teaspoon salt
1 cup dried cranberries
⅔ cup white chocolate chips

Preheat oven to 350°. In a large bowl, beat together butter, sugar and eggs until smooth and creamy. In a separate bowl, mix together the cinnamon, flour, oats, baking soda and salt until well combined. Gradually add the dry mixture to the butter mixture. Continue to mix until an even consistency is reached; add the dried cranberries and white chocolate chips, stirring to blend. Drop dough by rounded teaspoons onto a non-stick cookie sheet, or a cookie sheet lightly coated with a non-stick spray; bake for 10 to 12 minutes. The cookies should be refrigerated in an airtight container and serve chilled.

Yield: 3 dozen

If you would like to add a decorative touch of color, a glaze can be made to drizzle over the top. Mix together 1½ cups of confectioners' sugar and 2 tablespoons water, along with a few drops of food coloring (start with 3 drops and increase to get the desired color).

PIGNOLI COOKIES

4 egg whites
½ teaspoon cream of tartar
1½-1⅓ cups confectioners sugar
1 pound almond paste
1-1½ pounds Pignoli nuts, crushed
Parchment paper

*P*reheat oven to 375°. With an electric mixer, beat egg whites with cream of tartar until stiff peaks form; add confectioners' sugar. Break up almond paste and add to the mixture and blend well (the dough will be sticky). Using a teaspoon, take a small amount and roll in nuts and shape into crescents. Place on cookie sheet lined with parchment paper. Bake for 10 to 12 minutes on center rack of oven.

Yield: 3-4 dozen

WHITE CHOCOLATE MACADAMIA NUT COOKIES

½ cup butter or margarine, softened
½ cup shortening
¾ cup firmly packed brown sugar
½ cup granulated sugar
1 large egg
1½ teaspoons vanilla extract
2 cups all-purpose flour
1 teaspoon baking soda
½ teaspoon salt
6 ounces white chocolate-flavored baking bars, cut into small chunks
1 (7-ounce) jar macadamia nuts, coarsely chopped

*P*reheat oven to 350°. Beat butter and shortening at medium speed with an electric mixer until soft and creamy; gradually add sugars, beating well. Add egg and vanilla; beat well. Combine flour, soda and salt; gradually add to butter mixture, beating well. Stir in white chocolate chunks and nuts. Drop dough by rounded teaspoonfuls, 2 inches apart, onto lightly greased cookie sheets. Bake for 8-10 minutes. Cool slightly on cookie sheets; remove to wire racks, and let cool completely.

Yield: 5 dozen

KILLER CUPCAKES

8 ounces cream
  cheese, softened
1 egg
⅓ cup sugar
⅛ teaspoon salt
12 ounces semi-sweet
  chocolate chips
1½ cups flour
1 cup sugar
¼ cup cocoa
1 teaspoon baking
  soda
½ teaspoon salt
1 cup water
⅓ cup vegetable oil
1 teaspoon vanilla
  extract
½ cup ground pecans,
  optional

*P*reheat oven to 350°. Combine cream cheese, egg, sugar and salt; mix well. Blend in chocolate chips; set aside. Sift together flour, sugar, cocoa, soda and salt. Stir in water, oil and vanilla. Line miniature cupcake pans with paper liners. Fill each cup ⅓ full with cocoa mixture, then top with one generous teaspoon cheese mixture. Sprinkle with ground nuts, if desired. Bake for 20 minutes.

Yield: 4 dozen

A favorite for kids and adults alike!

CHEESE CAKE COOKIES

⅓ cup brown sugar
½ cup chopped nuts
1 cup flour
⅓ cup melted butter
8 ounces cream
  cheese, softened
¼ cup sugar
1 egg
1 tablespoon lemon
  juice
1 teaspoon vanilla
  extract
2 tablespoons milk

*P*reheat oven to 350°. With an electric mixer, mix brown sugar, nuts, flour and butter until mixture resembles fine crumbs. Reserve ½ cup to be used as a topping. Place remainder in a greased 8 x 8 inch square pan and press firmly. Bake for 12 to 15 minutes. Blend cream cheese and sugar until smooth. Beat in egg, lemon juice, vanilla extract and milk. Pour onto baked crust; top with reserved crumbs and bake 25 minutes. Cool thoroughly and cut into squares. Keep refrigerated.

Yield: 2 dozen

CHOCOLATE CHERRY BROWNIES

¾ cup unsalted butter
6 ounces unsweetened chocolate, chopped
2½ cups sugar
4 eggs
1 egg yolk
1½ teaspoons vanilla extract
½ teaspoon almond extract
1 cup plus 2 tablespoons all-purpose flour
1 teaspoon ground cinnamon
1 cup halved, dried, sour or Bing cherries or chopped pitted prunes
1 cup semi-sweet chocolate chips

*P*reheat oven to 350°. Butter and flour a 13 x 9 inch glass baking dish. Melt butter and unsweetened chocolate in heavy saucepan over low heat, stirring until smooth. Remove from heat and blend in sugar. Add eggs one at a time, then egg yolk. Add vanilla and almond extracts, flour and cinnamon; stir until just blended. Stir in cherries and chocolate chips. Spread batter in prepared pan. Bake until brownies are firm around edges and tester inserted into center comes out with a few crumbs; approximately 35 minutes. Cool on rack then cut into 16 or 32 pieces.

Yield: 16 or 32 pieces

Can be prepared 2 days ahead. Wrap brownies individually and store in airtight container.

WHITE CHOCOLATE BROWNIES

½ cup unsalted butter
8 ounces white chocolate chips, divided
2 large eggs
⅛ teaspoon salt
½ cup sugar
½ teaspoon vanilla extract
1 cup all-purpose flour
8 ounces semi-sweet chocolate chips
Parchment paper

*P*reheat oven to 350°. Lightly butter an 8 inch square pan and line bottom with parchment paper; lightly butter paper. Melt butter in small heavy saucepan over low heat. Remove pan from heat and add one half of the white chocolate, do not stir. Using electric mixer, beat eggs with salt in large bowl until frothy. Gradually add sugar and beat until pale yellow. Add butter/white chocolate mixture, vanilla, salt and flour; mix until just combined. Stir in semi-sweet chips and remaining white chocolate chips. Spoon mixture into prepared pan. Bake until tester comes out almost clean (25-35 minutes). Cover top with foil if it becomes too brown during baking.

Yield: 16 brownies

White Chocolate Raspberry Cheesecake

CRUST
1 cup vanilla wafer crumbs

½ cup ground almonds

2 tablespoons sugar

⅛ teaspoon almond extract

3 tablespoons butter or margarine, melted

FILLING
4 ounces white chocolate, chopped

16 ounces cream cheese, softened

3 large eggs

¾ cup sugar

2 teaspoons flour

1 teaspoon vanilla

GLAZE
¼ cup heavy cream

4 ounces white chocolate, chopped

SAUCE
12 ounces frozen raspberries

½ cup white wine

⅓ cup sugar

Fresh raspberries for garnish (optional)

*P*reheat oven to 350°. To prepare the crust, combine all ingredients in a small bowl or food processor until mixture resembles coarse crumbs. Press into bottom of an 8 or 9 inch springform pan. Bake for 10 minutes; cool completely. Reduce oven temperature to 325°.

For the filling, melt white chocolate in double boiler. Cool to lukewarm. In a medium bowl, beat cream cheese with electric mixer until smooth. Add eggs, one at a time, mixing well after each addition. Mix in sugar, flour and vanilla. Gently but thoroughly blend in melted white chocolate. Pour filling over crust. Bake until cheesecake hardens around edges, but still moves slightly in center when gently shaken (approximately 40 minutes); cool completely. Cover and refrigerate 8 hours or overnight.

To glaze, in small saucepan, bring cream to simmer over low heat. Add white chocolate and stir until smooth. Spread glaze evenly over top of cooled cheesecake. Refrigerate until set. Cake may be made ahead to this point up to 2 days in advance.

Prepare sauce by thawing raspberries in a sieve placed over a bowl, reserving juice. In a small saucepan, boil wine and sugar until reduced to ¼ cup (approximately 10 minutes). Puree thawed berries in a food processor. Press puree through a sieve to remove seeds. Sweeten puree with 2 tablespoons each wine syrup and reserved raspberry juice, adding more to taste. To serve; spoon a pool of raspberry sauce onto individual plates. Slice cheesecake and place on top of sauce. Drizzle more sauce over top, if desired. Garnish plates with fresh berries.

Yield: 12-16 slices

LEMON CHEESECAKE

CRUST

¾ cup graham cracker crumbs

2 tablespoons sugar

1 tablespoon ground cinnamon

1 tablespoon butter or margarine, softened

FILLING

5 (8-ounce) packages cream cheese, softened

1 ⅔cups sugar

5 eggs

⅛ teaspoon salt

1½ teaspoons vanilla extract

¼ cup fresh lemon juice

To prepare crust, combine graham cracker crumbs, sugar, and cinnamon. Stir well and set aside. Grease bottom and sides of a 10 inch springform pan with the butter. Add the crumb mixture, tilting pan to coat sides and bottom. Refrigerate.

Preheat oven to 300°. Beat cream cheese with an electric mixer at medium speed until light and fluffy; add sugar, beating well at high speed. Add eggs one at a time, beating well after each egg. Stir in salt, vanilla and lemon juice. Pour into prepared crust. Bake for 1 hour and 20 minutes (center may be soft but will set when chilled). Cool on a wire rack. Cover and chill at least 8 hours.

Yield: 12-16 slices

COCONUT BANANA CAKE

CAKE
¾ cup shortening

1½ cups sugar

2 eggs

1 cup mashed bananas

½ teaspoon salt

2 cups sifted cake flour

1 teaspoon baking soda

1 teaspoon baking powder

½ cup buttermilk

1 teaspoon vanilla

½ cup chopped pecans

1 cup flaked coconut

CREAMY NUT FILLING
½ cup sugar

2 tablespoons flour

½ cup heavy cream

2 tablespoons butter

½ cup chopped pecans

¼ teaspoon salt

1 teaspoon vanilla

WHITE SNOW FROSTING
1 egg white

¼ cup shortening

¼ cup butter

½ teaspoon coconut extract

½ teaspoon vanilla

2 cups sifted confectioners sugar

*P*reheat oven to 375°. To prepare cake, cream together shortening and sugar until fluffy. Add eggs; beat 2 minutes at medium speed. Add bananas and beat 2 minutes longer. In a separate bowl, sift together dry ingredients. Add to creamed mixture along with buttermilk and vanilla; beat 2 minutes. Stir in nuts.

Pour batter into 2 greased and floured 9 inch round layer cake pans. Sprinkle ½ cup coconut on each layer. Bake for 25 to 30 minutes. Remove from pan and cool layers on racks, coconut side up.

Meanwhile, prepare filling by combining sugar, flour, cream and butter in a heavy saucepan. Cook over medium heat until thickened. Add pecans, salt and vanilla; cool.

When cake layers are cool, place first layer coconut side down on cake plate. Spread with filling. Top with second layer, coconut side up.

For frosting, cream the egg white, shortening, butter, coconut extract and vanilla until well blended. Gradually add confectioners sugar and beat until light and fluffy. Frost on the sides and 1 inch around the top edge of cake, leaving the center unfrosted.

Yield: 12-16 slices

COSTA RICAN RUM CREAM CAKE

CAKE
1 package yellow cake mix with pudding
1 cup water
⅓ cup vegetable oil
3 eggs
1 (14-ounce) can sweetened condensed milk
1 (12-ounce) can evaporated milk

SAUCE
1 cup whipping cream
⅓ cup rum or 1 teaspoon rum extract

TOPPING
1 cup whipping cream
⅓ cup coconut, toasted
⅓ cup macadamia nuts, chopped

*P*reheat oven to 350°. In a large bowl, combine cake mix, water, oil, eggs, sweetened condensed milk and evaporated milk and beat at low speed until moistened. Beat for two minutes at high speed. Pour into a greased 13 x 9 inch baking pan. Bake for 25-30 minutes or until toothpick inserted in center comes out clean.

While cake is baking, combine all sauce ingredients in a large bowl; blend well. Remove cake from oven and cool 5 minutes. Using a long tined fork, pierce hot cake every 1 to 2 inches. Slowly pour sauce mixture over the cake. Refrigerate cake at least 3 hours to chill and allow sauce to absorb.

Before serving, in a small bowl, beat 1 cup whipping cream until stiff peaks form; spread over cold cake. Sprinkle with coconut and macadamia nuts. Store in refrigerator.

Yield: 12-15 servings

To toast coconut, spread on cookie sheet; bake at 350° for 7-8 minutes or until light golden brown, stirring occasionally. Or, spread a thin layer in microwave safe pie pan. Microwave on low for 4 ½ to 8 minutes or until light golden brown, tossing with a fork after each minute.

Ultimate Poppy Seed Cake

1 cup buttermilk

¾ cup poppy seeds

1 teaspoon almond extract

1 cup butter, softened

2¼ cups sugar, divided

5 eggs, separated

2½ cups flour

1 teaspoon baking powder

1 teaspoon baking soda

1 teaspoon cinnamon

*P*reheat oven to 350°. Grease and flour a 10 inch bundt pan. Mix buttermilk, poppy seeds and almond extract in a medium bowl and set aside. Cream butter with 1½ cups sugar in large bowl. Beat in egg yolks 1 at a time, mixing well after each addition. Continue beating until pale yellow and fluffy. Sift together flour, baking powder and baking soda. Add dry ingredients to butter alternating with buttermilk mixture. In separate bowl, beat egg whites until stiff but not dry. Fold into batter.

Spoon half of batter into prepared pan. Sprinkle with remaining sugar and then cinnamon. Add remaining batter and spread top evenly. Bake 50-60 minutes or until tester inserted in center comes out clean. Cool in pan 20 minutes. Invert cake onto platter. Serve at room temperature.

Yield: 12 slices

Nutrition Analysis per slice:

saturated fat -	13.4 g	sodium -	340.8 mg
calories -	482	fiber -	0
fat -	23.0 g	cholesterol -	158.2 mg
carbohydrate -	60.7 g	sugar -	36.8 g

This cake is even better the next day!

Italian Cream Cake

CAKE

- 2 cups sugar
- ½ cup butter
- ½ cup shortening
- 5 eggs, separated
- 1 teaspoon baking soda
- 1 cup buttermilk
- 2 cups flour
- ½ teaspoon salt
- 1 tablespoon vanilla
- 1 cup coconut
- 1 cup chopped pecans

CREAM CAKE ICING

- 8 ounces cream cheese, softened
- ½ cup butter
- 1 pound confectioners' sugar
- 1 teaspoon vanilla

*P*reheat oven to 325°. Cream sugar, butter and shortening. Add egg yolks one at a time, beating well after each addition. Stir soda into buttermilk and let sit for 10 minutes. Meanwhile, beat egg whites until stiff peaks form; set aside. Sift together flour and salt and add to the sugar and butter mixture alternating with buttermilk. Add vanilla, coconut and pecans. Gently fold in egg whites. Pour batter into 3 greased and floured 9 inch cake pans. Bake for 35 minutes. Meanwhile, beat all icing ingredients until smooth. Ice between layers and on outside of cooled cake.

Yield: 12-16 slices

TROPICAL CARROT CAKE

CAKE
1½ cups vegetable oil
4 eggs
2 cups sugar
2 cups flour
2 teaspoons baking powder
1½ teaspoons baking soda
2 teaspoons cinnamon
1 teaspoon salt
3 cups grated carrots
8 ounces pineapple, crushed and drained
1 cup chopped pecans

ICING
½ cup margarine, softened
1 pound confectioners' sugar
8 ounces cream cheese, softened
1 teaspoon vanilla
½ cup pecan halves, optional

*P*reheat oven to 350°. Grease and flour three 9-inch cake pans. Mix together oil, eggs and sugar; beat well. Add dry ingredients and mix well. Add carrots, pineapple and chopped pecans; mix thoroughly. Pour batter into cake pans and bake for 35 to 40 minutes or until cake tester comes out clean. Cool cakes at least 20 minutes. Prepare icing by mixing margarine, confectioners' sugar and cream cheese together with an electric mixer. Add vanilla and mix well. Ice between layers and entire cake.

Yield: 12 slices

For presentation, place pecan halves in a decorative design on top of cake.

Brown Sugar Pound Cake

CAKE
- 1 cup butter
- ½ cup shortening
- 1 pound light brown sugar
- 1 cup sugar
- 5 eggs
- 1 teaspoon baking powder
- ½ teaspoon salt
- 3 cups sifted flour
- 1 cup milk
- 1 teaspoon vanilla
- 1 cup chopped pecans (optional)

BROWN SUGAR GLAZE
- 2 tablespoons shortening
- 2 tablespoons butter
- ½ cup brown sugar, packed
- ½ teaspoon salt
- 2 tablespoons milk
- 1 teaspoon vanilla
- ½ cup chopped pecans

*P*reheat oven to 350°. To prepare cake, beat together butter and shortening. Gradually add sugars, creaming until light and fluffy. Beat in eggs one at a time. Sift dry ingredients and add to batter, alternating with the milk and vanilla; stir in pecans. Pour batter into a greased bundt pan. Bake for 1 hour and 15 minutes. Cool in pan for 10 minutes, then remove.

To prepare the glaze, combine shortening, butter, brown sugar, salt and milk in a saucepan and place over medium heat. Stir constantly until sugar is melted and smooth. Remove from heat and add the vanilla and pecans. Pour the glaze over cake and broil under preheated broiler until the glaze is bubbly.

Yield: 20 slices

SOUR CREAM POUND CAKE

3 cups sugar
1 cup butter, creamed
½ cup shortening
6 eggs
3 cups sifted flour
1 cup sour cream
¼ teaspoon baking soda
1 teaspoon vanilla
1 teaspoon almond extract
2 teaspoons imitation butter extract
1 teaspoon lemon juice

*P*reheat oven to 350°. Combine sugar, butter and shortening. Add eggs one at a time. Add flour alternating with sour cream. Add baking soda, vanilla, almond extract, butter extract and lemon juice; mix well. Pour batter into a greased and floured tube or bundt pan. Bake for 1¼ to 1½ hours.

Yield: 16-20 slices

Sift confectioners' sugar lightly over cake for a finishing touch.

FRENCH CHOCOLATE CAKE

1 pound sweet or semi-sweet chocolate
1 teaspoon water
1 tablespoon flour
1 tablespoon sugar
11 tablespoons butter, softened
4 eggs, separated
Confectioners' sugar for garnish
1 cup whipped cream

*P*reheat oven to 425°. Grease a 9 inch cake or springform pan. Line the pan with waxed paper, carefully smoothing edges. Melt chocolate and water in a double boiler over simmering water. Do not let water boil. Remove from heat and stir in flour, sugar and butter; blend well. Beat egg yolks and gradually add to chocolate mixture. Beat egg whites until stiff and gently fold into batter. Pour batter into prepared pan. Bake 20 to 25 minutes; cake will continue to firm while cooling. When completely cooled, remove from pan and sprinkle with confectioners' sugar. Top with whipped cream and cut into thin slices.

Yield: 10-12 slices

Try placing a doily on cake before sprinkling with confectioners' sugar. Remove doily after sprinkling for a lacy appearance. A chocoholics dream!

BLACK RUSSIAN CAKE

CAKE
- 1 (18½ -ounce) chocolate cake mix
- ½ cup vegetable oil
- 1 (3.9-ounce) package instant chocolate pudding mix
- 4 eggs, room temperature
- ¾ cup strong brewed coffee
- ⅓ cup Kahlúa liqueur
- ⅓ cup Creme de Cacao liqueur

TOPPING
- 1 cup confectioners' sugar
- 2 tablespoons strong brewed coffee
- 2 tablespoons Kahlúa liqueur
- 2 tablespoons Creme de Cacao liqueur

*P*reheat oven to 350°. Combine cake mix, oil, pudding mix, eggs, coffee and liqueurs in a large bowl. Beat for 4 minutes at medium speed. Spoon into well greased bundt pan. Bake for 45 minutes. Remove cake from pan when cool.

Prepare topping by combining confectioners' sugar, coffee and liqueurs in small bowl. Using a long tined fork, pierce cake every few inches and spoon topping over cake. Let cake absorb flavors for one hour before serving.

Yield: 12 slices

Nutrition Analysis per slice:

saturated fat -	2.7 g	sodium -	305.1 mg
calories -	422	fiber -	0
fat -	14.2 g	cholesterol -	91.3 mg
carbohydrate -	62.6 g	sugar -	37.7 g

Hot Fudge Sundae Cake

1 cup flour
¾ cup granulated sugar
¼ cup plus 2 tablespoons cocoa, divided
2 tablespoons baking powder
¼ teaspoon salt
½ cup milk
2 tablespoons vegetable oil
1 teaspoon vanilla
1 cup chopped pecans, optional
1 cup packed brown sugar
1¾ cups very hot tap water
Ice cream

*P*reheat oven to 350°. Combine flour, sugar, 2 tablespoons cocoa, baking powder and salt in an ungreased 9 inch square baking pan. Add milk, oil and vanilla; stir with a fork until smooth. Stir in nuts, if desired. Spread batter evenly in pan. Sprinkle batter with brown sugar and ¼ cup cocoa. Pour hot water over batter. Bake for 40 minutes. While warm, spoon into dessert dishes and top with ice cream. Spoon sauce from pan onto each serving.

Yield: 9 servings

Nutrition Analysis per serving:

saturated fat -	1.5 g	sodium -	502.4 mg
calories -	283	fiber -	0.8 g
fat -	9.5 g	cholesterol -	0
carbohydrate -	49.2g	sugar -	32.1 g

CHUCK & HAROLD'S KEY LIME PIE

PASTRY
1½ cups graham
   cracker crumbs
3 tablespoons sugar
3 tablespoons
   unsalted butter,
   melted

PIE
10 egg yolks
2 (14-ounce) cans
   sweetened
   condensed milk
1¼ cups Key lime juice
   Whipped cream for
   garnish
1 lime, cut into
   wedges for garnish

*P*reheat oven to 325°. Mix crumbs, sugar and melted butter together and press evenly on sides and bottom of a 10 inch pie pan. Bake for 10 minutes; set aside.

In a large bowl, whisk together egg yolks and condensed milk until smooth and glossy. Blend in the lime juice. (Note: It is critical that the lime juice is added last. Otherwise, the acid of the juice will curdle the egg yolks.) Pour mixture into baked pie shell. Bake for 15-20 minutes. Cool at room temperature and refrigerate at least five hours or, preferably, overnight. Garnish with whipped cream and lime slices and serve.

Yield: 8-10 slices

Key Lime Pie is as much a Florida tradition as is Chuck and Harold's Restaurant on Palm Beach! This recipe can be made ahead, frozen or doubled.

FRESH STRAWBERRY PIE

1 quart large, whole
   strawberries,
   divided
3 tablespoons
   cornstarch
⅓ cup water
1 tablespoon lemon
   juice
¼ teaspoon salt
1 cup sugar
1 9 inch baked pastry
   shell
Whipped cream

*W*ash and hull strawberries. Blend cornstarch and water in a small bowl; mix in half of the strawberries. Puree in blender or food processor. Add lemon juice, salt and sugar. Microwave on high, stirring every minute until mixture thickens, approximately 6 minutes; cool. Arrange remainder of the strawberries in baked pastry shell. Cover with cooked mixture. Chill until set. Garnish with whipped cream.

Yield: 8 slices

Nutrition Analysis per slice:

saturated fat -	0	sodium -	243.6 mg
calories -	275	fiber -	1.6 g
fat -	8.3 g	cholesterol -	16.3 mg
carbohydrate -	51.3 g	sugar -	32.6 g

For a taller pie, increase the amount of whole strawberries in pastry shell.

KEY LIME RUM PIE

PASTRY

2 cups finely crushed chocolate wafers (65 cookies)

½ cup unsalted butter, melted

FILLING

1 (14-ounce) can sweetened condensed milk

⅓ cup fresh lime juice (preferably Key lime)

1 tablespoon grated lime rind, divided

3 eggs, separated

½ teaspoon salt

1 cup heavy cream, whipped

2 tablespoons sugar

1 tablespoon dark rum

Shaved chocolate for garnish

*P*reheat oven to 350°. Place wafers in strong plastic bag and crush finely with rolling pin. Add melted butter; blend well. Press mixture firmly to sides and bottom of 9-inch pie plate. Bake for 10 minutes. Cool on rack for 30 minutes.

Reduce oven temperature to 250°. Mix condensed milk with lime juice, 1½ teaspoons of lime rind and beaten egg yolks. In a separate bowl, beat egg whites and salt until stiff; fold into lime and egg yolk mixture. Pour into shell and bake for 10 minutes. Cool 30 minutes. Chill in refrigerator 30 minutes. Add sugar and rum to whipped cream. Top pie with whipped cream. Sprinkle with shaved chocolate and remaining lime rind. Refrigerate until serving time.

Yield: 10-12 slices

PEAR~APPLE CRUMB PIE

1 9-inch unbaked pastry shell (see page 259 for basic pastry recipe)

⅓ cup sugar

2 tablespoons flour

½ teaspoon cinnamon

¼ teaspoon salt

3 cups sliced canned pears, drained

2 cups sliced tart apples (Granny Smith)

½ cup raisins

½ teaspoon lemon peel

1 tablespoon lemon juice

TOPPING

½ cup flour

½ cup brown sugar

½ teaspoon salt

½ cup chopped pecans or walnuts

4 tablespoons butter, diced

*P*reheat oven to 400°. Combine sugar, flour, cinnamon, salt, pears and apple slices; mix well. Add raisins, lemon peel and lemon juice; mix well. Pour into pie crust.

Combine topping ingredients until coarse and crumbly. Sprinkle topping over pie and bake for 15 minutes. Cover with foil and continue to bake for 20-30 minutes until apples are tender.

Yield: 8 slices

Nutrition Analysis per slice:

saturated fat -	4.7 g	sodium -	484.7 mg
calories -	491	fiber -	3.3 g
fat -	18.8 g	cholesterol -	35.1 mg
carbohydrate -	82.2 g	sugar -	49.5 g

GINGERSNAP BERRY PIE

PASTRY

1 cup finely crushed gingersnaps (15 cookies)

¾ cup finely crushed vanilla wafers (18 wafers)

¼ cup finely chopped walnuts

⅓ cup melted butter

FILLING

1 envelope unflavored gelatin

1¾ cups unsweetened white grape juice

8 ounces cream cheese, softened

¼ cup sugar

1 teaspoon vanilla

2½ cups blueberries

1½ cups sliced strawberries

Citrus leaves for garnish

*P*reheat oven to 375°. In a medium mixing bowl, combine crushed gingersnaps, crushed vanilla wafers and walnuts. Add butter and stir with a fork until mixture resembles coarse crumbs. Press crumb mixture onto bottom and 1½ inches up sides of a 9 inch springform pan. Bake for 5 minutes and let cool.

In a medium saucepan, combine gelatin with grape juice and let sit for 5 minutes. Stir over low heat until gelatin dissolves. Chill 40-50 minutes or until partially set, stirring occasionally until it reaches the consistency of unbeaten egg whites. In a small mixing bowl, beat the cream cheese, sugar and vanilla with an electric mixer until smooth. Spread mixture over bottom of prepared crust. Spoon half of the gelatin mixture over cream cheese layer. Top with 1½ cups of the blueberries, all of the sliced strawberries and then the remaining blueberries. Spoon the remaining gelatin mixture over berries. Chill 4-6 hours or until set. To serve, loosen crust with a narrow spatula; remove the sides of the spring form pan. Garnish with citrus leaves.

Yield: 12 slices

Nutrition Analysis per slice:

saturated fat -	6.5 g	sodium -	155.2 mg
calories -	723	fiber -	1.5 g
fat -	12.5 g	cholesterol -	29.5 mg
carbohydrate -	23.6 g	sugar -	13.9 g

RHUBARB-RASPBERRY PIE

1¾ cups sugar

1 teaspoon cinnamon

6 tablespoons all-purpose flour

4 cups chopped fresh rhubarb or frozen rhubarb (see note)

1 cup raspberries

1 medium cooking apple, peeled and shredded

2 9-inch unbaked pastry shells

*P*reheat oven to 375°. In a large mixing bowl, stir together the sugar, cinnamon and flour. Stir in rhubarb, raspberries and apples. Transfer to a pastry-lined 9 inch pie plate. Trim pastry to the rim of the plate. Cut slits in the second pastry and place on top of the fruit filled pie. Seal and flute the edge. Cover edges with foil; bake for 25 minutes. Remove foil and bake an additional 20-25 minutes or until top is golden and fruit is tender. Cool and serve.

Yield: 8 slices

Nutrition Analysis per slice:

saturated fat -	0	sodium -	322.5 mg
calories -	514	fiber -	0
fat -	16.4 g	cholesterol -	32.6 mg
carbohydrate -	29.9 g	sugar -	44.4 g

If using frozen rhubarb, add two more tablespoons of flour and mix rhubarb with the sugar and flour; let mixture stand until the fruit is partially thawed. Add the raspberry and apple. Cook for 50 minutes instead of 25 minutes and remove foil; bake for an additional 10-20 minutes until golden and tender.

APPLE-CRANBERRY STREUSEL PIE

PIE

¾ cup boiling water

½ cup dried cranberries or dried tart cherries

6 large apples, peeled, cored and sliced (6 cups)

¾ cup sugar

3 tablespoons all-purpose flour

1 teaspoon apple pie spice

¼ teaspoon salt

⅓ cup half-and-half or light cream

1 9-inch deep-dish unbaked pastry shell

TOPPING

⅓ cup all-purpose flour

⅓ cup toasted pecans or walnuts, finely chopped

⅓ cup packed brown sugar

¼ teaspoon ground nutmeg

3 tablespoons margarine

*P*reheat oven to 375°. Pour boiling water over cranberries to cover; let stand for 5 minutes and drain. Mix cranberries and apples; place in pastry shell. Combine sugar, flour, apple pie spice and salt. Stir in half-and-half or cream and pour over fruit.

For topping, combine ⅓ cup flour, nuts, brown sugar and nutmeg. With a blender or fork, cut in butter until the pieces are the size of small peas; sprinkle over filling. Cover edge of pie with foil and bake for 25 minutes. Remove foil and bake another 20-25 minutes. Cool pie for 45 minutes.

Yield: 8 slices

Nutrition Analysis per slice:

saturated fat -	1.9 g	sodium -	250 mg
calories -	439	fiber -	3.0 g
fat -	16.6 g	cholesterol -	20.6 mg
carbohydrate -	72.8 g	sugar -	48.5 g

FRESH PEACH PIE

PASTRY
1 cup blanched almonds
1 cup flaked coconut
¼ cup sugar
¼ cup butter or margarine

FILLING
1 cup sour cream
6 tablespoons confectioners' sugar, divided
1 teaspoon orange juice
1 teaspoon shredded orange rind
1 teaspoon vanilla
3 cups sliced fresh peaches
½ cup whipping cream
Dash of salt

*P*reheat oven to 375°. To prepare crust, process almonds in food processor until medium fine; mix with coconut. Work in sugar and butter with fingers or spoon; reserve 3 tablespoons for topping. Press evenly in bottom and sides of an ungreased 9-inch glass pie plate. Bake for 10-12 minutes or until light golden brown. To prevent edges from burning, cover edges with foil leaving center uncovered. Place remaining crumb mixture in shallow pan and bake for 5-6 minutes while pie shell is baking.

To prepare filling, beat sour cream; add salt, 4 tablespoons of confectioners' sugar, orange juice, rind and vanilla. Spread on bottom and sides of shell. Cover with attractively arranged peaches. Whip cream; fold in remaining 2 tablespoons confectioners' sugar. Cover peaches with the whipped cream. Sprinkle toasted coconut mixture over top. Chill and serve.

Yield: 8 slices

Confectioners' sugar may be adjusted to taste depending on sweetness of fresh peaches.

MANGO PIE

PASTRY

2½ cups all-purpose flour

12 tablespoons cold butter, cut into ¼ inch pieces

4 tablespoons cold vegetable shortening

Pinch of salt

6 tablespoons ice water

FILLING

2 (14-ounce) packages frozen mangoes, thawed and pureed or 2 cups fresh mango puree

1 tablespoon fresh lime juice

1 cup sugar

¼ cup sifted all-purpose flour

¼ cup evaporated milk

Pinch of salt

Pinch of nutmeg

2 eggs, separated

*I*n a large bowl, combine flour, butter, shortening and salt and blend until the mixture resembles coarse meal. Add the ice water and toss with a fork just until the water is incorporated. Form the dough into a ball, flattening it somewhat. Dust lightly with flour. Cover in plastic wrap or waxed paper and refrigerate for 1 hour. On a floured surface, roll half of the dough out into a ⅛ inch thick circle. Fit dough into a 9 or 10 inch pie dish. Trim any excess dough and press edges with the back of a fork. Chill for 1 hour before filling. Roll out remaining dough ⅛ inch thick and cut into 1 inch wide strips using a pastry cutter. Place strips on waxed paper, cover and refrigerate for 1 hour before using.

Preheat oven to 350°. In a medium saucepan, heat mango puree and lime juice. Add sugar, flour, milk, salt and nutmeg and cook, over medium heat, for 3 minutes; remove from heat. In a medium bowl, beat egg yolks and fold into mango mixture. Beat egg whites until soft peaks form and fold into mango mixture. Spread in pie shell and decorate with strips of pastry dough. Bake for 40 minutes or until filling is set. Let cool before serving.

Yield: 8 slices

A sensational end to lunch!

PECAN PIE

1 9-inch unbaked
   pastry shell
3 large eggs
¾ cup dark corn
   syrup
¾ cup sugar
2 teaspoons melted
   butter or margarine
1 teaspoon vanilla
1 teaspoon maple
   extract
⅛ teaspoon salt
1 cup pecan halves

*P*reheat oven to 400°. Roll out pie dough to an 11-12 inch circle and fit into 9 inch tart or quiche pan with removable bottom. Press dough gently against bottom and sides of pan, then roll rolling pin over top of pan to trim off excess crust. Freeze shell for 10 minutes. Press square of aluminum foil down into tart shell and fill with beans, rice or pie weights. Bake for 5 minutes. Remove tart shell from oven, take out foil and beans and reduce oven temperature to 350°.

In a large bowl, beat eggs, corn syrup, sugar, butter, vanilla, maple extract and salt at medium speed until smooth and well blended. Stir in pecan halves, then pour filling into tart shell and bake 45-50 minutes until outer edges are set but center is still slightly soft.

Yield: 10 slices

CHOCOLATE-PECAN-OATMEAL PIE

¾ cup coarsely
   chopped pecans
¾ cup quick cooking
   oatmeal
¾ cup semi-sweet
   chocolate chips
½ cup light corn
   syrup
½ cup sugar
2 large eggs
¼ cup unsalted butter,
   melted
1 9-inch unbaked
   pastry shell
Whipped cream for
   topping, if desired

*P*reheat oven to 325°. Sprinkle pecans, oatmeal and chocolate over bottom of pie shell. In a medium bowl, mix syrup, sugar and eggs; stir in butter until well blended. Pour over mixture in pie shell. Bake for one hour or until filling is set. Cool on wire rack. Top with whipped cream.

Yield: 10-12 slices

A tradition with a twist!

Exquisite Pie

2 eggs
1 cup sugar
½ cup melted butter
   or margarine
1 teaspoon vanilla
½ cup coconut
½ cup pecans
½ cup golden raisins
1 9-inch unbaked
   pastry shell

*P*reheat oven to 350°. Beat eggs slightly with a fork. Add sugar and beat again. Add butter and vanilla; blend well. Fold in coconut, pecans and raisins. Pour into pastry shell and bake for 35 minutes.

Yield: 8-10 slices

German Chocolate Pie

4 ounces sweet
   cooking chocolate
¼ cup margarine or
   butter
1 (14-ounce) can
   sweetened
   condensed milk
½ cup unsifted flour
1 teaspoon vanilla
   extract
⅛ teaspoon salt
2 eggs, beaten
1⅓ cups flaked
   coconut, divided
1 cup chopped
   pecans
1 9-inch unbaked
   pastry shell
Whipped cream,
   optional

*P*reheat oven to 350°. In heavy saucepan, over low heat, melt chocolate and margarine or butter; remove from heat and cool to room temperature. Combine milk, flour, vanilla, salt, beaten eggs and chocolate mixture; mix well. Reserving ¼ cup coconut for garnish, stir in remaining coconut and nuts. Pour into pastry shell; garnish with remaining coconut. Bake 40-50 minutes until top is firm and coconut is lightly browned. Cool thoroughly before cutting. Garnish with whipped cream, if desired.

Yield: 10 slices

PEANUT BUTTER PIE

½ cup creamy peanut butter

¾ cup confectioners' sugar

⅓ cup flour

½ cup sugar

⅛ teaspoon salt

2 cups milk

2 egg yolks, slightly beaten

2 teaspoons margarine or butter

1 teaspoon vanilla extract

1 large banana, sliced

1 9-inch baked pastry shell

1 cup heavy whipping cream, whipped (optional: add 2-3 tablespoons granulated sugar while whipping)

Mix peanut butter and confectioners' sugar until crumbly. Spread on the bottom of cooled pastry shell. Mix flour, sugar, salt and milk in saucepan until it comes to a rolling boil, stirring constantly. Add a tablespoon of mixture to beaten egg yolks and mix; continue adding several more tablespoons of mixture then place egg mixture back into saucepan. Remove from heat; add margarine or butter and vanilla. Arrange banana slices in pastry shell.

Pour filling in shell and let cool. Chill in refrigerator for at least 6 hours. Spread whipped cream over filling.

Yield: 8-10 slices

GRAND MARNIER DIP FOR FRUIT

3 egg yolks, lightly
  beaten
⅓ cup sugar
¼ teaspoon salt
¼ cup Grand Marnier
  or other orange-
  flavored liqueur
2 cups whipping
  cream, whipped
Assorted fresh fruit
  (strawberries,
  raspberries, melons,
  kiwi, etc.)

*C*ombine egg yolks, sugar and salt in a small saucepan; cook over medium heat, stirring constantly, until temperature reaches 160°. Stir in liqueur; let cool. Fold whipped cream into liqueur mixture. Cover and chill up to 4 hours. Serve with assorted fresh fruit.

Yield: 4 ¾ cups

CITRUS SAUCE FOR FRESH FRUIT

¼ cup sugar
¼ teaspoon grated
  orange rind
¼ teaspoon grated
  lemon rind
⅓ cup fresh orange
  juice
¼ cup fresh lemon juice
2 egg yolks, beaten
2 cups heavy cream,
  whipped
Assorted fresh fruit
  (strawberries,
  raspberries,
  pineapple, papaya,
  melons, etc.)

*I*n the top of a double boiler, combine and heat sugar, rinds and juices. When hot, pour 3 tablespoons of this mixture into beaten egg yolks, stirring constantly. Then slowly beat egg mixture into sugar mixture. Stirring constantly, cook over simmering water until thickened and mixture coats spoon. Cool to room temperature. Fold a large spoonful of the egg and sugar mixture into whipped cream. Then fold whipped cream into remaining sauce. Mix well and chill.

Yield: 3 cups

CAFE CHARDONNAY'S TIRAMISU

1 cup Italian mascarpone cheese

7 ounces sugar, divided

4 ounces amaretto, divided

1 cup pastry cream (see page 245)

1 cup sweetened whipping cream, whipped

1 cup brewed espresso or strong coffee

1 package Italian lady fingers

15 Amaretto cookies, crumbled

1 small piece of bittersweet chocolate

ESPRESSO SABAYON

6 egg yolks

½ cup sugar

3 ounces espresso syrup

1 cup heavy cream, whipped

½ pint raspberries or blackberries and mint leaves for garnish

Confectioners' sugar or cocoa powder for garnish

*I*n a mixing bowl, blend the mascarpone, 3 ounces sugar, 2 ounces Amaretto and the pastry cream. Fold in the whipped cream and refrigerate until needed. This can be done up to 3 hours ahead. Combine the espresso, 4 ounces sugar and remaining Amaretto in a small pan and simmer for 5 minutes. When the syrup has cooled, layer the bottom of a large glass trifle bowl with half the lady fingers. Brush them with enough espresso syrup to soften. Spread a layer of the mascarpone filling over the lady fingers, ½ inch thick. Top this with another layer of lady fingers, syrup and then mascarpone filling. Reserve 3 ounces of espresso syrup for Sabayon. Smooth the top with a spatula. Sprinkle the top with the crumbled cookies and grate the chocolate over the top. Set in the refrigerator for 3 hours before serving.

To make the Espresso Sabayon, place eggs, sugar and syrup in a stainless steel bowl. Place the bowl over a pot of simmering water. Whip the mixture with a thin wire whisk over the water until it is thick and you can see the bottom of the bowl while whipping. While whipping over the hot water, you must be whipping constantly or the eggs will cook too quickly. If you must stop, remove the bowl from the heat. Cool over a bowl of ice, stirring occasionally. When cool, fold the whipped cream into the eggs.

To serve, place a tablespoon of Espresso Sabayon on a plate. Spoon a piece of Tiramisu from the dish and place on the Sabayon. Garnish with berries and mint leaves. Dust the plate with confectioners' sugar or cocoa powder.

Yield: 10-12 servings

Cafe Chardonnay of Palm Beach Gardens is known for this Tiramisu. It is as much fun to make as it is to eat!

Pastry Cream

1 cup milk
½ cup sugar
2 tablespoons cornstarch
2 egg yolks
½ vanilla bean
1 tablespoon unsalted butter
⅛ teaspoon salt

Combine milk, sugar, cornstarch, egg yolks and seeds from vanilla bean in a medium saucepan. Cook over low heat until thick and lightly bubbling, stirring constantly. Remove from heat; add butter and salt. Transfer to a clean bowl and cover with plastic wrap, placing wrap on surface of cream. Cool to room temperature then refrigerate one hour minimum before using.

Cremé Brulée with Belgian Chocolate and Raspberry Mint Sauce

BRULEE
8 egg yolks
¾ cup heavy cream
2 cups half-and-half
18 tablespoons sugar, divided
Seeds of ½ vanilla bean
4 tablespoons Belgian chocolate, made into curls

RASPBERRY SAUCE
4 tablespoons fresh raspberries
1 tablespoon raspberry syrup
1 teaspoon fresh mint leaves, shredded
Mint leaves for garnish

Preheat oven to 300°. Combine egg yolks, heavy cream, half-and-half, 6 tablespoons of sugar and vanilla bean seeds in a bowl. Whisk until well blended. Pour into individual 6-ounce ramekins or custard cups. Sprinkle with chocolate curls. Place ramekins in a 13 x 9 inch baking dish and surround with warm water. Bake until custard is just set, approximately 40 minutes. Remove ramekins and allow custards to cool. Refrigerate for 4 to 6 hours or overnight.

To make the Raspberry Sauce, combine raspberries, syrup and shredded mint in a small bowl. Gently stir until evenly mixed.

To serve, sprinkle a layer of sugar (about 2 tablespoons each) on each custard. Caramelize sugar with a propane torch or place under the broiler watching carefully until lightly browned. Spoon one tablespoon Raspberry Sauce on top of each brulee and garnish with a mint leaf.

Yield: 4 servings

CHAMPAGNE SORBET

1 cup sugar
¼ cup water
1 cup fresh orange juice
½ cup fresh lemon juice
16 ounces champagne
Fresh strawberries to garnish

*C*ombine sugar and water in a saucepan and bring to a boil over medium heat. Reduce heat and simmer 5 minutes; cool. Blend in remaining ingredients and freeze in individual fluted glasses. Garnish with fresh strawberries.

Yield: 8 cups

Nutrition Analysis per serving:

saturated fat -	0	sodium -	3.3 mg
calories -	150	cholesterol -	0 mg
fat -	0	fiber -	0 g
carbohydrate -	29.9 g	sugar -	28.1 g

Try sorbet with one cup of fresh pureed strawberries combined with the cooled mixture. The strawberries will float to the top when placed in individual fluted glasses.

FLORIDA FLAN

1 cup sugar, divided
4 large eggs
2 cups half-and-half
1 tablespoon dark rum
1 teaspoon vanilla extract

*P*reheat oven to 300°. Heat ½ cup sugar in saucepan over medium heat until melted and amber in color. Immediately pour into six 6-ounce custard cups and arrange cups in a 13 x 9 inch baking pan. Whisk eggs with ½ cup sugar in medium bowl. Whisk in half and half, rum and vanilla. Pour into prepared custard cups. Pour hot tap water into baking pan to reach halfway up sides of cups. Bake 35-40 minutes or until knife inserted in center comes out clean. Remove cups from water. Refrigerate up to 4 hours. To serve, invert onto dessert plates.

Yield: 6 servings

BREAD PUDDING WITH
RUM SAUCE

BREAD PUDDING

½ cup raisins

3 tablespoons rum (or whiskey)

1 loaf French Bread, torn into chunks

1 quart milk

2 cups sugar

2 tablespoons vanilla extract

3 eggs

1 cup peeled and diced apples or 1 cup sliced bananas

3 tablespoons butter, melted

SAUCE

½ cup butter

1 cup sugar

1 teaspoon vanilla

1 egg

Soak raisins in rum for 10 minutes. Soak bread in milk for 30 minutes. Preheat oven to 350°. Remove raisins from rum and set rum aside for sauce. Mix together sugar, vanilla, eggs, apples or bananas and raisins. Combine with bread chunks. Spread melted butter on bottom of 13 x 9 inch baking pan. Add bread mixture. Bake uncovered for 30 minutes or until bubbly hot. Prepare sauce by creaming together butter and sugar; add vanilla. Slowly stir in egg; then add rum. Heat and stir over low heat about 5 minutes. Place slices of bread pudding on plate. Spoon sauce over top.

Yield: 15 servings

POACHED PEACHES AND RASPBERRY SAUCE

1 cup water
1½ cups sugar, divided
2 cups dry white wine
6 large peaches, peeled but not cored
1 pint fresh raspberries
¼ cup framboise or kirsch (optional)
Juice from ½ lemon

*B*oil water, 1 cup sugar and wine uncovered for 20 minutes in a large deep pot. Reduce heat, add whole peaches and cook, covered, for 4 minutes. Remove from heat and let stand until cool; refrigerate. Blend raspberries, ½ cup sugar and framboise until smooth. Strain well and discard seeds. Stir in lemon juice. Refrigerate, covered, until ready to use. To serve, drain peaches; stand each on a plate and top with ¼ cup sauce.

Yield: 6 servings

Nutrition Analysis per serving:

saturated fat -	0	sodium -	4.8 mg
calories -	394	cholesterol -	0
fat -	1.0 g	fiber -	6.0 g
carbohydrate -	84.3 g	sugar -	71.6 g

BAVARIAN APPLE TORTE

PASTRY
½ cup margarine
⅓ cup sugar
¼ teaspoon vanilla
1 cup flour

FILLING
8 ounces cream cheese, softened
¼ cup sugar
1 egg
½ teaspoon vanilla

TOPPING
⅓ cup sugar
½ teaspoon cinnamon
4 cups peeled apple slices
¼ cup sliced almonds

*T*o prepare pastry, cream margarine, sugar and vanilla; blend in flour. Spread dough onto bottom and up the sides of a greased 9-inch spring-form pan.

Prepare filling by combining cream cheese and sugar; mix well. Blend in egg and vanilla. Pour in pastry lined pan.

Preheat oven to 450°. To prepare topping, combine sugar and cinnamon. Toss apples in mixture. Arrange apples over cream cheese layer; sprinkle with almonds. Bake for 10 minutes, reduce heat to 400°; continue baking for 25 minutes. Cool before removing rim of pan.

Yield: 8-10 servings

RASPBERRY PEARS

¾ cup frozen
  raspberries
⅛ cup brown sugar
⅛ cup granulated
  sugar
2 teaspoons lemon
  rind
4 medium pears,
  peeled but not
  cored, stems intact
1 teaspoon cornstarch

*I*n a blender, puree frozen raspberries until smooth; press through sieve set over a 2-quart casserole; discard seeds. Into puree, add sugars and grated lemon peel and stir. Arrange pears in puree with stems toward the center; spoon puree on the pears. Cook uncovered in microwave on high 10 to 12 minutes, until tender. Turn pears over halfway through cooking. With slotted spoon, remove pears and set aside. Stir cornstarch into the puree. Cook on high 1-2 minutes until boiling and thickened. Refrigerate pears in puree. Serve chilled.

Yield: 4 servings

Nutrition Analysis:

saturated fat -	0	sodium -	3.8 mg
calories -	146	cholesterol -	0
fat -	0.8 g	fiber -	5.2 g
carbohydrate -	37.1 g	sugar -	27.2 g

LEMON CUPS

1 cup sugar
4 tablespoons flour
⅛ teaspoon salt
2 tablespoons melted
  butter
5 tablespoons lemon
  juice
Grated rind of 1
  lemon
3 egg yolks, beaten
1½ cups milk
3 egg whites

*P*reheat oven to 350°. Blend sugar, flour and salt; add melted butter. Add lemon juice and rind and blend well. Add egg yolks and milk; stir well. In separate bowl, beat egg whites until stiff; fold into lemon mixture. Pour into 8 ungreased custard cups or ramekins placed in a 13 x 9 inch baking pan. Fill pan with hot water until half way up the sides of the custard cups. Bake for 45 minutes. Each cup will have custard on the bottom with sponge cake on top.

Yield: 8 servings

Nutrition Analysis per serving:

saturated fat -	3.1 g	sodium -	111.7 mg
calories -	194	cholesterol -	121.9 mg
fat -	6.1 g	fiber -	0.1 g
carbohydrate -	31.3 g	sugar -	25.9 g

ORANGE ALASKAS

ORANGE ALASKAS
3 oranges
1 pint orange sherbet
3 egg whites
6 tablespoons sugar, divided

ORANGE CUSTARD SAUCE
3 tablespoons sugar
1 tablespoon cornstarch
¼ teaspoon salt
1 cup fresh orange juice, strained

Halve oranges; juice and remove pulp. Set juice aside for custard sauce. Fill each orange shell with scoops of sherbet and freeze. Prepare meringue by beating egg whites until stiff but not dry. Gradually add 6 tablespoons of sugar and continue to beat until very stiff. Remove sherbert shells from freezer and spread meringue completely over shells. Return to freezer until ready to use.

To make Orange Custard Sauce, mix 2 tablespoons sugar, cornstarch, salt and orange juice in a double boiler until thick and smooth.

Preheat broiler. Remove sherbert shells with meringue from freezer. Broil 1-2 minutes until meringue is a delicate brown. Drizzle the orange custard sauce over Alaskas fresh from the oven and serve.

Nutrition Anaylsis per serving:

saturated fat -	0.8 g	sodium -	151 mg
calories -	223	cholesterol -	4.7 mg
fat -	1.4 g	fiber -	1.7 g
carbohydrate -	52 g	sugar -	0

CHERRY CREPES JUBILEE

CREPES
1 egg
1 cup milk
3 tablespoons butter, divided
1 cup sifted flour

ALMOND CREAM FILLING
1 cup sugar
¼ cup flour
1 cup milk
2 eggs
2 egg yolks
½ cup finely chopped toasted almonds
3 tablespoons butter
2 teaspoons vanilla
¼ teaspoon almond extract

BRANDIED CHERRY SAUCE
1 (21-ounce) can cherry pie filling
3 tablespoons brandy
2 tablespoons butter
½ teaspoon grated lemon peel
1 tablespoon lemon juice
Dash of nutmeg

*T*o prepare crepes, beat egg just enough to blend. Add milk, one tablespoon butter and flour. Beat until smooth. Lightly grease an 8-inch skillet and heat. Remove from heat and pour in ¼ cup batter, tilt from side to side until batter covers bottom, return to heat. Brown on one side only. Turn out on paper towel. Repeat and stack with waxed paper between each crepe.

To prepare Almond Cream Filling, combine sugar and flour in a medium saucepan. Add milk and cook and stir until thickened and bubbly. Cook and stir 2 minutes more. Beat whole eggs and egg yolks slightly. Stir small amount of hot mixture into eggs. Return all to hot mixture. Cook and stir to boiling. Remove from heat. Beat until smooth. Stir in remaining ingredients. Cover with waxed paper and cool.

To prepare Brandied Cherry Sauce, combine all sauce ingredients in a saucepan and warm over medium heat until heated through.

Preheat oven to 350°. Spread ¼ cup Almond Cream Filling on unbrowned side of each crepe. Roll up and place side by side in a 13 x 9 inch baking dish. Melt remaining 2 tablespoons butter and brush over crepes. Bake for 20-25 minutes. To serve, spoon Brandied Cherry Sauce on top of baked crepes in baking dish.

Yield: 10-12 crepes

Option for entertaining: Heat 3-4 tablespoons brandy in small pan, flame and pour over cherries. A delicious and showy dessert for entertaining.

RASPBERRY VELVET TART

PASTRY
- ¾ cup cake flour
- ¾ cup all-purpose flour
- ¼ cup sugar
- ½ cup unsalted butter, chilled, cut into pieces
- 1 egg yolk
- 1 tablespoon whipping cream
- 2 tablespoons cold water

FILLING
- 12 ounces good quality white chocolate, chopped
- ½ cup hot whipping cream
- ¼ cup unsalted butter, room temperature
- 2 cups fresh raspberries

WHITE CHOCOLATE LEAVES
- 3 ounces good quality white chocolate, chopped
- 16 small, thick, freshly picked leaves, such as rose, gardenia, lemon or camellia, with ⅛ inch stems

To prepare pastry, mix flours and sugar in large bowl. Add butter and cut in until mixture resembles coarse meal. Beat egg yolk with cream to blend. Pour over flour mixture and stir until dough comes together, adding water to bind dough, if necessary. Gather dough into ball and flatten into a disk. Wrap in plastic and refrigerate 30 minutes. (Can be prepared one day ahead. Let dough soften slightly before continuing.) Roll dough out on lightly floured surface to a ⅛ inch thick round. Roll dough up on rolling pin and transfer to 9-inch tart pan with removable bottom. Trim and finish edges. Refrigerate crust for 30 minutes. Preheat oven to 350°. Line pastry with foil or parchment and fill with dried beans or pie weights. Bake 15 minutes. Remove beans and foil and continue baking crust until golden brown, approximately 15 minutes. Cool crust completely on wire rack.

To prepare filling, melt white chocolate in top of double boiler over simmering water, stirring until smooth. Mix in cream and butter. Remove from double boiler. Distribute raspberries evenly over bottom of prepared crust, reserving a few for garnish. Pour chocolate mixture over berries, filling crust completely. Refrigerate until firm, about one hour. (Can be prepared 1 day ahead; let stand at room temperature one hour before serving).

To prepare white chocolate leaves, melt white chocolate in top of double boiler over simmering water, stirring until smooth. Spread in thin layer over veined underside of leaves being careful not to drip on the edges. Refrigerate until firm, about 30 minutes. Gently peel off leaves, starting at stem end. (Can be prepared one week ahead. Cover in airtight container and refrigerate.) Arrange leaves and reserved berries decoratively on top of tart. Sift confectioners' sugar lightly over and serve.

Yield: 8 servings

OLD-FASHIONED PUMPKIN TORTE

TORTE

2⅔ cups toasted slivered almonds

1 cup graham cracker crumbs

1¼ teaspoons baking soda

1¼ teaspoons pumpkin pie spice

¾ teaspoon finely shredded orange peel

8 eggs, separated

1⅓ cups sugar, divided

1 cup canned pumpkin

1½ teaspoon vanilla

FILLING

16 ounces cream cheese, softened

⅔ cup packed light brown sugar

2 teaspoons vanilla

½ teaspoon pumpkin pie spice

⅔ cup finely chopped pitted dates or raisins

½ cup chunky style applesauce

TOPPING

½ cup whipping cream

2 teaspoons sugar

½ teaspoon finely shredded orange peel

*G*rease and flour three 8-inch round baking pans; set aside. In food processor or blender, chop almonds in small batches until finely ground. In mixing bowl, stir in graham cracker crumbs, baking soda, pumpkin pie spice, almonds and orange peel; set aside.

Preheat oven to 350°. Beat egg yolks and ⅔ cup of sugar with electric mixer on high speed for 6 minutes. Stir in pumpkin and vanilla and fold in nut mixture; set aside. In large mixing bowl, beat egg whites on medium speed until soft peaks form. Gradually add remaining ⅔ cup sugar, 2 tablespoons at a time, beating until stiff. Fold 1 cup of the egg white mixture into the pumpkin mixture. Fold the pumpkin mixture into remaining egg white mixture. Spread evenly in prepared pans. Bake for 20-25 minutes. Cool on racks for 10 minutes. Remove from pans.

To prepare filling, beat cream cheese until fluffy. Add brown sugar, vanilla and pumpkin pie spice; beat well. Stir in dates or raisins and applesauce. Cover and chill.

To prepare topping, beat whipping cream and sugar in a chilled mixing bowl at medium speed. Add orange peel and beat until stiff.

To assemble torte, split each cake layer in half horizontally. Place bottom of split layer on decorative serving plate. Spread with ⅔ cup of filling. Repeat with remaining torte layers and filling, ending with torte. Spoon topping over top layer.

Yield: 10-12 servings

Spicy Apple Dumplings

4 baking apples (2 pounds)

2 tablespoons sugar

1½ teaspoons ground cinnamon, divided

¼ teaspoon nutmeg

⅛ teaspoon ground cloves

1 teaspoon grated orange rind

¼ cup toasted chopped walnuts

2 tablespoons raisins

2 tablespoons light brown sugar

2 tablespoons melted butter

1 sheet puff pastry dough or combined dough of 2 unbaked pastry shells

1 egg yolk mixed with 1 tablespoon of water

𝒫reheat oven to 450°. Grease a 12 x 8 inch dish. Peel and core apples. Mix sugar and 1 teaspoon of cinnamon on wax paper; roll apples in mixture to coat. Combine ½ teaspoon cinnamon, nutmeg, cloves, orange rind, walnuts, raisins, brown sugar and butter; set aside. Combine 2 pastry shells together and divide dough into 5 equal pieces. Roll 4 pieces into 8-inch rounds. Place 1 apple on center of each pastry round and top with a quarter of the nut mixture. Gather and press pastry on top of each apple. Place in dish. With extra pastry dough, roll out and cut out leaf shapes. Brush with egg mixture. Place leaves on top of pastry covered apples to look like a just-picked apple. Bake for 15 minutes and then reduce to 350° and bake for 30 minutes.

Yield: 8 servings

Nutrition Analysis per serving:

saturated fat -	2.25 g	sodium -	313.7 mg
calories -	339	cholesterol -	79 mg
fat -	19.5 g	fiber -	1.6 g
carbohydrate -	42.2 g	sugar -	16.6 g

BAKLAVA

4 cups walnuts, finely chopped

½ cup sugar

1 teaspoon ground cinnamon

1 pound phyllo dough (strudel leaves)

1 cup butter or margarine, melted

1 (12-ounce) jar honey

*P*repare 2½ hours before serving or early in day. Grease a 13 x 9 inch baking dish. In large bowl with spoon, mix chopped walnuts, sugar and cinnamon until blended. Cut phyllo into 13 x 9 inch rectangles. In baking dish, place 1 sheet of phyllo; brush with melted butter or margarine. Repeat to make 5 more layers of phyllo; sprinkle with 1 cup walnut mixture. Place 1 sheet of phyllo in baking dish over walnut mixture; brush with butter or margarine. Repeat entire layering process, overlapping any small strips of phyllo to make rectangles, if necessary. Repeat layering two more times. Place remaining phyllo on top of last walnut layer; brush with butter or margarine.

Preheat oven to 300°. With a sharp knife, cut just halfway through layers in triangle pattern to make 24 servings. Bake for 1 hour and 25 minutes or until top is golden brown.

Meanwhile, in small saucepan over medium-low heat, heat honey until hot but not boiling. Spoon hot honey over Baklava. Cool in pan on wire rack at least 1 hour, then cover and leave at room temperature until serving. With sharp knife, finish cutting through layers.

Yield: 24 servings

PLUM TORTE

1 cup sugar
½ cup butter, softened
1 cup flour
1 teaspoon baking
  powder
⅛ teaspoon salt
2 eggs, slightly beaten
12 Italian plums,
  halved and pitted
½ cup sugar
1 lemon, juiced
1 tablespoon
  cinnamon

*P*reheat oven to 350°. Cream sugar and butter and set aside. Mix flour, baking powder, salt and eggs; add to butter mixture. Pour and smooth into a greased 9-inch springform pan. Cover with plum halves, arranging them with the skin side up. In a separate bowl, mix the sugar, lemon juice and cinnamon. Sprinkle on top of torte and bake for one hour.

Yield: 8-10 servings

BLUEBERRY SAUCE

1 pint blueberries
½ cup sugar
1 teaspoon ground
  cinnamon
½ teaspoon ground
  nutmeg
1 tablespoon
  cornstarch
⅓ cup orange juice

*C*lean blueberries. Combine sugar, cinnamon, nutmeg and cornstarch in medium saucepan. Stir in cornstarch and orange juice; add blueberries. Cook over medium heat, stirring frequently, until thick and bubbly (approximately 5 minutes). Cool and refrigerate until use.

Yield: 1½ to 2 cups

This elegant sauce has an endless variety of uses. Try serving over lemon ice cream, pound cake or fresh strawberries.

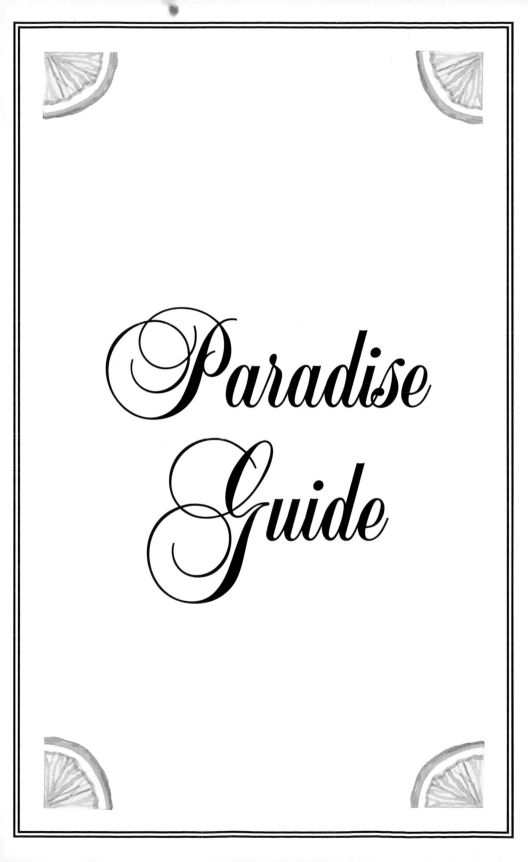

Paradise Guide

THE WILDLIFE OF PARADISE

From the beaches along the east coast, to the shore of Lake Okeechobee on the west, Palm Beach County provides a mosaic of natural habitats for wildlife. Saltwater waterways to freshwater marshes, sandhill scrub to pine flatwoods, tropical hammocks to mangrove estuaries, create a paradise for our fellow South Florida inhabitants.

Imagine one summer night walking along the beach when a large shape materializes at the edge of the water and lumbers up on the beach. It's a sea turtle beginning the ritual of digging a nest in the sand to lay her precious eggs. Imagine the thrill later that summer, one morning before sunrise, observing baby sea turtles emerging from their eggs and the sand, instinctively scrambling across the beach to the ocean's edge.

Along the Intracoastal Waterway, the gentle manatees can be seen feeding in the warm waters while Great Blue Herons, Wood Storks and aerial diving Kingfishers lurk nearby. The awesome alligator, the ancient Gopher Tortoise and the beautiful Indigo Snake are among the more mysterious members of our animal society. From the endangered Florida Panther to the abundant mischievous racoons, South Florida is paradise to an endless variety of species.

ROASTED PEPPERS

$\mathcal{M}$any popular recipes call for roasted peppers. Roasted peppers may be substituted for fresh peppers in many recipes, adding a more mild, sweet flavor.

To roast peppers, cut peppers in half and remove seeds and core. Place on a baking sheet, cut side down. Bake at 450-500° for 5-10 minutes or until the skin is charred and blackened. Remove from oven and seal in a zipped plastic bag for 10 minutes or in a brown paper bag for 15 minutes. Remove peppers from bag; loosened skins will easily peel away.

BASIC PASTRY/PIE CRUST

SINGLE CRUST
1½ cups sifted flour
½ teaspoon salt
½ cup shortening
Ice and water

$\mathcal{F}$ill a small glass with ice cubes and water; set aside. Combine flour and salt. Add shortening, combining with a fork until dough forms pea size pieces. If a food processor is available, use a steel blade and on/off strokes. Using a tablespoon measure, add iced water one spoon at a time blending with a fork or using on/off strokes in a food processor. Add water just until dough is moistened, then form into a ball. When using a food processor, add water until dough forms one complete ball.

Lightly flour a flat surface and lightly flour ball of dough. Using a floured rolling pin, roll dough ball from middle to edge until it is ⅛ inch thick. Place rolled crust into pie or quiche plate. Gently press into plate, trim excess edge and flute edge with a pinching style or using the tine of a fork.

For a pre-baked crust, preheat oven to 450°. Using a fork, prick the entire crust every ½-1 inch. Bake for 10-12 minutes or until just beginning to brown.

TWO CRUST/TOPPED
PIE CRUST
2 cups sifted flour
1 teaspoon salt
⅔ cup shortening
Ice and water

$\mathcal{R}$epeat steps above, splitting dough ball into two pieces prior to rolling.

HERB BUTTER

½ cup butter, softened
3-5 drops fresh lemon
juice
2-3 tablespoons
chopped fresh
herbs (basil, chives,
dill, fennel, parsley
or watercress)

*I*n a small bowl, blend butter and lemon juice with a fork until fluffy. Add the herbs and blend well. Spoon butter into a mold, small bowl or roll into a thin log. Wrap with plastic wrap and refrigerate until ready to use.

Yield: ½ cup

This delicious butter has an endless number of uses. Try it with grilled meats, poultry and fish, sandwiches, vegetables or on thick slices of toasted bread.

HERB MAYONNAISE

2 cups mayonnaise
⅓ cup chopped fresh
herbs (basil,
tarragon, rosemary,
parsley or oregano)

*G*ently combine ingredients in a small bowl with a whisk. Refrigerate until ready to use.

Herb Mayonnaise adds a special touch to any sandwich. Try it when mayonnaise is called for in any of your favorite salad recipes.

For a unique and attractive alternative, substitute pureed roasted red peppers for the fresh herbs. The mayonnaise will be light pink in color with a flavor that enhances any dish.

HERB VINEGAR

Fresh herbs of choice
Vinegar (cider, wine
or rice variety)

*L*ightly pack a glass jar or bottle with fresh herbs. When using herbs straight from the garden, be certain to pick them early in the morning when the flavor is best. Fill the jar or bottle with vinegar and seal. Let vinegar steep in a dark cupboard for 2-3 weeks then strain vinegar into a clean jar or bottle, discarding the herbs. Place 1-2 new herb sprigs in vinegar and use in your favorite recipes. The proportion of herbs to vinegar varies as widely as tastes; sample the vinegar throughout the steeping process to achieve desired flavor.

Have fun experimenting with different combinations of herbs. When using garlic, peel each clove and score it with a paring knife to release the flavor.

CHICKEN STOCK

6 pounds chicken wings, backs, or a mixture of wings, backs, necks and giblets (except livers)

32 cups cold water, divided

4 medium onions, peeled and quartered

4 medium carrots, peeled and quartered

4 bay leaves

20 stems parsley (without leaves)

1 teaspoon black peppercorns

1 teaspoon dried thyme

Put chicken pieces in a large stockpot. Add enough cold water to cover chicken. Bring to a boil; add more cold water to reduce to below boiling; stir. Bring back to a boil, lower heat to very low so that liquid bubbles gently. Continually skim off foam that collects on surface. Add onions, carrots, bay leaves, parsley stems, peppercorns and thyme. Adjust heat to keep surface just breaking with bubbles, but not boiling. Partially cover and cook, 2 to 3 hours, skimming foam and fat occasionally. Strain stock through a colander lined with several thicknesses of damp cheesecloth, discarding solids. If stock is not to be used immediately, cool to lukewarm. Refrigerate until fat rises to the surface and congeals (approximately 8 hours). If stock is to be used within 3 to 5 days, leave fat and skim off when ready to use or freeze.

Yield: 20 cups of stock

FISH STOCK

2 pounds fish bones, tails and heads (mild fish only)

1 tablespoon unsalted butter

1 medium onion, sliced

½ cup dry white wine

7½ cups cold water

1 stalk celery, cut in 2-inch pieces

1 bay leaf

8 stems parsley (without leaves)

½ teaspoon dried thyme

Put fish bones in a large bowl in sink. Let cold water run over bones for 5 minutes. Melt butter in a large stockpot over low heat. Add onion and cook, stirring often, until soft. Add fish bones, wine, water, celery, bay leaf, parsley and thyme. Mix well. Bring just to a boil and skim top to remove foam. Reduce heat to low and simmer, uncovered, skimming occasionally, for 20 minutes. Pour contents through a fine strainer, discard solids. If not using immediately, cool to room temperature. Pour into 1 or 2 cup containers. Refrigerate, covered, up to 2 days or freeze up to 3 months.

Yield: 6 cups fish stock

If fish bones are not available, substitute 1½ pounds of mild fish pieces.

BEEF STOCK

8 pounds beef soup bones, chopped in pieces by the butcher

4 medium onions, unpeeled, root end cut off, quartered

4 medium carrots, scrubbed but not peeled, quartered

4 stalks celery, cut in 2 inch pieces

4 bay leaves

20 stems parsley (without leaves)

8 garlic cloves, unpeeled

1 teaspoon black peppercorns

1 teaspoon dried thyme

32 cups cold water (approximately), divided

*P*reheat oven to 450°. Roast bones in a roasting pan, turning occasionally until they begin to brown, about 30 minutes. Add onions, carrots and celery; roast until browned; approximately 30 minutes. Drain fat. Transfer bones and vegetables to a large stockpot. Add bay leaves, parsley stems, garlic, peppercorns, thyme and enough of the cold water to cover. Bring to boil. Add more cold water to reduce to below boiling; stir once. Bring back to a boil and reduce heat to very low so that liquid bubbles very gently. Skim off foam that collects on surface. Partially cover and cook, skimming foam and fat occasionally, for 4 to 6 hours. During first 2 hours of cooking, add hot water occasionally to keep ingredients covered. Strain stock through a colander lined with several thicknesses of dampened cheesecloth, discarding solids. If stock is not to be used immediately, cool to lukewarm. Refrigerate until fat rises to the surface and congeals (about 8 hours). If stock will be used within 3 to 5 days, leave fat; skim fat when ready to use. If stock is to be frozen, skim fat.

Yield: 16 cups

Vegetable Stock

2 leeks, cleaned and cut into ½ inch pieces (white and soft green portions only)

2 tablespoons vegetable oil

2 yellow onions, peeled and chopped into ½ inch pieces

9 garlic cloves, peeled and finely chopped

2 small carrots, peeled and cut into ½ inch rounds

1 parsnip, peeled and cut into ½ inch rounds

3 small potatoes, quartered

2 stalks celery, cut into ½ inch pieces

½ pound mushrooms, halved

1 teaspoon dried thyme

1 bay leaf

1 teaspoon dried oregano

4 sprigs of parsley

10 cups cold water

2 teaspoons kosher salt

½ teaspoon pepper

*H*eat oil in a large stockpot over medium heat. Add leeks, onions and garlic. Stir to coat with oil and cook 5 minutes. Add remaining ingredients. Bring to a boil, skim impurities from the surface; reduce heat to low. Cook for 30 minutes. Strain into a large bowl; discard vegetables. Stock can be stored in the refrigerator in a covered container for up to 5 days or freeze for up to 1 month.

Yield: 10 cups

RECIPE NUTRITION GUIDE

Fat
Fat Free - less than 0.5 gm of fat per serving
Low Fat - 3 gm or less per serving
Reduced Fat - less than 10 gm of fat per serving

Cholesterol
Low Cholesterol - less than 60 mg of cholesterol per serving

Sodium
Low Sodium - less than 140 mg sodium per serving

Fiber
High fiber - 5 gm or more of dietary fiber per serving
Good Source - 2.5 to 4.9 gm of dietary fiber per serving

Healthy Food
No more than 3 gm of fat, 1 gm of saturated fat, 350 mg of sodium and/or 60 mg cholesterol per serving.

Nutrition analysis of selected recipes by Barbara Eldridge, RD, LD

Resources:
Food Values of Portions Commonly Used
by Jean A. T. Pennington,
Harper Perennial, 15th ed., 1989

Nutritive Value of American Foods,
United States Department of Agriculture
Handbook No. 456, November 1975

Krauses Food, Nutrition and Diet Therapy,
L. K. Mahan and S. E. Scott-Stump, 9th ed., 1996, Appendix 41 and 42, pages 1016-1095

American Heart Association pamphlet,
The New Food Label, 1995

Following is a guide for ingredients listed in this cookbook unless otherwise indicated:

Butter is lightly salted, not whipped or pre-softened.

Brown sugar refers to light brown sugar.

Eggs are all large eggs.

Flour is unsifted, all-purpose flour.

Milk is whole milk; buttermilk is 3.5% buttermilk.

Sugar refers to granulated sugar.

METRIC CONVERSION GUIDE

Weight Equivalents

1 ounce	=	30 grams
2 ounces	=	55 grams
3 ounces	=	85 grams
4 ounces	=	115 grams
5 ounces	=	140 grams
6 ounces	=	170 grams
7 ounces	=	200 grams
8 ounces	=	225 grams
9 ounces	=	250 grams
10 ounces	=	285 grams
11 ounces	=	310 grams
12 ounces	=	340 grams
13 ounces	=	370 grams
14 ounces	=	400 grams
15 ounces	=	425 grams
16 ounces	=	450 grams

Granulated Sugar

1 teaspoon	=	4 grams
1 tablespoon	=	12 grams
¼ cup	=	50 grams
⅓ cup	=	65 grams
½ cup	=	95 grams
1 cup	=	190 grams

Flour

1 tablespoon	=	8.75 grams
¼ cup	=	35 grams
⅓ cup	=	45 grams
½ cup	=	70 grams
1 cup	=	140 grams
1½ cups	=	210 grams
2 cups	=	280 grams
3 cups	=	420 grams

Volume Equivalents

¼ teaspoon	=	1.25 milliliters (ml)
½ teaspoon	=	2.5 ml
1 teaspoon	=	5 ml
1 tablespoon	=	15 ml
¼ cup	=	60 ml
⅓ cup	=	80 ml
½ cup	=	125 ml
1 cup	=	250 ml
250 ml	=	2.5 deciliters
2.5 deciliters	=	¼ liter
2 cups	=	500 ml
500 ml	=	½ liter
4 cups	=	1 liter

EQUIVALENT MEASURES

dash	=	less than ⅛ teaspoon
1 teaspoon	=	60 drops
1 teaspoon	=	⅓ tablespoon
1 tablespoon	=	3 teaspoons
2 tablespoons	=	1 fluid ounce
4 tablespoons	=	¼ cup
8 tablespoons	=	½ cup or 4 ounces
12 tablespoons	=	¾ cup
1 cup	=	½ pint or 8 fluid ounces
2 cups	=	1 pint
4 cups	=	1 quart
1 pint	=	16 fluid ounces
1 quart	=	2 pints
2 quarts	=	½ gallon
4 quarts	=	1 gallon
8 quarts, dry measure	=	1 peck
4 pecks, dry measure	=	1 bushel
1 pound	=	16 ounces
1 pound	=	2 cups liquid

Fahrenheit to Centigrade:
Subtract 32 from Fahrenheit degree,
multiply by 5 and divide by 9.

Centigrade to Fahrenheit:
Multiply Centigrade degree by 9,
divided by 5 and add 32.

THE PARADISE FISH GUIDE

*I*nformation on how to purchase and prepare fresh fish could fill volumes! The following suggestions will help you, the home cook, select and prepare fish successfully with little effort.

Because of their bone structure, all fish can be classified as either round or flat. Roundfish (such as salmon, swordfish and kingfish) can be cooked whole, cut into fillets or cut crosswise into steaks. Flatfish (such as flounder, catfish, snapper, grouper and dolphin) should be cut into fillets because they can not satisfactorily be cut into steaks.

Lean fish, such as flounder, snapper, grouper and dolphin are suited to cooking with some sort of fat or liquid (poaching, steaming or sautéing) because their flesh dries out more quickly than an oily fish. If they are basted frequently, they may also be baked, broiled or grilled. An oily fish, such as tuna, pompano, trout, swordfish, catfish and salmon contain more fat. Because of the high fat content, they tend to stay moist when grilled, baked or broiled with little or no added fat or liquid.

A truly fresh fish should not smell fishy in any way! A fresh fish has a mild odor and firm, elastic flesh that bounces back when pressed. The scales should be shiny and tight to the skin.

If the fish you are purchasing has been frozen, ask your fishmonger how long it has been defrosted. Do not buy any fish that has been defrosted for more than two days!

Freshness in fish fillets is often harder to detect; avoid fillets that are turning yellow or brown around the edges. Look for flesh on the fish to have a natural sheen. Avoid buying fish that has been frozen, defrosted and frozen a second time. A good sign of a twice-thawed fillet is the package will contain "bloody" ice.

To store fresh fish, rinse with water; pat dry. Arrange in one layer in a baking dish lined with paper towels. Cover with plastic wrap and refrigerate. Prepare as soon as possible. Never re-freeze thawed fish. The best way to freeze a whole fish is to ice glaze it. Set whole fish on baking sheet and freeze until firm. Dip frozen fish into ice water; glaze will form immediately. Return fish to freezer to solidify glaze. Repeat glazing steps until glaze is approximately 1 inch thick. Place in a freezer bag and store in freezer no longer than two months for oily fish and six months for lean fish. To freeze fillets or steaks, wrap individually in heavy foil or plastic wrap, or stack between sheets of freezer wrap. Freeze oily fillets no longer than one month, lean fillets no longer than three months.

The opacity test is the most reliable way to determine if the fish is done. Insert a sharp knife into the thickest portion of the fish. If the fish is ready to be removed from the heat, it will be opaque and flesh will not stick to the bones. Poached or fried fish will cook quicker because water and oil transfer heat faster. Fish will continue to cook after removed from heat source; be careful not to overcook!

Catfish is a moderately oily freshwater fish that is best served baked, broiled, grilled or panfried.

Grouper is a lean saltwater fish that is best served baked, broiled, fried, grilled or poached.

Florida Pompano is a moderately oily saltwater fish that is best served baked, broiled, grilled, fried or sautéed.

Red Snapper is a lean saltwater fish that is best served baked, broiled, grilled, panfried, poached or sautéed.

Salmon is a moderately oily both salt and freshwater fish that is best served baked, broiled, grilled, poached, smoked, or steamed.

Swordfish is a moderately oily saltwater fish that is best served baked, broiled or grilled.

Trout is a moderately oily freshwater fish that is best served baked, broiled, grilled, poached, sautéed or smoked.

Tuna is an oily saltwater fish that is best served baked, broiled, grilled or sautéed.

Watch for the season of your favorite Florida fish:

Florida Lobster	August 1 to March 31
Oyster and Florida Pompano	Late November to Mid-March
Florida Yellow Tail Snapper	Mid-May to December
Stone Crab	October 15 to May 1
Shrimp	Year Round
Mahi Mahi (Dolphin)	Year Round

Tropical Fruits

South Florida is known throughout the country for its tropical fruits, such as citrus, mango and avocado. The following list includes these and a number of lesser known varieties. Regardless of the type, fruit delicacies can be included in a wide range of recipes or merely eaten in their natural state. When you find these delights in the grocery store, fruit stand or gourmet market, enjoy them as we in the Palm Beaches do!

Avocado

1 cup equals 190 calories

Avocados come in different shapes, sizes, and a variety of green shades and are generally available in the cooler months. There are 67 varieties of the Florida avocado. All have a delicate nut-like flavor and a smooth creamy texture. Florida avocados are lower in calories than any other domestically grown avocados; many claim they are superior in taste.

Avocados are handpicked from the tree when mature but are "eating ripe" at their best at a later time when they have lost their feeling of firmness and yield to gentle pressure of the hand. To speed ripening, place the avocado in a brown paper bag.

To split an avocado in half, simply cut lengthwise around the seed. Turn halves in opposite directions to separate. Lift out the seed and peel the skin off the avocado with knife or fingers. To prevent discoloration if you're not using it right away, sprinkle cut surface with lemon or lime juice, leave the seed in place, and cover the avocado with plastic or foil. Ripe avocados, whole or cut, can be stored in the refrigerator for several days. However, cooking at high temperatures is not advised as avocados contain tannin and will develop a very bitter flavor. Whole or sliced, avocados do not freeze well. However, they may be frozen in a puree form.

Avocadoes are best served with salads, split and stuffed with crab or chicken and as the main ingredient in guacamole. Or, for the purist, sliced avocado with salt and pepper is wonderful by itself.

Banana

1 medium banana equals 101 calories

The banana is one of the most important and widely grown fruits with roughly 300 varieties in existence. Bananas are divided into two main types: sweet eating bananas and cooking bananas known as plantains. For the people of the tropics, the plantain replaces the potato. This fruit is longer than the sweet banana, its skin is thick and clings tightly to the fruit. It is deeper yellow in color and the fruit tapers sharply at the base and tip.

Bananas have many uses, depending on the type. They are good raw, cooked, baked, broiled, boiled or frozen. They may be used in a large variety of beverages, entrees, breads, salads and desserts.

Plantains are most often served fried. Peel and slice fruit into thin wafers and fry in deep fat to produce "chips". As an alternative, peel and slice fruit lengthwise and fry in a greased skillet. This makes a tasty, sweet and nutritious addition to a menu.

To bake bananas, peel and arrange in a greased baking pan. Brush well with melted butter. Sprinkle lightly with salt. Bake at 450° for 10-12 minutes or until bananas are tender.

Broiled bananas are a true delight. To broil, peel and arrange on a broiler rack or pan. Coat with butter and salt lightly. Broil 3 or 4 inches from heat element approximately 5 minutes on each side, or until browned and tender.

To freeze banana puree, mash or puree bananas, working quickly to avoid darkening of the fruit. Two or 3 bananas yield 1 cup of puree. Add one tablespoon of prepared syrup for each banana used. Mix, package and freeze. Frozen puree may be used in many recipes calling for mashed bananas.

CALAMONDIN

Calamondin is a citrus fruit, grown in South Florida and generally in season from November through March. It is a small, 1½ inch diameter, thin-skinned orange-colored fruit that resembles a miniature orange. The inner white pith is not bitter as in other citrus fruits. However, it is very acidic in flavor, which prevents most people from eating it in its natural state. Calamondins are also used decoratively as well as for the fruit.

After discarding the seeds, the entire fruit may be used in making marmalade. Other uses include desserts, sauces and preserves. Halves of calamondin are a treat served with seafood. Thin slices attractively garnish punch, tea or salad dressings. The juice, which is highly prized for drinks, can also be frozen in cubes and used as desired.

CARAMBOLA

*1 average carambola
equals 20 calories*

The carambola, often called star fruit, is a very interesting fruit, long a favorite of Southern China. South Florida's tropical climate is well suited to the production of carambola trees with a number of varieties, the best known being the Golden Star.

Carambolas average 4 to 5 inches in length and 2 inches in diameter. The fruit is most unusual as it is star-shaped when sliced. A crisp, waxy, golden-yellow skin encloses the juicy pulp that in some varieties is very sour while in others is almost sweet.

Carambolas may be pickled, frozen or preserved. However, they develop a bitter taste if cooked. The delicate, distinctive flavor is far best when used fresh. Carambolas may be refrigerated for a week or more, but the sooner this fruit is eaten, the better. Thin slices of sweet carambola are sparkling stars which enchant menus. Slice fruit crosswise and use in the following ways: dip in sugar, chill and serve as snacks; add to fresh fruit salads; float slices in a punch bowl or garnish baked meats.

To freeze carambola, cover fresh slices with cold syrup made of equal parts of water and sugar. Pack in an airtight container, leaving ½ inch headspace. Use the frozen slices as garnishes.

COCONUT

*1 cup packed grated fresh coconut
equals 440 calories*

The coconut palm is a symbol of tropical South Florida and has been a source of nourishment for centuries.

A good fresh coconut is heavy for its size. Shake it to make sure it contains milk and avoid cracked coconuts and those with wet, moldy eyes.

To open a fresh coconut, remove the outer husk and puncture the "eyes" of the nut with a nail or ice pick. Drain the milk to drink fresh or save it and use later in recipes.

To remove the shell, bake the drained coconut at 350° for 20-30 minutes, or put it in the freezer for an hour. Then, place the coconut on a firm surface and tap the shell lightly with a hammer in several places until it cracks. Separate the pieces of meat from the shell and trim off the brown layer with a sharp knife.

Coconut milk may be used fresh or frozen in puddings or desserts. Coconut meat may be grated, using a medium blade in a food chopper. One medium-size coconut equals about 3 cups of packed grated coconut or 5 cups of unpacked coconut.

Cleaned whole pieces of coconut may be

sprinkled lightly with sugar (1 tablespoon to about 1 quart of pieces) and packed into airtight containers for freezing.

To grated coconut, add 2 tablespoons of sugar. Mix well and pack firmly into airtight containers, pressing out air before sealing. Coconut may be kept in the freezer for 8-12 months.

GRAPEFRUIT

1 white grapefruit equals 88 calories
1 pink grapefruit equals 92 calories
1 cup juice equals 96 calories

The sunshine state of Florida produces almost 45% of the world's grapefruit. Available year-round, Florida grapefruit has become a versatile fruit no longer used just for breakfast. There are two types of grapefruit: white-fleshed and pink-fleshed. The white grapefruit has honey-colored meat and bright yellow skin. The pink grapefruit has pink meat and a pink blush to the skin.

When choosing a grapefruit, the heavier for the size, the juicier it will be. Varying shades of yellow or green coloring in the grapefruit peel are determined by temperature. Cool weather gives the fruit a colorful blush and warm weather may cause the fruit to remain green even though it is fully mature.

One grapefruit produces 10-12 sections. One medium grapefruit produces ⅔ cup of juice.

GUAVA

1 guava equals 70 calories

Guava trees grow in South Florida as a cultivated tree and also widely in a semi-wild condition, with fruit maturing practically year-round. The fruit can be round, oval, or pear-shaped. Its weight when ripe can be from 1 ounce to as much as 1 pound. Skin color is usually yellow with flesh ranging from white, yellow, pink to red. The fruit can be thin-shelled with many seeds to thick-shelled with few seeds. Flavor ranges from sweet to highly acidic while the aroma of ripe guavas varies from strong and penetrating to mild and pleasant. Guavas are high in vitamin C content, making them an excellent substitute for orange or tomato juice.

Guavas cut in half, peeled if desired and with the seedy central pulp scooped out are called guava shells and have many uses. The fruit may be mashed, strained and used to make delicious ice cream, juice, jelly, chutney and punches.

JABOTICABA

The jaboticaba tree is native to southern Brazil and produces one of its most popular fruits. In South Florida this fruit is still rather uncommon, but can be grown with success. It has been tried in the markets and has been well received.

One of the most spectacular of all tropical fruit trees, jaboticabas grow directly upon the trunk and larger branches, individually or in clusters, from the ground up. Each fruit is grape-like in appearance, with ½-inch round shapes. When ripe, jaboticabas are dark maroon to almost black in color. The pulp is whitish and translucent, contains 1 to 4 seeds and is quite juicy and flavorful.

Jaboticabas are produced most of the year. They can be eaten fresh or made into jellies, syrups, jams or wine. Both the juice and the fruit freeze well.

KUMQUAT

5-6 kumquats
equal 65 calories

There are 3 species of the kumquat grown in Florida. Nagami is the most common and also the most successful in the southern end of the state. It is oblong and approximately 1½ inches in length. The orange fleshy peel is sweet and aromatic, while the pulp is quite acidic.

The Marumi variety is round, slightly over 1 inch in diameter and deep orange in color when ripe. The juice is quite acidic, while the peel is sweet and spicy. Maiwa kumquats also are round, about 1½ inches in diameter, and the peel is orange-yellow in color when ripe. The juice is essentially non-acidic, and the peel is sweet.

The kumquat is a good fruit for candying, as it crystallizes well. Also frequently used as an ornamental, the kumquat is excellent for garnishes, marmalades, preserves, appetizers, salads or just plain. Fresh kumquats will keep in the refrigerator for about 1 month.

Preserved kumquats are delicious in various forms as meat accompaniments.

Lemon

1 medium lemon equals 20 calories
1 cup juice equals 61 calories

Lemons are versatile in use, reasonable in price and deliciously refreshing. They can add color, cheer and good eating to every day of the year. Lemons range in size from small ones to the Ponderosa variety, which is similar in size to a grapefruit. Favorite varieties include Meyer, an orange-lemon cross; Bearss, a heavy fruit with very tough skin and high oil content and Ponderosa, which is actually a citran-lemon cross that is quite large and can be used as a lemon substitute.

When choosing lemons, avoid those with bruised or wrinkled skins. Lemons keep at room temperature for 7-10 days. In the refrigerator, place them in a plastic bag and store in the vegetable crisper and they will keep for at least a month.

Six medium lemons produce one cup of juice.

One medium lemon produces 3 teaspoons of grated rind.

The following are some ideas for lemons:

• Roll a lemon several times and insert a toothpick in one end. Remove the pick, give food a few squirts for flavor and replace the toothpick. Store the lemon in the refrigerator until the next fresh squeeze is needed.
• Add fresh grated peel to puddings, cakes, sugar, icings or salad dressing to give them a personal touch and add flavor.
• Substitute lemon juice for vinegar in many recipes for a fresher taste.
• Make your own buttermilk by adding 1 tablespoon of lemon juice to 1 cup of milk. Let stand 5 minutes before using.
• Squeeze fresh lemon juice into the poaching liquid of fish to season and to keep fish white in color.
• Place thick strips of lemon peel in a warm oven for a few minutes to dispel unwanted odors.
• Cut lemons in half and scoop out the pulp. Fill with lemon sherbet and serve as a palate refresher.

Lime

1 medium lime equals 10 calories
1 cup juice equals 64 calories

Most limes grown in Florida are either of the small Key or Mexican or the larger Persian or Tahiti variety. The Key lime is a small, greenish-yellow, round lime approximately 1½ inches in diameter. It is very popular in South Florida in drinks and the famous Key Lime Pie. The green Persian lime is the one most often found in the market.

A wedge of fresh lime can go any place a lemon goes, but with perhaps a bit more flare.

Lime juice may be substituted for lemon in any recipe, but use only 2/3 to 3/4 as much, due to its higher acidity. Fresh lime juice is used in place of vinegar in dressings, marinades and sauces.

Lime wedges offer extra zest to iced tea, cold drinks and tomato juice. Squeezed on salads, lime juice adds zip but very few calories. Since there is very little sodium in fresh lime juice, it can make salt free diets interesting again. Lime juice squeezed over fresh fruit adds a nice taste and also keeps the fruit from turning dark.

LOQUAT

10 loquats equal 59 calories
The loquat, also called Japanese plum, is a small delicious, oval-shaped fruit 1½-2 inches long. It contains two or three large brown seeds. Color varies from pale yellow to light orange when ripening. The tough, slightly wooly, thick skin is easily peeled from the juicy, firm flesh of the fruit. The flavor is mildly acidic, resembling that of an apple or a peach and can be used much like an apple in baking or preserving. Florida loquats usually ripen from February through April.

Loquats are good to eat out of hand, in pies, cakes, jellies and jams. They can also be frozen. They can be refrigerated for a short time but do bruise easily.

As an average, 14-16 seeded and peeled loquats equal 1 cup.

LYCHEES

10 lychees equal 58 calories
Be prepared for a taste thrill when you first eat one of these most esteemed of all fruits. The origin of the lychee goes back 3,500 years. Today, this exotic fruit grows in Florida, rich in flavor, color and natural beauty.

Lychees look like clusters of rough red cherries or strawberries hanging form twigs of handsome dark green trees. These approximately 1 inch round-to-oval fruits must ripen on the tree for best flavor. The red skin is thin and leathery, forming a shell, but easily pulls away with the fingers to expose a delicate white flesh surrounding a single, shiny dark brown seed.

The slightly acidic flavor of a lychee is difficult to describe. Think of the sweetest, juiciest, most fragrant grape you can imagine, then try to make it even sweeter. Some varieties contain more sugar than others and are an excellent source of vitamin C. Lychees may be successfully refrigerated in plastic containers for 2 or 3 weeks.

Approximately 20-35 lychees, depending on their size, equal 1 cup of peeled and seeded fruit. Lychees are most frequently served fresh, eaten out of the shell or shelled and added to fruit salads.

To enjoy a fresh lychee, hold it with the stem end up and gently break the skin with your fingernail. Peel the shell down and take a bite of juicy flesh.

Peeled, pitted lychees may be frozen in a sugar syrup. Slight toughening occurs, but the flavor remains excellent. Freezing a lychee in its shell seems to produce a fruit as tender as the fresh product.

A wonderful flavor combination is lychee with papaya and pineapple.

MANGO

1 mango equals, 152 calories
The mango is often called the apple of the south and may be of more importance to people of the tropics than the apple and peach are to those living in more temperate areas. It is a medium size fruit, from 2-5 inches in width and 2-10 inches long. The skin is smooth and thick and, as it ripens, it turns to yellow-green or yellow-orange, often with splashes of crimson or russet red. The flesh may be light lemon to dark apricot in color. The better varieties of mango have a rich aromatic flavor and are juicy and delicious. The most prized varieties are not very fibrous and have flesh that separates easily from the hairy seed.

If you have never handled or eaten a mango before, approach with caution, as some people are allergic to them. Mangos may be picked at the mature green stage. After they have ripened, they should not be refrigerated in temperatures under 50 degrees. The mango is good both at the green stage and when ripe. Green mangos can be substituted for apples or peaches in any recipes. When green, the mango is best for cooking. It can be used for mock green apple pie, pickles or mock applesauce. Ripe mangos are good in salads, pies, sauces, breads, chutneys and cakes. The ripe fruit can also be pickled, preserved, canned, frozen, pureed, dried or eaten just plain. Mangos are excellent sliced and served with cream and sugar or served with cottage cheese or ice cream. Bite-size frozen slices make a deliciously refreshing sweet treat!

ORANGE

1 orange equals 73 calories
1 cup juice equals 112 calories
Any way you slice them, oranges are delicious. Each variety has a delightful aroma, beautiful color and distinctive flavor all its own. Technically, the orange is a berry. Florida Indians, during Spanish settlement times, were particularly fond of the bright-colored sour oranges, piercing their skins and filling them with honey.

Navel oranges are one of the most popular varieties because they are large and seedless. The navel has a thick skin, is easy to peel and is widely used for orange sections. Hamlin oranges are very popular for juice. Pineapple oranges are medium sized, moderately seedy and prized for both juice and fresh eating. Valencia oranges mature later than all others. They are nearly seedless, medium large in size, possess a tough rind and produce the best juice for freezing. Temple oranges are of medium size with few seeds and are actually a cross between a tangerine and an orange. Honeybell (or Minneola) oranges are actually tangelos. This delicious fruit with a season from January to

March is a cross between a Duncan grapefruit and a Dancy tangerine. The rind is deep orange in color and the flesh is very juicy with few seeds.

PAPAYA

1 medium size papaya equals 119 calories
There are many strains and varieties of this melon-like tropical fruit, and the variation in size, form and color is remarkable. Some papayas resemble small watermelons, while others are quite small and almost round. The skin is smooth and thin and the colors range from deep orange to green. The flesh of papaya is white before maturity, turning to a rich yellow-orange as the fruit ripens. The center cavity contains pea-sized grayish-black seeds. Papaya is produced on trees year-round in tropical Florida, and depending on the temperature, may ripen without coloring, so softening is the key to ripeness. At warmer temperatures, 65 degrees or over, a yellow blush is associated with ripening.

Papaya may be eaten "on the half shell" with lemon or lime juice generously sprinkled over it or combined with citrus fruits in salads. The pulp, combined with cream, makes a delicious frozen dessert. Sliced and seasoned like peaches, papaya may be used in pies.

PINEAPPLE

1 pound of pineapple equals 236 calories
1 cup juice equals 138 calories
There were pineapple farms in the Palm Beaches during the 1930s, but it was generally discovered that the climate was not suited to large scale commercial production of pineapples. Three varieties of pineapple that are grown in Florida and known for their distinct characteristics are Red Spanish, Smooth Cayenne and Natal Queen. Size varies from 1-10 pounds or

more, oval to cylindrical in shape and color varies from yellowish to orange in color.

Pineapples should ripen on the plant for maximum flavor and sugar content. It does not increase in sweetness after it has been harvested. Judging the degree of ripeness of a pineapple requires experience and knowledge of a particular variety. Pineapple is usually sweeter in the summer months. A yellow rind is not necessarily an indication of a sweet or ripe pineapple. A first-quality, well-developed pineapple is one in which the crown is small and compact. The sound test is the most dependable guide for choosing a good pineapple. Snap the fruit with thumb and forefinger. If you get a hollow sound, the fruit is sour. If you get a dull, solid sound, the fruit is sweeter and full of juice.

SEAGRAPE

20-25 seagrapes
equal 26 calories

The seagrape is one of South Florida's most desirable ornamental trees. In the late summer, the berries grow in long grape-like clusters but are in no way related to the grape. The fruit hangs from branches in abundance and ripens from September through October. The single stone in the fruit is large. The velvet skin has a slightly salty flavor and a light or dark purple color. The pulp is thin.

To pick seagrapes, hold a pail under a cluster and gently run a hand over them, dislodging only the ripe fruit. Seagrapes contain just enough pectin to produce a jelly of unusual flavor. The fruit is also used for juice, syrup and wine.

STRAWBERRY

1 cup strawberries
equals 55 calories

Although not exclusively a tropical plant, strawberries have been popular in

Florida for many years and are grown on about 2,600 acres annually. This glossy red fruit is unique because it is the only one with seeds on its outside. Several varieties are grown in Florida with ranges in shape, size and degrees of tartness. The harvest season is late December through April. Botanically speaking, the strawberry is neither a berry nor a fruit. It is the enlarged stem end of the small white blossom of the plant and a member of the rose family.

Berries with large uncolored or large seedy areas should be avoided, as they will be poor in flavor and texture. A dull, shrunken appearance or softness indicates over-ripeness or decay. Do not wash or stem strawberries before storing in a refrigerator and use within one or two days, as strawberries are very delicate and highly perishable.

For unsweetened frozen strawberries, wash the berries, remove the caps and drain in a colander. Pack the berries into a container. For better color, cover with water containing 1 teaspoon crystalline ascorbic acid for each quart of water. Leave ½ inch space at the top, seal, label and freeze.

TANGERINE

1 tangerine equals 39 calories
1 cup juice equals 106 calories

Tangerines are related to the mandarin orange, and most are smaller than other common citrus. They are considerably easier to peel and section than oranges. The Robinson variety is one of Florida's largest tangerines with the flesh and peel a deep orange in color. This fruit matures as early as October.

Dancy tangerines mature during December, have a very loose peel and are of excellent quality. The Dancy variety has a highly colored orange peel and dark orange flesh with a small amount of seeds.

Tangerine juice may be substituted in recipes calling for orange juice.

CRYSTALLIZED CITRUS PEEL

2 cups thick fruit peel, cut into ¼ to ½ inch wide strips
2 quarts water
⅔ cup corn syrup
1⅓ cups sugar
1⅓ cups water
½ teaspoon salt
Sugar

Simmer strips of peel for 30 minutes in 2 quarts water, adding more water as necessary. Discard water. Add fresh water and repeat procedure twice. Combine corn syrup, sugar, 1 ⅓ cups water and salt in a saucepan; bring to a boil. Add fruit peel and boil gently for 30 minutes. Reduce heat and cook slowly 30-40 minutes or until all syrup has been absorbed. Roll peel in granulated sugar. Place on rack to cool.

Package peel in airtight containers and freeze for long storage, or store in boxes lined with waxed paper. You may also store in jars with a few air holes in the lid. Peel will keep 2-3 months. Serve as candy or where candied fruit is used in recipes. Makes a beautiful garnish for cakes and pies.

CANDIED DRIED KUMQUATS

1 quart kumquats
1 tablespoon baking soda
Water
2½ cups sugar, divided
2 cups water
½ cup corn syrup

Sprinkle kumquats with baking soda. Cover with water and let soak in the soda solution 20 minutes. Drain, rinse in several changes of cold water. Make a slit in each kumquat, through to the seeds.

Dissolve 2 cups of the sugar in 2 cups water and bring to a boil. Add kumquats and simmer 30 minutes. Remove from heat, weigh the fruit down with a plate to keep it submerged; let cool and plump for 24 hours.

Drain off the syrup and add it to remaining ½ cup of sugar and the corn syrup. Bring to a boil and simmer until kumquats are plump and transparent. Again submerge the fruit in the syrup and let it plump for 24 hours. Reheat kumquats in syrup, boil for 30 minutes, and cool.

Lift kumquats from syrup and place on racks to dry in sun or in a cool oven, 100°. The kumquats may then be stuffed with fondant or nutmeats and rolled in granulated sugar, or dipped in glaze.

SEND A SLICE OF PARADISE TO YOUR FAMILY AND FRIENDS...

$\mathcal{R}$olling orange groves in full bloom bring the sweet smell of spring to South Florida. The ability to walk into your garden and pick fresh oranges to squeeze for morning juice is one reason that Palm Beach County is paradise to its residents. The Cushman Fruit Company has been bringing a slice of this paradise to those around the world who enjoy "handpicked" quality for over 50 years. Fruits are an integral part of the recipes in this carefully assembled cookbook and the family-owned Cushman Fruit Company can bring them to your doorstep. Nothing can better represent the fresh inviting flavors of the Palm Beaches than fresh fruit.

To place an order or to receive your free catalogue call toll free 1-800-776-7575 or Fax 1-800-776-4329.

Cushman's

Limited Edition Fruit®...Since 1945

Index

A

Almond Orange Garden Salad 72
Angel Hair Pasta with Fresh Tomato Sauce 108
Appetizers
  Baked Brie 18
  Basil Tomato Tart 15
  Bruschetta with Arugula and Smoked
    Mozzarella 11
  Bruschetta with Matchstick Pepper Strips 12
  Bull's-Eye Chili Dip 18
  Caramel Butter Brie 19
  Cheddar Artichoke Crescents 25
  Cheese and Onion Rolls 25
  Chicken Fajita Pizza 194
  Chili Rellenos Squares 11
  Chutney Cashew Dip 15
  Crab Stuffed Mushrooms 24
  Crabmeat Imperial on Melba Rounds 23
  Gouda Cheese Puff 13
  Herbed Spinach Balls 27
  Hot Artichoke Crostini 13
  Hot Artichoke Spinach Dip 14
  Layered Sun-Dried Tomato and Pesto Spread 22
  Oriental Chicken Wings 27
  Paradise Cheese Ball 20
  Peppercorn Spread 23
  Reuben Dip 19
  Shrimp Mousse 21
  Smoked Fish Dip 17
  Smoked Salmon Spread 12
  Snappy Sunshine Salsa 26
  Spicy Seafood Dip 16
  Summer Vegetable Medley 14
  Sweet Bacon Wraps 26
  Vegetables with Avocado Anchovy Dip 17
  White Cheddar Rollups 24
Apple
  Apple-Cranberry Streusel Pie 237
  Appleanna Bread 43
  Bavarian Apple Torte 248
  Pear-Apple Crumb Pie 234
  Spicy Apple Dumplings 254
Apple Pecan Winter Squash 144
Apple-Cranberry Streusel Pie 237
Appleanna Bread 43
Apricot Cornish Hens 195
Artichoke
  Artichoke Quiche 54
  Hot Artichoke Crostini 13
  Hot Artichoke Spinach Dip 14
  Shrimp and Artichoke Vinaigrette 94

Artichoke Quiche 54
Asparagus
  Dijon Asparagus Salad 89
  Marinated Asparagus 133
AuGratin Tomatoes 146
Avocado
  Avocado Layered Soup 62
  Avocado Salad with Spicy Dressing 80
  Saffron Rice with Avocado 156
Avocado Layered Soup 62
Avocado Salad with Spicy Dressing 80
Vegetables with Avocado Anchovy Dip 17

B

Baked Bananas 151
Baked Brie 18
Baked Chicken Piquant with Rice 179
Baked Rice, Tomatoes and Cheese 153
Baked Scallops with Cream 203
Baked Stuffed Lobster 200
Baklava 255
Banana
  Appleanna Bread 43
  Baked Bananas 151
  Banana Poppy Seed Dressing 88
  Banana Zinger 33
  Coconut Banana Cake 223
Banana Poppy Seed Dressing 88
Banana Zinger 33
Barbecued Chicken Marinade 184
Basic Pastry/Pie Crust 259
Basil Grilled Chicken 186
Basil Tomato Tart 15
Bavarian Apple Torte 248
Beachfront Bean Medley 85
Beans
  Beachfront Bean Medley 85
  Black Bean and Chicken Chili 70
  Black Bean and Corn Salad 83
  Bull's-Eye Chili Dip 18
  Penne Pasta with Black Beans and Mango 127
  Rice and Black Beans 155
Béchamel Lasagna Rolls 110
Beef
  Beef Tenderloin with Peppercorns 168
  Bull's-Eye Chili Dip 18
  Ginger-Orange Barbecued Beef Back Ribs 165
  Grilled Pineapple Burgers 104
  Herbed Eye Roast Sandwiches 104
  Lemon Dill Meatballs in Creamy
    Tomato Sauce 120

Mango Beef Stir-fry 167
Marinated Steak and Spinach Salad 91
Picadillo 166
Ropa Vieja 164
Sauté de Boeuf 169
Steak Rolls in Red Wine Sauce 163
Beef Stock 262
Beef Tenderloin with Peppercorns 168
Beverages
Banana Zinger 33
Chocolate Coffee Royale 32
Cranberry Cinnamon Punch 31
Fresh Lemonade 28
Frosted Orange Drink 29
Mango Frozen Daiquiris 29
Mint Tea 34
Mocha Cream Liqueur 33
Pineapple Smoothie 29
Ruby Fruit Sangria 30
Seaside Mist 28
Spiced Cranberry Tea 34
Strawberry Daiquiri Punch 31
Sunrise Coffee Punch 32
Sustainer Slush 30
Toasted Almond 33
Tropical Champagne Punch 32
Black Bean and Chicken Chili 70
Black Bean and Corn Salad 83
Black Russian Cake 230
Blackened Pompano 197
Blue Cheese Bubble Bread 50
Blue Cheese Coleslaw 76
Blueberry
Blueberry Orange Muffins 40
Blueberry Sauce 256
Bow Ties with Spinach Sauce and Cheese 107
Bread Pudding with Rum Sauce 247
Breads
Appleanna Bread 43
Blue Cheese Bubble Bread 50
Blueberry Orange Muffins 40
Bruschetta with Arugula and Smoked
  Mozzarella 11
Bruschetta with Matchstick Pepper Strips 12
Caramel Cinnamon Rolls 48
Caraway Soda Bread 39
Cheddar Dill Bread 49
Creamy Caramel-Pecan Rolls 46
Florida Orange Bread 41
Focaccia 48
Hot Artichoke Crostini 13
Jalapeño Cornbread 50
Key Lime Bread 42
Key Lime Danish 37
Mango Nut Bread 41
Orange Rolls 38

Overnight Refrigerator Rolls 47
Pancakes
Ricotta Cheese Pancakes 53
Pecan French Toast 52
Rolls and Muffins
Blueberry Orange Muffins 40
Caramel Cinnamon Rolls 48
Creamy Caramel-Pecan Rolls 46
Herbed Buttermilk Biscuits 51
Orange Rolls 38
Overnight Refrigerator Rolls 47
Strawberry Orange Muffins 39
Strawberry Orange Muffins 39
Streusel Coffee Cake 45
Sweet Walnut Bread 44
Toasted Coconut Bread 42
Tropical Loaf 44
Brie Pasta 113
Broccoli
Broccoli Puff 134
Lemon Broccoli with Garlic 133
Broccoli Puff 134
Broiled Swordfish with Mint and Lime 210
Brown Sugar Pound Cake 228
Brunch
Artichoke Quiche 54
Cheese and Egg Strata 53
Pecan French Toast 52
Ricotta Cheese Pancakes 53
Seafood Quiche 55
Tomato and Basil Quiche 56
Zucchini Frittata 52
Bruschetta with Arugula and Smoked Mozzarella ... 11
Bruschetta with Matchstick Pepper Strips 12
Bull's-Eye Chili Dip 18

C

Cabbage
Crunchy Cabbage Salad 80
Cafe Chardonnay's Tiramisu 244
Cakes
Black Russian Cake 230
Brown Sugar Pound Cake 228
Coconut Banana Cake 223
Costa Rican Rum Cream Cake 224
French Chocolate Cake 229
Hot Fudge Sundae Cake 231
Italian Cream Cake 226
Lemon Cheesecake 222
Sour Cream Pound Cake 229
Streusel Coffee Cake 45
Tropical Carrot Cake 227
Ultimate Poppy Seed Cake 225
White Chocolate Raspberry Cheesecake 221
Candied Dried Kumquats 275

Caramel Butter Brie 19
Caramel Cinnamon Rolls 48
Caraway Soda Bread 39
Carrots
   Carrot Cups with Summer Sauce 141
   Ginger Carrots 135
Cauliflower
   Scalloped Cauliflower 134
Celery Seed Dressing 79
Champagne Sorbet 246
Cheddar Artichoke Crescents 25
Cheddar Dill Bread 49
Cheese and Egg Strata 53
Cheese and Onion Rolls 25
Cheese Cake Cookies 219
Cheeses
   Baked Brie 18
   Blue Cheese Bubble Bread 51
   Blue Cheese Coleslaw 76
   Brie Pasta 113
   Bruschetta with Arugula and Smoked
      Mozzarella 11
   Caramel Butter Brie 19
   Cheddar Artichoke Crescents 25
   Cheddar Dill Bread 49
   Cheese and Egg Strata 53
   Cheese and Onion Rolls 25
   Chick Pea and Cheese Salad 84
   Chili Cheese Casserole 152
   Creamy Double Cheese Soup 69
   Dried Cherry and Goat Cheese Salad ... 74
   Endive and Gorgonzola Salad 73
   Gorgonzola and Pistachio Fettucine ... 111
   Gouda Cheese Puff 13
   Layered Sun-dried Tomato and Pesto Spread 22
   Open-Face Gorgonzola Cheese,
      Tomato and Basil Sandwich 97
   Paradise Cheese Ball 20
   Peppercorn Spread 23
   Reuben Dip 19
   Ricotta Cheese Pancakes 53
   Summer Feta Salad 73
   Sweet Bell Pepper and Feta Salad 82
   Sweet Corn and Cheddar Chowder 60
   White Cheddar Rollups 24
Cherry
   Cherry Crepes Jubilee 251
Chevré Stuffed Tomatoes 147
Chewy Brown Sugar Cookies 216
Chick Pea and Cheese Salad 84
Chicken
   Baked Chicken Piquant with Rice 179
   Barbecued Chicken Marinade 184
   Basil Grilled Chicken 186
   Black Bean and Chicken Chili 70
   Chicken and Artichokes 188

Chicken and Spinach Pasta Salad 87
Chicken Breasts Stuffed with Feta and Dried
   Tomato 189
Chicken Cutlets Italienne 183
Chicken Fajita Pizza 194
Chicken in Tomato Sauce with Dill and Feta
   Cheese 117
Chicken Puffs 192
Chicken Ratatouille 182
Chicken Sautéed with Balsamic Vinegar 191
Chicken Stock 261
Chicken with Tarragon and Wine 190
Creamy Chicken with Angel Hair Pasta 118
Grilled Chicken Breast Sandwiches With
   Coleslaw 102
Grilled Chicken Kabobs 187
Jambalaya 177
Lime Barbecued Chicken
   with Black Bean Sauce 185
Mandarin Almond Chicken 178
Marinated Chicken Breasts in Pepper Sauce on
   Fettucine 115
Moore-Betty Chicken 193
Orange Chicken 179
Oriental Chicken Salad Pitas 101
Oriental Chicken Wings 27
Pasta with Chicken and Peanut Sauce 116
Pasta with Chicken, Peas and Sun-Dried
   Tomatoes 114
Pecan Chicken 194
Raspberry Chicken 180
Tortellini Chicken Salad with Sun-Dried Tomato
   Vinaigrette 86
Chili Cheese Casserole 152
Chili Rellenos Squares 11
Chocolate
   Black Russian Cake 230
   Chocolate Cherry Brownies 220
   Chocolate Coffee Royale 32
   Chocolate-Pecan-Oatmeal Pie 240
   Cranberry and White Chocolate Chip
      Cookies 217
   French Chocolate Cake 229
   German Chocolate Pie 241
   Hot Fudge Sundae Cake 231
   Killer Cupcakes 219
   Mocha Cream Liqueur 33
   White Chocolate Brownies 220
   White Chocolate Macadamia Nut Cookies 218
   White Chocolate Raspberry Cheesecake 221
Chocolate Cherry Brownies 220
Chocolate Coffee Royale 32
Chocolate-Pecan-Oatmeal Pie 240
Chuck & Harold's Key Lime Pie 232
Chutney Cashew Dip 15
Cinnamon Raisin Souffle 156

great for Brunch

Citrus Salad with Banana Poppy Seed Dressing 88
Citrus Sauce For Fresh Fruit 243
Coconut
  Coconut Banana Cake 223
  Toasted Coconut Bread 42
Coconut Banana Cake 223
Coconut Crisps 215
Coconut Fried Shrimp 203
Cold Cream of Tomato Soup with Mint,
  Avocado and Cucumber 64
Confetti Squash Casserole 146
Cookies
  Cheese Cake Cookies 219
  Chewy Brown Sugar Cookies 216
  Chocolate Cherry Brownies 220
  Coconut Crisps 215
  Cranberry and White Chocolate Chip Cookies .. 217
  Killer Cupcakes 219
  Lime Delights 216
  Oatmeal Coconut Cookies 215
  Pignoli Cookies 218
  Sugar and Spice Cookies 217
  White Chocolate Brownies 220
  White Chocolate Macadamia Nut Cookies 218
Corn
  Black Bean and Corn Salad 83
  Crabmeat Corn Soup 68
  Curried Corn and Sweet Peppers 135
  Paraguayan Corn Souffle 136
  Sweet Corn and Cheddar Chowder 60
Cornish Hens
  Apricot Cornish Hens 195
Costa Rican Rum Cream Cake 224
Crab and Angel Hair Pasta 121
Crab and Lobster Lasagna 122
Crab Cakes with Mustard Sauce 196
Crab Stuffed Mushrooms 24
Crabmeat Corn Soup 68
Crabmeat Imperial on Melba Rounds 23
Cranapple and Honey Baked Pork Chops 170
Cranberry
  Apple-Cranberry Streusel Pie 237
  Cranberry Cinnamon Punch 31
  Hot Cranberry Casserole 151
Cranberry and White Chocolate Chip Cookies 217
Cranberry Cinnamon Punch 31
Cranberry Orange Lamb Chops 175
Creamy Caramel-Pecan Rolls 46
Creamy Chicken with Angel Hair Pasta 118
Creamy Clam Sauce with Linguine 123
Creamy Double Cheese Soup 69
Cremé Brulée with Belgian Chocolate and
  Raspberry Sauce 245
Crunchy Cabbage Salad 80
Crystallized Citrus Peel 275

Curried Apple Rice 153
Curried Corn and Sweet Peppers 135
Curried Lentil Pockets 98
Curried Watercress and Orange Salad 74

D

Deep Sea Pesto Pasta 126
Desserts
  Baklava 255
  Bavarian Apple Torte 248
  Blueberry Sauce 256
  Bread Pudding with Rum Sauce 247
  Cafe Chardonnay's Tiramisu 244
  Caramel Butter Brie 19
  Champagne Sorbet 246
  Cherry Crepes Jubilee 251
  Citrus Sauce For Fresh Fruit 243
  Cremé Brulée with Belgian Chocolate and
    Raspberry Sauce 245
  Florida Flan 246
  Grand Marnier Dip For Fruit 243
  Lemon Cups 249
  Old-Fashioned Pumpkin Torte 253
  Orange Alaskas 250
  Pastry Cream 245
  Plum Torte 256
  Poached Peaches and Raspberry Sauce 248
  Raspberry Pears 249
  Raspberry Velvet Tart 252
  Spicy Apple Dumplings 254
Dijon Asparagus Salad 89
Dill Dressing 95
Dried Cherry and Goat Cheese Salad 74

E

Eggplant
  Eggplant Casserole 136
Eggs
  Artichoke Quiche 54
  Cheese and Egg Strata 53
  Cinammon Raisin Souffle 156
  Seafood Quiche 55
  Tomato and Basil Quiche 56
Embassy Risotto with Porcini 158
Endive and Gorgonzola Salad 73
Equivalent Measures 265
Exquisite Pie 241

F

Fettuccine with Chardonnay Red Pepper Sauce 112
Fish Stock 261
Floribbean Shrimp 202
Florida Flan 246
Florida Orange Bread 41

Focaccia 48
French Chocolate Cake 229
Fresh Lemonade 28
Fresh Lobster Salad 96
Fresh Peach Pie 238
Fresh Spinach Salad 78
Fresh Strawberry Pie 232
Fried Rice 152
Frosted Orange Drink 29
Fruit Salad with Celery Seed Dressing 79
Fruits
    Fruit Salad with Celery Seed Dressing ... 79
    Tropical Champagne Punch 32
    Tropical Loaf 44
Fruit Shipping 276

G

Garlicky Potatoes 140
Gazpacho 65
German Chocolate Pie 241
Ginger Carrots 135
Ginger-Orange Barbecued Beef Back Ribs ... 165
Gingersnap Berry Pie 235
Gold Coast Spinach Salad 77
Gold Coast Sweet Potatoes 142
Gorgonzola and Pistachio Fettucine 111
Gouda Cheese Puff 13
Gourmet Spinach Soup 61
Grand Marnier Dip For Fruit 243
Grecian Snapper with Feta Cheese 208
Green Beans
    Green Beans in Basil and Walnut Sauce ... 137
    Green Beans with Warm Mustard Vinaigrette ... 138
Green Beans in Basil and Walnut Sauce 137
Green Beans with Warm Mustard Vinaigrette ... 138
Grilled Chicken Breast Sandwiches With Coleslaw 102
Grilled Chicken Kabobs 187
Grilled Marinated Leg of Lamb 174
Grilled Mushroom Sandwiches 99
Grilled Pineapple Burgers 104
Grilled Pork Tenderloin 171
Grilled Swordfish with Avocado Sauce 211
Grilled Tuna with Ginger Cream Sauce 212
Grilled Vegetable Salad 149

H

Herb Butter 260
Herb Butter Zucchini Fans 144
Herb Mayonnaise 260
Herb Vinegar 260
Herbed Buttermilk Biscuits 51
Herbed Eye Roast Sandwiches 104
Herbed Pork Tenderloin 172
Herbed Spinach Balls 27

Honey Dressing 75
Honey Grilled Shoulder of Lamb 174
Honey Mustard Chicken Sauce 188
Hot Artichoke Crostini 13
Hot Artichoke Spinach Dip 14
Hot Cranberry Casserole 151
Hot Fudge Sundae Cake 231

I

Italian Cream Cake 226
Italian Crescent Sandwiches 97
Italian Sausage Soup 67

J

Jalapeño Cornbread 50
Jambalaya 177

K

Key Lime Bread 42
Key Lime Danish 37
Key Lime Rum Pie 233
Killer Cupcakes 219

L

Lamb
    Cranberry Orange Lamb Chops 175
    Grilled Marinated Leg of Lamb 174
    Honey Grilled Shoulder of Lamb 174
    Low-fat Lamb Kabobs 175
    Peach Glazed Leg of Lamb 176
Layered Sun-dried Tomato and Pesto Spread ... 22
Lemon
    Fresh Lemonade 28
    Lemon Cheesecake 222
    Lemon Cups 249
Lemon Broccoli with Garlic 133
Lemon Cheesecake 222
Lemon Cups 249
Lemon Dill Meatballs in Creamy Tomato Sauce ... 120
Lentil Soup 59
Lime
    Chuck & Harold's Key Lime Pie 232
    Key Lime Bread 42
    Key Lime Danish 37
    Key Lime Rum Pie 233
    Lime Delights 216
Lime Barbecued Chicken with Black
    Bean Sauce 185
Linguine with Garlic and Rosemary Oil 112
Low-fat Lamb Kabobs 175

M

Macadamia Crusted Yellowtail Snapper
    with Tropical Fruit Salsa 206

Mahi Mahi with Mango Salsa 198
Mandarin Almond Chicken 178
Mango
    Mango Frozen Daiquiris 29
    Mango Nut Bread 41
    Mango Pie 239
Mango Beef Stir-fry 167
Mango Frozen Daiquiris 29
Mango Nut Bread 41
Mango Pie 239
Mango Salsa 198
Mango Snapper 209
Marinated Asparagus 133
Marinated Chicken Breasts in Pepper Sauce
    on Fettucine 115
Marinated Steak and Spinach Salad 91
Metric Conversion Guide 265
Mile Marker Snapper 205
Mint Tea 34
Mocha Cream Liqueur 33
Moore-Betty Chicken 193
Mountain Top Marinated Tomatoes 148
Mushroom
    Spinach, Bacon and Mushroom Gratin 143
    Grilled Mushroom Sandwiches 99
Mustard Sauce 197

N

Nuts
    Almond Orange Garden Salad 72
    Baklava 255
    Chocolate-Pecan-Oatmeal Pie 240
    Chutney Cashew Dip 15
    Gorgonzola and Pistachio Fettucine 111
    Mango Nut Bread 41
    Pecan Chicken 194
    Pecan French Toast 52
    Pecan Pie 240
    Sweet Walnut Bread 44

O

Oatmeal Coconut Cookies 215
Old-Fashioned Pumpkin Torte 253
Onions
    Cheese and Onion Rolls 25
    Seasonal Peas and Onions 140
    Sweet Scalloped Onions 139
Open-Face Gorgonzola Cheese, Tomato
    and Basil Sandwiches 97
Orange
    Almond Orange Garden Salad 72
    Blueberry Orange Muffins 40
    Curried Watercress and Orange Salad 74
    Florida Orange Bread 41
    Frosted Orange Drink 29

Orange Alaskas 250
    Strawberry Orange Muffins 39
Orange Alaskas 250
Orange Chicken 179
Orange Rolls 38
Oriental Chicken Salad Pitas 101
Oriental Chicken Wings 27
Oven Roasted Vegetables 150
Oven-Baked French Fries 137
Overnight Refrigerator Rolls 47

P

Paella Salad 92
Palm Beach Pasta Salad 90
Paradise Cheese Ball 20
Paradise Fish Guide 266
Paraguayan Corn Souffle 136
Pasta
    Angel Hair Pasta with Fresh Tomato Sauce 108
    Béchamel Lasagna Rolls 110
    Bow Ties with Spinach Sauce and Cheese 107
    Brie Pasta 113
    Chicken and Spinach Pasta Salad 87
    Chicken in Tomato Sauce with Dill and
        Feta Cheese 117
    Crab and Angel Hair Pasta 121
    Crab and Lobster Lasagna 122
    Creamy Chicken with Angel Hair Pasta 118
    Creamy Clam Sauce with Linguine 123
    Deep Sea Pesto Pasta 126
    Fettuccine with Chardonnay Red
        Pepper Sauce 112
    Gorgonzola and Pistachio Fettucine 111
    Lemon Dill Meatballs in Creamy
        Tomato Sauce 120
    Linguine with Garlic and Rosemary Oil 112
    Marinated Chicken Breasts in Pepper Sauce
        on Fettucine 115
    Palm Beach Pasta Salad 90
    Pasta Primavera 129
    Pasta with Chicken and Peanut Sauce 116
    Pasta with Chicken, Peas and
        Sun-Dried Tomatoes 114
    Pasta with Shrimp and
        Jalapeño Orange Sauce 124
    Penne and Fresh Tuna with Raisin and
        Almond Sauce 125
    Penne from Heaven 119
    Penne Pasta with Black Beans and Mango 127
    Pesto Fettuccine with Chicken and
        Asparagus 130
    Rigatoni a la Vodka 109
    Sun-Dried Tomato Fettucine 107
    Tortellini Chicken Salad with Sun-Dried
        Tomato Vinaigrette 86

Tortellini Soup 62
Vegetable Carbonara 118
Vegetarian Pasta 128
Pasta Primavera 129
Pasta with Chicken and Peanut Sauce 116
Pasta with Chicken, Peas and
    Sun-Dried Tomatoes 114
Pasta with Shrimp and Jalapeño Orange Sauce 124
Pastry Cream 245

Peach
Fresh Peach Pie 238
Poached Peaches and Raspberry Sauce 248
Peach Glazed Leg of Lamb 176
Peanut Butter Pie 242

Pear
Pear-Apple Crumb Pie 234
Raspberry Pears 249
Pear-Apple Crumb Pie 234

Peas
Chick Pea and Cheese Salad 84
Curried Lentil Pockets 98
Lentil Soup 59
Sautéed Peas with Basil 143
Seasonal Peas and Onions 140
Pecan Chicken 194
Pecan French Toast 52
Pecan Pie 240
Penne and Fresh Tuna with Raisin and
    Almond Sauce 125
Penne from Heaven 119
Penne Pasta with Black Beans and Mango 127
Peppercorn Spread 23

Peppers
Chili Rellenos Squares 11
Curried Corn and Sweet Peppers 135
Fettuccine with Chardonnay Red
    Pepper Sauce 112
Red Pepper Soup 69
Roasted Red Pepper Salad 81
Sweet Bell Pepper and Feta Salad 82
Turkey and Roasted Pepper Sandwich 103
Pesto Fettuccine with Chicken andAsparagus 130
Picadillo 166

Pies
Apple-Cranberry Streusel Pie 237
Basic Pastry-Pie Crust 259
Chocolate-Pecan-Oatmeal Pie 240
Chuck & Harold's Key Lime Pie 232
Exquisite Pie 241
Fresh Peach Pie 238
Fresh Strawberry Pie 232
German Chocolate Pie 241
Gingersnap Berry Pie 235
Key Lime Rum Pie 233
Mango Pie 239
Peanut Butter Pie 242

Pear-Apple Crumb Pie 234
Pecan Pie 240
Rhubarb-Raspberry Pie 236
Pignoli Cookies 218

Pineapple
Grilled Pineapple Burgers 104
Pineapple Smoothie 29
Plum Torte 256
Poached Peaches and Raspberry Sauce 248
Poached Salmon with Raspberry Sauce 201
Poppy Seed Dressing 77

Pork
Cranapple and Honey Baked Pork Chops 170
Grilled Pork Tenderloin 171
Herbed Pork Tenderloin 172
Italian Sausage Soup 67
Pork Loin with Orange Marmalade Glaze 170
Pork Tenderloins with Roasted Bell Peppers
    and Tomatoes 173
Sausage Grits 154
Stuffed Pork Chops 171
Sweet Bacon Wraps 26

Potatoes
Garlicky Potatoes 140
Gold Coast Sweet Potatoes 142
Oven-Baked French Fries 137
Rosemary Potatoes 142

Poultry – see Chicken, Cornish Hens, Turkey

Pumpkin
Old-Fashioned Pumpkin Torte 253
Pumpkin Squash Bake 145

R

Raspberry
Raspberry Pears 249
Raspberry Poppy Seed Dressing 89
Raspberry Velvet Tart 252
Raspberry Vinaigrette 71
Red Leaf Raspberry Salad 71
Rhubarb-Raspberry Pie 236
Splendid Raspberry Spinach Salad 76
Raspberry Chicken 180
Raspberry Pears 249
Raspberry Poppy Seed Dressing 89
Raspberry Sauce 201
Raspberry Velvet Tart 252
Raspberry Vinaigrette 71
Ratatouille Sandwiches 100
Recipe Nutrition Guide 264
Red Leaf Raspberry Salad 71
Red Pepper Soup 69
Reuben Dip 19
Rhubarb-Raspberry Pie 236

Rice
Baked Rice, Tomatoes and Cheese 153

Curried Apple Rice 153
Embassy Risotto with Porcini 158
Fried Rice 152
Rice and Black Beans 155
Risotto with Gorgonzola Cheese 157
Saffron Rice with Avocado 156
Vegetable Brown Rice 154
Rice and Black Beans 155
Ricotta Cheese Pancakes 53
Rigatoni a la Vodka 109
Risotto with Gorgonzola Cheese 157
Roasted Peppers 259
Roasted Red Pepper Salad 81
Ropa Vieja 164
Rosemary Potatoes 142
Ruby Fruit Sangria 30

S

Saffron Rice with Avocado 156
Salads
Almond Orange Garden Salad 72
Avocado Salad with Spicy Dressing 80
Beachfront Bean Medley 85
Black Bean and Corn Salad 83
Blue Cheese Coleslaw 76
Chick Pea and Cheese Salad 84
Chicken and Spinach Pasta Salad 87
Citrus Salad with Banana Poppy Seed Dressing . 88
Crunchy Cabbage Salad 80
Curried Watercress and Orange Salad 74
Dijon Asparagus Salad 89
Dried Cherry and Goat Cheese Salad 74
Endive and Gorgonzola Salad 73
Fresh Lobster Salad 96
Fresh Spinach Salad 78
Fruit Salad with Celery Seed Dressing 79
Gold Coast Spinach Salad 77
Marinated Steak and Spinach Salad 91
Oriental Chicken Salad Pitas 101
Paella Salad 92
Palm Beach Pasta Salad 90
Red Leaf Raspberry Salad 71
Roasted Red Pepper Salad 81
Seafood Salad with Dill Dressing 95
Shrimp and Artichoke Vinaigrette 94
Shrimp and Scallop Salad 96
Splendid Raspberry Spinach Salad 76
Summer Feta Salad 73
Summer Shrimp and Olive Salad 93
Sunset Salad 75
Sweet Bell Pepper and Feta Salad 82
Tortellini Chicken Salad with Sun-Dried
Tomato Vinaigrette 86
Salad Dressings
Banana Poppy Seed Dressing 88

Celery Seed Dressing 79
Dill Dressing 95
Honey Dressing 75
Poppy Seed Dressing 77
Raspberry Poppy Seed Dressing 89
Raspberry Vinaigrette 71
Spicy Dressing 81
Sunlight Salad Dressing 72
Vinaigrette Dressing 93
Salmon en Croute 202
Sandwiches
Curried Lentil Pockets 98
Grilled Chicken Breast Sandwiches With
Coleslaw 102
Grilled Mushroom Sandwiches 99
Grilled Pineapple Burgers 104
Herbed Eye Roast Sandwiches 104
Italian Crescent Sandwiches 97
Open-Face Gorgonzola Cheese, Tomato and
Basil Sandwiches 97
Oriental Chicken Salad Pitas 101
Ratatouille Sandwiches 100
Turkey and Roasted Pepper Sandwich 103
Sauces and Salsas
Blueberry Sauce 256
Mango Salsa 198
Raspberry Sauce 201
Tropical Fruit Salsa 207
Vegetable Salsa 199
Honey Mustard Chicken Sauce 188
Mustard Sauce 197
Snappy Sunshine Salsa 26
Sausage Grits 154
Sauté de Boeuf 169
Scalloped Cauliflower 134
Scallopini of Veal 162
Seafood
Clam
Creamy Clam Sauce with Linguine 123
Crab
Crab and Angel Hair Pasta 121
Crab and Lobster Lasagna 122
Crab Cakes with Mustard Sauce 196
Crab Stuffed Mushrooms 24
Crabmeat Corn Soup 68
Crabmeat Imperial on Melba Rounds 23
Veal Escallops Stuffed with Crab 163
Fish
Blackened Pompano 197
Broiled Swordfish with Mint and Lime 210
Grecian Snapper with Feta Cheese 208
Grilled Swordfish with Avocado Sauce 211
Grilled Tuna with Ginger Cream Sauce 212
Macadamia Crusted Yellowtail Snapper
with Tropical Fruit Salsa 206
Mahi Mahi with Mango Salsa 198

Mango Snapper 209
Mile Marker Snapper 205
Penne and Fresh Tuna with Raisin and
    Almond Sauce 125
Poached Salmon with Raspberry Sauce 201
Salmon en Croute 202
Smoked Fish Dip 17
Smoked Salmon Spread 12
Tortilla Crusted Dolphin 199
Lobster
Baked Stuffed Lobster 200
Crab and Lobster Lasagna 122
Fresh Lobster Salad 96
Mixed Seafood
Deep Sea Pesto Pasta 126
Seafood Quiche 55
Seafood Salad with Dill Dressing 95
Spicy Seafood Dip 16
Scallops
Baked Scallops with Cream 203
Shrimp and Scallop Salad 96
Shrimp
Coconut Fried Shrimp 203
Floribbean Shrimp 202
Jambalaya 177
Pasta with Shrimp and Jalapeño
    Orange Sauce 124
Shrimp and Artichoke Vinaigrette 94
Shrimp and Basil Soup 63
Shrimp and Scallop Salad 96
Shrimp Enchiladas 204
Shrimp Mousse 21
Summer Shrimp and Olive Salad 93
Seafood Quiche 55
Seafood Salad with Dill Dressing 95
Seaside Mist 28
Seasonal Peas and Onions 140
Snappy Sunshine Salsa 26
Soups
Avocado Layered Soup 62
Black Bean and Chicken Chili 70
Cold Cream of Tomato Soup with Mint,
    Avocado and Cucumber 64
Crabmeat Corn Soup 68
Creamy Double Cheese Soup 69
Gazpacho 65
Gourmet Spinach Soup 61
Italian Sausage Soup 67
Lentil Soup 59
Red Pepper Soup 69
Shrimp and Basil Soup 63
Sweet Corn and Cheddar Chowder 60
Tortellini Soup 62
Turkey Vegetable Soup 66
Vichyssoise 64
Sour Cream Pound Cake 229

Spiced Cranberry Tea 34
Spicy Apple Dumplings 254
Spicy Dressing 81
Spicy Seafood Dip 16
Spinach
Bow Ties with Spinach Sauce and Cheese 107
Chicken and Spinach Pasta Salad 87
Fresh Spinach Salad 78
Gold Coast Spinach Salad 77
Gourmet Spinach Soup 61
Herbed Spinach Balls 27
Hot Artichoke Spinach Dip 14
Marinated Steak and Spinach Salad 91
Spinach, Bacon and Mushroom Gratin 143
Splendid Raspberry Spinach Salad 76
Spinach, Bacon and Mushroom Gratin 143
Splendid Raspberry Spinach Salad 76
Squash
Apple Pecan Winter Squash 144
Confetti Squash Casserole 146
Pumpkin Squash Bake 145
Steak Rolls in Red Wine Sauce 163
Strawberry
Fresh Strawberry Pie 232
Strawberry Daiquiri Punch 31
Strawberry Orange Muffins 39
Strawberry Daiquiri Punch 31
Strawberry Orange Muffins 39
Streusel Coffee Cake 45
Stuffed Pork Chops 171
Stuffed Zucchini 145
Sugar and Spice Cookies 217
Summer Feta Salad 73
Summer Shrimp and Olive Salad 93
Summer Vegetable Medley 14
Sun-Dried Tomato Fettucine 107
Sunlight Salad Dressing 72
Sunrise Coffee Punch 32
Sunset Salad 75
Sustainer Slush 30
Sweet Bacon Wraps 26
Sweet Bell Pepper and Feta Salad 82
Sweet Corn and Cheddar Chowder 60
Sweet Scalloped Onions 139
Sweet Walnut Bread 44

T

Toasted Almond 33
Toasted Coconut Bread 42
Tomato
Angel Hair Pasta with Fresh Tomato Sauce 108
Basil Tomato Tart 15
Chevré Stuffed Tomatoes 147
Cold Cream of Tomato Soup with Mint,
    Avocado and Cucumber 64
Gazpacho 65

Layered Sun-dried Tomato and Pesto Spread 22
Mountain Top Marinated Tomatoes 148
Open-Face Gorgonzola Cheese, Tomato and
    Basil Sandwich 97
Snappy Sunshine Salsa 26
Sun-Dried Tomato Fettucine 107
Tomato and Basil Quiche 56
Tomato Pie 147
Tomato and Basil Quiche 56
Tomato Pie 147
Tortellini Chicken Salad with Sun-Dried Tomato
    Vinaigrette 86
Tortellini Soup 62
Tortilla Crusted Dolphin 199
Tropical Carrot Cake 227
Tropical Champagne Punch 32
Tropical Fruit Salsa 207
Tropical Fruit Reference 268
Tropical Loaf 44

Turkey

Turkey and Roasted Pepper Sandwich 103
Turkey Vegetable Soup 66

U

Ultimate Poppy Seed Cake 225

V

Veal

Scallopini of Veal 162
Veal Escallops Stuffed with Crab 163
Veal Escallops with Tomato Basil Cream Sauce . 161
Veal with Caramelized Onions 162
Vegetable Brown Rice 154
Vegetable Carbonara 118
Vegetable Salsa 199
Vegetable Stock 263

Vegetables

Apple Pecan Winter Squash 144
AuGratin Tomatoes 146
Broccoli Puff 134
Carrot Cups with Summer Sauce 141
Chevré Stuffed Tomatoes 147
Confetti Squash Casserole 146
Curried Corn and Sweet Peppers 135
Eggplant Casserole 136
Garlicky Potatoes 140
Ginger Carrots 135
Gold Coast Sweet Potatoes 142
Green Beans in Basil and Walnut Sauce 137
Green Beans with Warm Mustard Vinaigrette ... 138
Grilled Vegetable Salad 149
Herb Butter Zucchini Fans 144
Lemon Broccoli with Garlic 133
Marinated Asparagus 133
Oven-Baked French Fries 137
Oven Roasted Vegetables 150
Paraguayan Corn Souffle 136
Pumpkin Squash Bake 145
Rosemary Potatoes 142
Sautéed Peas with Basil 143
Scalloped Cauliflower 134
Seasonal Peas and Onions 140
Spinach, Bacon and Mushroom Gratin 143
Stuffed Zucchini 145
Sweet Scalloped Onions 139
Tomato Caprese 148
Tomato Pie 147
Vegetables with Avocado Anchovy Dip 17
Vegetarian Pasta 128
Vichyssoise 64
Vinaigrette Dressing 93

W

White Cheddar Rollups 24
White Chocolate Brownies 220
White Chocolate Macadamia Nut Cookies 218
White Chocolate Raspberry Cheesecake 221

Z

Zucchini

Herb Butter Zucchini Fans 144
Ratatouille Sandwiches 100
Stuffed Zucchini 145
Zucchini Frittata 52

A Slice of Paradise

Fresh and Inviting Flavors from the Junior League of the Palm Beaches

Please send _____ copies of *A Slice of Paradise* @ $19.95 each $ _____

Florida residents add 6% sales tax (or current tax rate) $ _____

Shipping and Handling   @ $ 3.50 ($1.00 for each additional book) $ _____

Total $ _____

Ship To:

Name _____ Phone _____

Address _____

City _____ State _____ Zip Code_____

Method of Payment   _____ Check   _____ Credit Card

Please make checks payable to Junior League Publications

Junior League of the Palm Beaches, Inc. • Attention: Cookbook Sales

470 Columbia Drive, Bldg. F • West Palm Beach, FL 33409 • 561-689-7562

Visa /MasterCard Number _____

Expiration Date _____

Signature _____

Credit card orders may be placed by calling 561-689-7562 or fax 561-640-3955

Proceeds from the sale of this book support the many projects of the Junior League of the Palm Beaches, Inc.

A Slice of Paradise

Fresh and Inviting Flavors from the Junior League of the Palm Beaches

Please send _____ copies of *A Slice of Paradise* @ $19.95 each $ _____

Florida residents add 6% sales tax (or current tax rate) $ _____

Shipping and Handling   @ $ 3.50 ($1.00 for each additional book) $ _____

Total $ _____

Ship To:

Name _____ Phone _____

Address _____

City _____ State _____ Zip Code_____

Method of Payment   _____ Check   _____ Credit Card

Please make checks payable to Junior League Publications

Junior League of the Palm Beaches, Inc. • Attention: Cookbook Sales

470 Columbia Drive, Bldg. F • West Palm Beach, FL 33409 • 561-689-7562

Visa /MasterCard Number _____

Expiration Date _____

Signature _____

Credit card orders may be placed by calling 561-689-7562 or fax 561-640-3955

Proceeds from the sale of this book support the many projects of the Junior League of the Palm Beaches, Inc.